Complexity Thinking in Physical Education

In the past two decades, complexity thinking has emerged as an important theoretical response to the limitations of orthodox ways of understanding educational phenomena. Complexity provides ways of understanding that embrace uncertainty, non-linearity and the inevitable 'messiness' that is inherent in educational settings, paying attention to the ways in which the whole is greater than the sum of its parts. This is the first book to focus on complexity thinking in the context of physical education, enabling fresh ways of thinking about research, teaching, curriculum and learning.

Written by a team of leading international physical education scholars, the book highlights how the considerable theoretical promise of complexity can be reflected in the actual policies, pedagogies and practices of physical education. It encourages teachers, educators and researchers to embrace notions of learning that are more organic and emergent, to allow the inherent complexity of pedagogical work in physical education to be examined more broadly and inclusively. In doing so, *Complexity Thinking in Physical Education* makes a major contribution to our understanding of pedagogy, curriculum design and development, human movement and educational practice.

Alan Ovens is a Principal Lecturer in the School of Curriculum and Pedagogy at the University of Auckland, New Zealand. His research interests are in the areas of teacher education and educational sociology. He coordinates the Faculty's Special Interest Network in Complexity (SINC) and leads a Research Network in HPE Teacher Education.

Tim Hopper is an Associate Professor in the School of Exercise Science, Physical and Health Education in the Faculty of Education at the University of Victoria, British Columbia, Canada. His research interests are in the areas of teacher education, physical education and how complexity thinking informs learning.

Joy Butler is an Associate Professor in the Department of Curriculum and Pedagogy at the University of British Columbia, Canada. Her research interests are in the areas of teacher education, constructivist learning theory, complexity thinking and situated ethics. She is active in international scholarship, organization and advocacy for TGfU.

Routledge Studies in Physical Education and Youth Sport

Series Editor: David Kirk, University of Bedfordshire, UK

The *Routledge Studies in Physical Education and Youth Sport* series is a forum for the discussion of the latest and most important ideas and issues in physical education, sport and active leisure for young people across school, club and recreational settings. The series presents the work of the best well-established and emerging scholars from around the world, offering a truly international perspective on policy and practice. It aims to enhance our understanding of key challenges, to inform academic debate and to have a high impact on both policy and practice, and is thus an essential resource for all serious students of physical education and youth sport.

Also available in this series

Children, Obesity and Exercise
A practical approach to prevention, treatment and management
of childhood and adolescent obesity
Edited by Andrew P. Hills, Neil A. King and Nuala M. Byrne

Disability and Youth Sport
Edited by Hayley Fitzgerald

Rethinking Gender and Youth Sport
Edited by Ian Wellard

Pedagogy and Human Movement
Richard Tinning

Positive Youth Development Through Sport
Edited by Nicholas Holt

Young People's Voices in Physical Education and Youth Sport
Edited by Mary O'Sullivan and Ann Macphail

Physical Literacy
Throughout the Lifecourse
Edited by Margaret Whitehead

Physical Education Futures
David Kirk

Young People, Physical Activity and the Everyday
Living Physical Activity
Edited by Jan Wright and Doune Macdonald

Muslim Women and Sport
Edited by Tansin Benn, Gertrud Pfister and Haifaa Jawad

Inclusion and Exclusion Through Youth Sport
Edited by Symeon Dagkas and Kathleen Armour

Sport Education
International Perspectives
Edited by Peter Hastie

Cooperative Learning in Physical Education
An International Perspective
Edited by Ben Dyson and Ashley Casey

Equity and Difference in Physical Education, Youth Sport and Health
A Narrative Approach
Edited by Fiona Dowling, Hayley Fitzgerald and Anne Flintoff

Game Sense
Pedagogy for Performance, Participation and Enjoyment
Richard Light

Ethics in Youth Sport
Policy and Pedagogical Applications
Stephen Harvey and Richard Light

Assessment in Physical Education
A Sociocultural Perspective
Peter Hay and Dawn Penney

Complexity Thinking in Physical Education
Reframing curriculum, pedagogy and research
Edited by Alan Ovens, Tim Hopper and Joy Butler

Complexity Thinking in Physical Education

Reframing curriculum, pedagogy and research

Edited by
Alan Ovens, Tim Hopper and Joy Butler

Routledge
Taylor & Francis Group

LONDON AND NEW YORK

First published 2013
by Routledge
2 Park Square, Milton Park, Abingdon, Oxfordshire OX14 4RN

Simultaneously published in the USA and Canada
by Routledge
711 Third Avenue, New York, NY 10017

First issued in paperback 2014

Routledge is an imprint of the Taylor & Francis Group, an informa business

British Library Cataloguing in Publication Data
A catalogue record for this book is available from the British Library

Library of Congress Cataloging-in-Publication Data
Complexity thinking in physical education: reframing curriculum, pedagogy and research/edited by Alan Ovens, Tim Hopper and Joy Butler.
p. cm. -- (Routledge studies in physical education and youth sport)
1. Physical education and training--Research. 2. Critical pedagogy.
I. Ovens, Alan. II. Hopper, Tim. III. Butler, Joy.
GV361.C635 2013
613.7'1--dc23
2012021940

ISBN 13: 978-0-415-50721-9 (hbk)
ISBN 13: 978-0-415-64517-1 (pbk)

Typeset in Goudy
by Integra Software Services Pvt. Ltd, Pondicherry, India

Contents

Figures

Tables

Contributors

Duarte Araújo is an Associate Professor in the Faculty of Human Kinetics at the Technical University of Lisbon, Portugal, where he directs the Laboratory of Sports Expertise (http://www.fmh.utl.pt/spertlab/). His research involves the study of the dynamics of expert decision-making, which led to him receiving the ECSS 2001 and ACAPS 2002 young researcher awards. He is a consultant for many different national sports associations, essentially about the training of individual (player, referee, coach) and collective decision-making in sports. He has written many articles and books about individual and team behaviours in sport, both in high-quality scientific journals and in the popular press, and he has been invited to teach and to present his work on expert performance in sport in several countries.

Matthew Atencio is an Assistant Professor in the Curriculum, Teaching and Learning group at the Singapore National Institute of Education. He is primarily interested in researching physical education pedagogy innovation and collaborative professional development, as well as socio-cultural discourses that influence young people's physical activity and health engagements. He is currently researching the impacts of holistic curricular guidelines on primary schools in Singapore and Scotland.

Joy Butler is an Associate Professor in the Department of Curriculum and Pedagogy (EDCP) at the University of British Columbia, Canada, coordinator of Physical Education Teacher Education (PETE), Outdoor Education & Health programmes and of M.Ed. Cohorts for Physical Educators. Her research and teaching have developed around constructivist learning theory, complexity thinking, situated ethics and community wellness. She is active in international scholarship, organization and advocacy for Teaching Games for Understanding (TGfU).

Chris Button is an Associate Professor in the School of Physical Education at the University of Otago, New Zealand. A common theme of his research is the application of movement science to sport within an ecological framework (a summary of much of this work can be found in the textbook *Dynamics of Skill Acquisition: A Constraints-Led Approach* by Davids, Button, & Bennett, 2007).

As well as carrying out teaching and research, he has provided consultancy with several sports, providing advice on biomechanics and skill acquisition to the likes of Netball NZ, NZ Football and Motorsport NZ. He also plays and coaches soccer and futsal.

Timothy Carroll is an Associate Professor at the Centre for Sensorimotor Neuroscience within the School of Human Movement Studies at the University of Queensland, Australia. His research interests span the fields of exercise science and integrative neuroscience, with a focus on determining how the central nervous system is reorganized as a consequence of motor learning and exercise. He has specific interests in revealing the brain mechanisms underlying transfer of skill between limbs and improvements in strength through resistance training. Much of his work combines non-invasive brain and nerve stimulation methods with behavioural observations in experiments involving human participants.

Nicola Carse is a doctoral student in the Institute for Sport, Physical Education and Health Sciences at the University of Edinburgh, Scotland. Her thesis is investigating the process of educational change within Scottish primary physical education from the perspective of individual teachers. In addition to her PhD study her research interests are in the areas of teacher professional learning, primary physical education curriculum development, pedagogy and sport education.

Ching-Wei Chang is an Assistant Professor at the National Taiwan Normal University, Taiwan, ROC. He received his PhD in both France and Taiwan and was involved as a physical education teacher trainer at the NTNU. He has also specialized in basketball. His research interests are on the study of student strategies and on cooperative learning, with a special interest in constructivist approaches to learning such as Teaching Games for Understanding. In the last three consecutive years, he has received a grant from NSC (National Scientific Council, Taiwan) for conducting an 'action-reflection' approach in PETE. He has been an active member of AIESEP for ten years and is a board member of the Taiwanese Association of Sport Pedagogy.

Jia-Yi Chow is an Assistant Professor in the Department of Physical Education and Sports Science at the National Institute of Education, Nanyang Technological University, Singapore. His area of specialization is in motor control and learning. His key research work includes nonlinear pedagogy, investigation of multi-articular coordination changes, analysis of team dynamics from an ecological psychology perspective and examining visual–perceptual skills in sports expertise.

Keith Davids is Professor of Motor Learning in the School of Exercise and Nutrition Science, Queensland University of Technology, Australia. He was a first-class honours graduate of the University of London and gained a PhD at the University of Leeds in 1986. Between 1993 and 1999, he led the Motor Control group in the Department of Exercise and Sport Science at Manchester

Metropolitan University, UK. Currently he supervises doctoral students from Portugal, UK, Australia and New Zealand. He is co-editor in chief of the *International Journal of Sport Psychology* and holds editorial board positions.

Brent Davis is Professor and Distinguished Research Chair in Mathematics Education at the University of Calgary, Canada. His research looks at the educational relevance of developments in the cognitive and complexity sciences, and he teaches courses at the undergraduate and graduate levels in curriculum studies, mathematics education, and educational change. Davis has published in the areas of mathematics learning and teaching, curriculum theory, teacher education, epistemology, and action research in journals that include *Science, Harvard Educational Review, Journal for Research in Mathematics Education, Mathematics Teacher, and Teaching Children Mathematics*. His most recent book is *The Math Teachers Know: Profound Understanding of Emergent Mathematics* (2013, Routledge).

Ricardo Duarte is Professor of Football Coaching Methods and investigator in the Laboratory of Expertise in Sports in the Faculty of Human Kinetics at the Technical University of Lisbon, Portugal. He recently finished his PhD in Sports Sciences in which he studied and developed tools to capture the interpersonal coordination tendencies of competing football players in different levels of game organization (from dyads to collectives). He is also a consultant on youth football and performance analysis fields. His current research interests focus on the behavioural dynamics of football players and teams from the perspective of complex systems, in which he is particularly interested in knowledge transfer.

Catherine Ennis is a Professor of Curriculum Theory and Development in the Department of Kinesiology at the University of North Carolina, Greensboro, USA. She has directed research examining relationships between student learning (knowledge and performance) and innovative approaches to curriculum and teaching. Recent mixed method research has investigated curricular impacts on student conceptual change with respect to social, cultural and instructional variables. She has collaborated on numerous school–university research projects, including serving as principal investigator in the US National Institutes of Health sponsored curricular research. Previously, she held professorial positions at the University of Wisconsin, Madison and the University of Maryland, College Park.

Katie Fitzpatrick is a Senior Research Fellow in the School of Curriculum and Pedagogy at the University, Auckland, New Zealand. Her research interests include critical approaches to health education and physical education; health policy and practice in schools; youth perspectives and experiences of ethnicity, class, gender and sexuality; and critical ethnography.

Kath Godber is a doctoral student in the School of Human Movement Studies at the University of Queensland, Australia. Her research interests include the life-worlds of elite female performers, specifically those of secondary school age, and the layering of converging and emerging influences synchronous with ecological and social network perspectives. Her doctoral work investigates the attainment levels of talented young female athletes in Australasia in order to raise awareness and to gain insights regarding the educational needs of young female athletes, the secondary school's role in offering appropriate provision, and whether the specific needs of the athletes as students and as elite sports-women, are being met. She also works as the Sports Manager at an independent girls' college in central Auckland.

Tim Hopper is an Associate Professor in the School of Exercise Science, Physical and Health Education in the Faculty of Education at the University of Victoria in British Columbia, Canada. His research interests are in the areas of teacher education, physical education and how complexity thinking informs learning. He has taught at all levels of the school curriculum both in Canada and the UK. He maintains strong links with local schools through a teacher education approach known as school-integrated teacher education. He has just completed a three-year study into the development of a teacher education programme-wide electronic portfolio process and is currently exploring the role of Inventing Games in physical education and the way video games inform our understanding of learning and civic responsibility.

Mike Jess is Senior Lecturer in Physical Education at the University of Edinburgh, Scotland, where he is director of the Developmental Physical Education Group and programme leader of the Postgraduate Certificate in 3–14 Physical Education. He is joint coordinator of the Scottish Primary Physical Education Project, a longitudinal project supported by the Scottish Government since 2006. He also directs the Basic Moves programme which is currently being delivered throughout the UK. His main research interests are in complexity theory, developmental curriculum and pedagogy innovation and teachers' professional learning. He has extensive experience teaching physical education in preschool, primary and secondary settings, has delivered many conference presentations and CPD sessions and has written extensively on children's physical education, sport and physical activity.

Alan Ovens is a Principal Lecturer in the School of Curriculum and Pedagogy at the University of Auckland, New Zealand. His research interests are in the area of teacher education and educational sociology where he explores the use of self-study methodologies as an opportunity to develop a reflective practice located at the intersection of complexity thinking, critical theory and everyday life experience. He coordinates the Faculty's Special Interest Network in Complexity (SINC) and leads a Research Network in HPE Teacher Education. His current research explores innovative pedagogies for implementing forms of democratic teaching in teacher education settings.

Pedro Passos is an Assistant Professor in the Faculty of Human Kinetics at the Technical University of Lisbon, Portugal. He attained his PhD in Sport

Sciences in 2008. His research involves the study of the dynamics of interpersonal coordination in team sports, which led him to produce book chapters and several papers accepted for publication in scientific journals as well as communications in scientific meetings. He currently maintains his research work regarding interpersonal coordination in social systems as team sports and extending the paradigm of analysis to video games cooperative tasks, searching for new methods of analysis and extending his collaborations with researchers in Portugal, across Europe, Australia and New Zealand. He supervises masters and doctorate students from Portugal. Parallel to research activity he was also the head coach of an under-18 rugby team.

Ian Renshaw is a Senior Lecturer in the School of Exercise and Nutrition Science at the Queensland University of Technology, Australia. His research interests include an ecological dynamics approach to understanding perception and action in sport with particular emphasis on developing effective learning environments. To that end, he is particularly interested in the development of a nonlinear pedagogy for talent development, teaching and coaching of sport. Current research projects include: psychology and metastability in nonlinear pedagogy; the implementation of nonlinear pedagogy in schools; emergent decision-making in football referees; and representative learning design in sporting run-ups.

Karen Pagnano Richardson is an Associate Professor and Graduate Coordinator in the Department of Movement Arts, Health Promotion and Leisure Studies at Bridgewater State University, MA. Her research interests are in the area of physical education teacher education where she explores conceptual approaches to teaching including Teaching Games for Understanding. Her current research has centred on using complexity thinking to understanding student learning during game play and on students' development of tactical decision-making competency.

Claire Robson is a sessional instructor in Integral Theory at the University of Calgary, Canada and writer-in-residence for Quirk-e (the Queer Imaging & Riting Kollective for Elders). Her main interests lie in critical biography—the use of personal narrative to investigate cultural structures and to construct identity and memory. She is also interested in constructivist and complexivist pedagogies across the disciplines.

Anthony Rossi is a Senior Lecturer and member of the Centre for Sport, Physical & Health Education Research in the School of Human Movement Studies at the University of Queensland, Brisbane, Australia. His current research interests are in professional learning in workplaces related to human movement and allied health professions. His forthcoming book *Workplace Learning in Physical Education* (Routledge) focuses on school physical education departments as sites of workplace learning for teachers. In addition, he is interested in the role and the politics of funded sport interventions in indigenous communities. His work is underpinned by social, political and increasingly economic theory.

Deborah Sheehy is an Associate Professor and Department Chairperson in the Department of Movement Arts, Health Promotion and Leisure Studies at Bridgewater State University, MA. She serves on the AIESEP TGfU SIG International Advisory Board. Her research involves examining physical education teacher education candidates' learning and implementation of Teaching Games for Understanding. Her current research has centred on using complexity thinking to understand student learning during game play.

Ellen Singleton recently retired as Professor Emerita in the Faculty of Education at the University of Western Ontario, Canada. Her current research focuses on how girls and young women are portrayed in vintage and contemporary juvenile sport fiction. She is co-editor, with her colleague Aniko Varpalotai, of two (text)books focused on contemporary social and cultural issues facing physical and health educators: *Stones in the Sneaker: Active Theory for Secondary School Physical and Health Educators* and *Pedagogy in Motion: A Community of Inquiry for Human Movement Studies*.

Wayne Smith is a Senior Lecturer in the School of Curriculum and Pedadgogy at the University of Auckland, New Zealand. His research interests focus on examining the nature and development of skilful movement. His work in complexity aims to bring educational sociology and skill acquisition theory into a useful synergy in order to deepen understanding of learning and learners in physical education. He is currently co-editing a book entitled *Bourdieu in Physical Education* which is due for publication in 2013.

Dennis Sumara is Dean of the Faculty of Education at the University of Calgary, Canada. Prior to this appointment, he held academic positions at University of British Columbia, University of Alberta, York University, and Simon Fraser University. He has taught undergraduate and graduate courses in language arts education, teacher education, curriculum theory, and qualitative research methods. He was Founding Editor of the *Journal of the Canadian Association for Curriculum Studies* and has served in the editorial capacity with numerous peer-reviewed journals. His specific areas of expertise include literacy education, teacher education and curriculum studies. His research programme focuses on the study of literary engagement and curriculum, analyses of normative and counter-normative discourses in teacher education, and the theoretical and practical implications of complexity science to the field of education. He is author or co-author of five books, including *Why Reading Literature in School Still Matters: Interpretation, Imagination, Insight*, which won the 2003 USA National Reading Conference's Ed Fry Book Award.

Clara Tan Wee Keat is a Senior Lecturer in the Department of Physical Education and Sports Science at the National Institute of Education, Nanyang Technological University, Singapore. Her area of specialization is in physical education pedagogy. Some of her research work relates to physical education pedagogy, Teaching Games for Understanding, children's perception of physical education and achievement motivation in physical education and sport settings.

Richard Tinning is Professor of Pedagogy in the School of Human Movement Studies at the University of Queensland, Australia. He is also Professor of Physical Education in the School of Curriculum and Pedagogy at the University of Auckland, New Zealand. His research interests are informed by a socially critical perspective and have focused on issues related to knowledge, identity and the professional development of HPE teachers. Since his early work in the late 1980s and early 1990s he has been an international leader in the development of critical pedagogy in physical education. His recent book *Pedagogy and Human Movement: Research, Practice, Theory* (Routledge, 2010) focuses on pedagogy across the field of human movement in relation to physical activity, the body and health.

Bruno Travassos is an Assistant Professor in the Department of Sport Sciences at the University of Beira Interior, Portugal and a member of the group of performance analysis at CIDESD—Research Centre in Sports, Health Sciences and Human Development, Portugal. His research interests are in the area of game analysis and also on the development of decision-making behaviour of players with special emphasis in futsal and soccer. His current research explores the concept of representative design to better understand the effects of practice tasks in performance achievement and skill acquisition. He is also a futsal coach.

Luís Vilar is an Assistant Professor in the Faculty of Human Kinetics at the Technical University of Lisbon and in the Faculty of Physical Education and Sports at the Lusófona University of Humanities and Technologies, both in Portugal. He recently finished his PhD in Sports Sciences, investigating the informational constraints on attacker and defender performance in futsal. His research activities are focused on football/futsal aiming to examine: (i) informational constraints on players' performances; (ii) the influence of small-sided and conditioned games on skill acquisition and decision-making; (iii) the influence of team cognition on performance; and (iv) interpersonal patterns of coordination through network analysis tools. He was a futsal player and currently he is a football coach.

Nathalie Wallian is a Professor in the Faculty of Teacher Education and Higher Education at the University of Franche Comté, France. She has been a successful elementary school teacher, a physical education teacher at the Strasbourg International College, a physical education teacher trainer and then Assistant Professor in the Department of Sport Sciences of Besançon. She works in the area of sport education and in educational sciences. She is the director of a research team on didactics and language sciences, her research interests are on student strategies in physical education. She is also President of the French-speaking International Association for Research on Intervention by Sports (ARIS), a member of AIESEP, and a jury member of estate concourses for physical education teacher enrolment.

Foreword

Brent Davis and Dennis Sumara

A few years ago while attending a conference in Denver, we found ourselves in a small urban park on a sunny Sunday afternoon. Heralded by radio announcers as the first 'summery weekend' of the year, the warmth of the day and the sudden greening of the park seemed to pull all manner of people out of stores and homes.

The park didn't invite everyone, however. Cyclists, bladers and boarders were expressly forbidden from riding along the park's paths. That proscription didn't stop a small group of boarders from having fun nearby. Across the street, in an alley parking-lot, half a dozen adolescents were testing their skills on makeshift ramps and platforms that they had assembled from crates and pallets.

It was only after a few moments of admiring the skill level of a few that we noticed that there was more going on than practising and showing off. They were playing a game. There were two teams, rules (albeit evolving ones), a scoring system and penalties. There was also teaching, with challenges, advice and nuanced feedback. It was a system in which possibilities arose that didn't previously exist.

As we have explained elsewhere (Davis, Sumara, & Luce Kapler, 2008; Davis & Sumara, 2006), these youths were demonstrating their involvement in a structure primarily oriented by 'enabling constraints'—that is, a productive structure that involves the unique utilization of the already known in order to create the not-yet-known. As an inherently creative act, the 'game' being created by the skateboarders involved a certain degree of randomness within coherence, specialization across phenomenal levels and the opportunity for a diversity of skills and capabilities to be used and developed as the game continued to emerge.

To be honest, we couldn't quite figure out everything that was going on. Even the object of the game was a little obscure. It wasn't as simple as 'score the most by doing the hardest tricks'—as points were awarded for simply trying, for novel moves and for constructive suggestions. As well, there seemed to be some kind of handicap scoring system in play. And to further complicate things, it appeared that team membership was regularly adjusted when one side or the other started to amass a significant advantage. On that count, it almost seemed that the simultaneous objects of the game were: (1) do your personal best and (2) maintain the most equitable team composition possible. Odd indeed, particularly when one considers that these youths were likely to have been socialized in physical education settings oriented by competition and ranking. One could argue that we were witnessing an important form of youth activism—one where matters of social justice and equity were being worked out in the social space of the game-inventing activity.

Such happenings are a boon to anyone with an interest in the socially-interactive dimensions of human learning. They offer sites for discerning how norms arise, how rules are negotiated, how identities are acted out and how collective possibilities are co-created. Certainly, we couldn't help but bring one of our favourite interpretive frames—complexity thinking—to bear on what was happening. As detailed in Chapter 1, the transdiscipline of complexity thinking is devoted to making sense of the emergence of coherences that transcend the agents they comprise—in the way that ant colonies include but exceed the ants that populate them, brains emerge in, but are more than, the networked activities of neurons, and nations arise from, but can in no way be reduced to, individual citizens.

For more than three decades, complexivists have been focusing their attentions on these sorts of dynamic, adaptive, learning systems. The field of education has been a relative late arriver to the discussions, but there has been a surge of interest over the past ten years, evidenced by the theme of that Denver conference we mentioned. It was the 2010 meeting of the American Educational Researchers Association—the largest of its type in the world—and its focus that year was on understanding some of the complex ecologies of the connected educational world.

There was more than a slight irony to be sitting out-of-doors that conference day, watching emergence happening. Thousands of our colleagues were in meeting rooms on the other side of the park, many ostensibly discussing how to occasion the very sort of learning system that was unfolding before our eyes. For us, nearly 20 years into the domain, the event we observed was a complex one, and complexity thinking had equipped us with some powerful strategies for observing and interpreting what was going on. We could see the roles of constraints (in space, in equipment and so on), of flexibility (in team composition, in individual expectations), of redundancy (in expectation, in interest), of diversity (in expertise, in imagination) and in the ways in which novel, new knowledge was emerging from this collective activity of improvisational game play.

However, as educational researchers, complexity thinking helped us to attend to this event for tips on how we might design learning settings that would allow for a similar outcome—that is, participants engaging to extend their own, personal skills within a collective, gaming context. In some ways, it was a bit of a revelation to us, this noticing of the importance of the structure of the *game* to engage, to support, to develop and to grow.

Of course, as this book demonstrates, we weren't exactly the first to reach this insight. As every soccer and hockey match demonstrates, the game is a complex phenomenon. It emerges in the joint actions of its players, but exceeds those actions. That excess can be a fecund place, and educators can and should exploit it. We thus applaud the efforts of Ovens, Hopper and Butler to assemble this volume. To our thinking, it represents an important and timely advance to educational thought.

We are deliberate in our previous sentence in our reference to 'education' rather than 'physical education'. The insights presented in this book are located in physical education, but their relevance for schooling extends far beyond the gymnasium or the playing field. This is a book about educational possibility, and we hope that it is read as such. It demonstrates the interpretive and pragmatic value of complexity thinking for education, inviting some fresh thinking to matters of research, teaching and curriculum.

Preface

When we began this project almost four years ago, the idea of editing a book on complexity thinking in physical education seemed somewhat far-fetched. While complexity was not a particularly new concept in the broader sciences and educational theory, it was only beginning to attract the attention of physical educators at the time. The idea for a book emerged from meetings and discussions where we realized that we shared a belief in the value of applying complexity thinking to our work as physical educators. Along the way the project enabled us to connect with like-minded academics from around the globe and to develop a network of support for our collective work. In addition, the project also provided a vantage point from which to observe the evolving nature of ideas in our field. What was once far-fetched has quickly become of interest to many and the collection of distributed individuals working with complexity ideas is quickly growing into a broad and enthusiastic community.

About this book

While books tend to be organized in a linear way, with chapters numbered sequentially to indicate the progressive unfolding of an argument, we feel a book on complexity can reflect alternative ways of structuring. As editors, our aim was to focus on the broad and growing interest in complexity in a range of different disciplinary areas, introducing it and making it accessible to physical education scholars in a way that could be reflected in the actual policies, pedagogies and practices of the field. What has emerged is a collection of contributions that reflect how complexity thinking might be applied at all levels of education, which is itself a key lacuna or void in critical research more generally. Consequently, the following discussion of the chapters outlines one possible journey through the collection. It represents our own tentative attempts to place some coherence around the contributing chapters. We encourage readers to find other useful trajectories.

The opening four chapters are united around the possibilities for reframing the nature of the physical education. Chapter 1 provides an introduction and overview of complexity thinking. In Chapter 2, Ennis acknowledges that most efforts to introduce innovative curriculum ideas into the unbending context of large urban school districts typically only result in modest changes. She draws on complexity thinking to describe the educational context that enables and constrains curriculum intervention and discusses the insights she has gained on how to interact with the complexity of open educational systems. In the following chapter, Jess, Attencio and Carse also consider the usefulness of complexity theory as a means of envisioning and structuring contemporary practice in physical education. They consider how a 'complex' primary physical education curriculum emphasizing children's self-emergent and adaptive learning can result in learning trajectories that approach the 'edge of chaos' within parameters that are ambiguously bounded. They suggest that there is much potential in supporting teachers to 'shift' towards more complexity-oriented practices. In Chapter 4, Fitzpatrick cautions that it is important not to lose sight of the social justice issues that lie within and are reproduced by the field of physical education. She questions how complexity thinking can address issues of marginality and exclusion, asking whether complexity thinking brings anything new to scholars working with critical and post-structuralist ways of doing research.

The next grouping of four chapters address the changing nature of the learner and learning in physical education. In Chapter 5, Ovens and Godber challenge the belief that the content, function, setting and acting person are independent of each other, suggesting instead the need for a sensitivity to the relational nature of what it means to act with embodied competence in complex, discursive movement settings. In Chapter 6, Smith acknowledges that contemporary thinking around the learner has made a valuable shift to focus on the performer–environment relationship and to view skilful action as emerging from the interactions of individuals within environmental constraints over time towards specific functional goals. At the same time, he questions the place and nature of intentionality in nonlinear and self-organizing systems such as the human body. In Chapter 7, Rossi and Carroll examine the nature of learning in relation to the human capacity to adapt to changing environments. Their discussion draws from a range of fields to help examine useful synergies between recent advances in pedagogy and motor control. They discuss some possible ideas for pedagogy within the sport and physical activity domains, the implications of which would require a rethink on how motor skill learning opportunities might best be facilitated. In Chapter 8, Singleton reflects on the changing nature of learning in physical education by examining the theoretical thinking in pedagogy found in textbooks produced for the physical education teacher since the time physical education was first recognized as a discrete subject of study.

The next cluster of chapters is oriented towards reframing the nature of pedagogy in physical education. In Chapter 9, Butler and Robson present an alternative to conventional pedagogy, in which the teacher selects games and encourages participation. They suggest that as teachers encourage students to invent games, they can provide them with opportunities to understand how the nature of games and ethical game play emerge from the constraints imposed by each game form. In Chapter 10, Chow, Renshaw, Button, Davids and Tan Wee Keat examine how the benefits espoused for a nonlinear pedagogical approach could be adopted to enhance the design of learning programmes for physical education in schools. In the final chapter in this cluster, Button and his colleagues examine the value of developing an awareness that the self-organizing tendencies in social groups or teams offers physical educators an exciting new perspective upon which to base a nonlinear pedagogical strategy for learning design in team sports. By blending spontaneous, self-regulated learning environments with structured games and instruction, they argue that practitioners can both promote and channel the self-organizing capacity of teams.

The next three chapters are oriented by a common focus on teacher education. In Chapter 12, Hopper considers how complexity thinking can be applied to the planning and instruction of physical education methods classes. He provides a detailed example of a teacher education course designed around a school-integrated teacher education model involving experiences in school with students systematically infused into the course design. He discusses how the key components of complexity thinking have informed the development of the course. He outlines how key aspects of the course create spaces that enable meaningful learning that transforms pre-service teachers' negative attitudes to physical education, from their marginalized experiences as physical education students, to one where they feel inspired to be physical education teachers and profess joy for doing physical education. In Chapter 13, Wallian and Chang outline seven properties that contribute to the complexity of the physical education lesson setting, then explore teaching/learning as a complex system. They discuss how the paradigm of complexity thinking links with physical education teacher education perspectives in France. To conclude this section, in Chapter 14 Richardson, Sheehy and Hopper consider the dual dilemma for educators of how to ensure students both learn in and enjoy playing a game despite competing against opponents' of different abilities. Referring to a study with a class of pre-service teachers they draw on complexity thinking to show how students respond to instruction informed by the concepts of 'modification by adaptation' and 'game as teacher' to understand how students learn (or re-learn) games. Critically they show how adding the condition to game play 'where the outcome of a game encounter results in the game becoming more challenging for the successful player' they show how games can become more challenging and engaging for players of all abilities.

The final chapter offers a cautionary, but optimistic, assessment of how complexity ideas might be able to add to the continuous debates within the field. In Chapter 15, Tinning and Rossi challenge the idea that complexity thinking can provide a generative way of theorizing pedagogy in physical education in ways that are advantageous over other ways of theorising physical education pedagogy. They position themselves as sceptics with a view not to discard complexity thinking but, rather, to seek its most viable attributes to help shape pedagogical practice in physical education. They ask whether the attractiveness (usefulness) of complexity thinking might be understood by considering it as a meme (the cultural equivalent of a gene) that happens to have gained attention at this particular point in time.

Overall, we believe that this volume of work constitutes a significant and exciting contribution to scholarship in physical education. Collectively, the chapters challenge the orthodox view inherent in much published research that educational phenomena can be understood in terms of a linear mechanics of cause and effect and, instead, promote a nonlinear dynamics of complex systems where the outcomes cannot be predicted in advance but, rather, emerge as the system evolves and learns. Collectively, the chapters embrace notions of research, curriculum and learning that are more organic and emergent, allowing the inherent complexity of pedagogical work in physical education to be examined more broadly and inclusively. Overall, we believe that the book explores complexity thinking in physical education and highlights its considerable theoretical promise to reframe curriculum, pedagogy and research.

Acknowledgements

No book writes itself and, as we have found out, an edited collection also doesn't come together without the collective efforts of many people. We greatly appreciate the encouragement and vision of Professor David Kirk who actively supported the proposal from the start. We also thank and acknowledge the authors who, amongst their many commitments and projects, have always approached the challenge of drafting and revising the chapters with such positivity. We also acknowledge the contribution provided by our wonderful proofreader, Christine Tennet. Affectionately known to us as 'Hawkeye', we thank Chris for her attention to detail, knowledge and time she has spent ensuring the text reflects the intellectual quality of the authors' work.

From the outset we wanted to have each chapter blind-reviewed by at least two people. To this end, we would like to acknowledge the professional and insightful feedback from our international panel of reviewers. Their willingness to share their time and expertise has contributed significantly to the quality of the chapters. The members of the panel were:

- Elizabeth Anderson, School of Curriculum and Pedagogy, University of Auckland, New Zealand
- Chris Button, School of Physical Education, University of Otago, New Zealand
- Timothy Carroll, School of Human Movement Studies, The University of Queensland, Australia
- Anthony Clark, Curriculum and Pedagogy, University of British Columbia, Canada
- Lissa D'Amour, University of Calgary, Alberta, Canada
- Brent Davis, University of Calgary, Alberta, Canada
- Fiona Ell, School of Learning, Development and Professional Practice, University of Auckland, New Zealand
- Dawn Garbett, School of Curriculum and Pedagogy, University of Auckland, New Zealand
- Geri Van Gyn, School of Exercise Science, Physical and Health Education, University of Victoria, Canada.
- Rena Heap, School of Curriculum and Pedagogy, University of Auckland, New Zealand

- Michael Hemphill, Department of Health and Human Performance, College of Charleston, South Carolina, USA
- John Meldrum, School of Exercise Science, Physical and Health Education, University of Victoria, Canada
- Molly Mullen, School of Critical Studies in Education, University of Auckland, New Zealand
- Wendy Neilson, Faculty of Education, Wollongong University, NSW, Australia
- Ian Renshaw, School of Exercise and Nutrition Science, Queensland University of Technology, Australia
- Rod Philpott, School of Curriculum and Pedagogy, University of Auckland, New Zealand
- Claire Robson, Faculty of Education, University of Calgary, Alberta, Canada
- Tony Rossi, School of Human Movement Studies, The University of Queensland, Australia
- Ritesh Shah, School of Critical Studies in Education, University of Auckland, New Zealand
- Wayne Smith, School of Curriculum and Pedagogy, University of Auckland, New Zealand
- Brian Storey, Douglas University, New Westminster, BC, Canada
- Nick Zepke, School of Educational Studies, Massey University, New Zealand.

1 Reframing curriculum, pedagogy and research

Alan Ovens, Tim Hopper and Joy Butler

This book is based on the premise that physical education phenomena are inherently complex and explores the possible relevancies that complexity thinking may have for the field of physical education. In one sense, complexity has always confronted those working in physical education. The issue is not that educational phenomena are complex, but about the appropriateness of the frameworks we use to make sense of the 'messiness' that is inherent in complex educational settings. As the subheading of this book indicates, complexity offers the opportunity to question how we frame the issues central to curriculum, pedagogy and research in physical education. The idea of frame draws attention to the interpretative process involved in constructing meaning or making sense of the world. Frames are tacit perceptual mechanisms that transform the unfamiliar into meaningful and normative categories (Lawson, 1984) that are, in turn, central to the construction of shared meanings typifying particular discursive fields (Bernstein, 2000). Our objective in supporting the possibility of reframing the field is not one linked to a representational epistemology of changing perspective to gain a more accurate understanding of reality. Rather, the meaning of the term 'reframe' that we hope to invoke is linked to a quest of finding more complex and creative ways of interacting with our reality, which we can then use to interact in yet more complex and creative ways (Osberg, Biesta, & Cilliers, 2008). From a complexity perspective, reframing implies there are no final solutions, only new ways to interact that lead to new emergent possibilities. This sort of project is anything but straightforward, particularly given the lack of clarity around the concept and the relative 'newness' that complexity has in physical education literature. But it is one in which we collectively hope to 'expand the space of the possible' (Davis & Sumara, 1997).

At the outset it is important to address two potential misconceptions that may arise for readers when presented with the claims that complexity offers something new to physical education scholarship. Firstly, it is important to state that complexity does not constitute a single body of thought or unified theory, either in the natural or social sciences. Despite the use of terms such as 'complexity science' and 'complexity theory', there is no consensus around matters of research approach or agreed body of knowledge (Alhadeff-Jones, 2008; Richardson & Cilliers, 2001). As noted by Mason (2008), ideas about complexity derive from disciplinary fields as diverse as physics, biology, economics, sociology and law. What complexivists do have in common is a broad agreement on what constitutes a complex phenomenon or entity. Consequently, rather than defining it by its modes of inquiry, complexity is "more appropriately characterized in terms of its objects of study" (Davis & Sumara, 2006, p. 5). Most commonly, the objects of study are modelled as a 'system' of interacting entities in which the 'system' is perpetually constructing its own future as continuity and transformation (Stacey, 2001). The critical aspect is not to focus on the system, but on the *process of interaction between the elements* that enables the emergent properties and forms that is the focus of our inquiry (Byrne, 2005). The potential of complexity for physical education, then, is not as some explanatory system or meta-discourse that provides a more complete or superior set of explanations, but rather in the way it presents as a source domain that is rich with possible analogies for understanding human action, knowledge, identity and learning (Stacey, 2001).

Secondly, it is important to dispel the notion that complexity represents either a regression to some form of naïve scientism or the importing of models and methods from the natural sciences that are inappropriate for educational inquiry. On the contrary, the perspective complexity represents is consistent with the evolution of post-enlightenment thought and emerges from the collective efforts of those philosophers and scientists working within both the natural and social sciences who are attempting to challenge a mechanistic, reductionist view of the world (Gare, 2000, p. 335). For example, postmodernism and complexity share a similar sense of the implausibility of grand narratives and the impossibility of independent objective observation (Kuhn, 2008). Complexity thinking pays attention to diverse disciplinary sensibilities while acknowledging the multidimensionality, non-linearity, interconnectedness and unpredictability encountered in human activity. It arises *among* rather than *over* other discourses and is oriented by the realization that the act of comparing diverse and seemingly unconnected phenomena is both profoundly human and, at times, tremendously fecund (Davis & Sumara, 2006, p. 8).

Our aim in this book is to promote discussion and reflection by both engaging scholars already employing complexity in their work and readers who are unfamiliar with it and still uncertain of its value. The aim of this initial chapter is to provide an overview of complexity and reflect on its possible value to physical education. It begins by providing an overview of what we mean by complexity thinking and it focuses on some of the themes that have been most used in education. This provides an introduction to complexity for the nonspecialist audience from which the following chapters may build. We also address the question of what complexity thinking may contribute to physical education scholarship by considering the discursive tensions in areas central to the field such as research, curriculum, learning, teaching and embodment.

What is complexity?

The task of trying to understand complexity is itself complex. Definitions, by their very nature, seek certainty and stability of meaning and the irony is that these are the very qualities that complexity seeks to challenge. Complexity is also not a field of study easily defined by its constituent concepts or contributing disciplines. Alhadeff-Jones (2008) suggests that disorder has often shaped the evolution of research focused on complexity, which has given rise to different generational forms and the heterogeneity of meaning and multiplicity of definitions and trends that currently exist. In their attempt to make sense of the field, Richardson and Cilliers (2001) define three different themes or communities: *hard complexity science*, which aims to uncover and understand the nature of reality; *soft complexity science*, which makes use of complexity as a metaphorical tool to understand and interpret the world; and *complexity thinking*, which adopts a philosophical approach to considering the implications of assuming a complex world. In a similar manner, Byrne (2005) explores some of the philosophical variations in the way that complexity is used and distinguishes between *simplistic* complexity, which has a focus on the general set of rules from which emergent complexity flows, and *complex* complexity that has a focus on the contingent and contextual nature of complex forms. Such classifications, while somewhat artificial, point to the way the varied discourses, histories and concepts that represent complexity are highly nuanced, intertwined and potentially inconsistent.

Our own preference lies with the idea of *complexity thinking* and the way it foregrounds this form of inquiry as an attitude which is potentially generative of, and pays attention to, diverse sensibilities without making claims to or being trapped by, universals or absolutes. It is a view that argues that, while complexity may not provide us with the conceptual tools to solve our complex problems, it "shows us (in a rigorous way) why these problems are so difficult" (Cilliers, 2005, p. 257). Complexity thinking, as Davis and Sumara (2006) point out, prompts a kind of "level jumping between and among different layers of organisation enabling attention to be oriented towards other dynamic, co-implicated and integrated levels, including neurological, the experiential, the contextual/material, the symbolic, the cultural, and the ecological" (p. 26). In other words, complexity thinking is transphenomenal (requires awareness of phenomena at different levels of organization), transdisciplinary (requires border crossing between theoretical frames) and interdiscursive (requires an awareness of how discourses intersect, overlap and interlace) (Davis, 2008; Davis & Phelps, 2005).

While acknowledging that the field of complexity is difficult to define, even to the point of questioning if it is a field, a starting point is to have a shared set of meanings of concepts and ideas that are frequently referred to. The following discussion provides an overview of some of the key themes that have the most frequent uptake in the educational literature, namely complex systems, emergence and adaptation.

Complex systems

A general starting point is that complexity generally exists in situations in which a large number of agents are connected and interacting with each other in dynamic ways (Mason, 2008). An agent is understood as something that takes part in an interaction of a system and is itself subsequently changed: a person, a society, a molecule, a plant, a nerve cell, a physical education student, a teacher, etc. The behaviour of these systems is said to be complex because the relationships between multiple elements give rise to emergent qualities that cannot be reduced to the sum of their constituent parts or to a central agent responsible for overall control of the system (Byrne, 2005; Cilliers, 1998). As a property of the system, complexity is situated between order and disorder. That is, complex systems are neither predictable nor regular in the way that they act. However, neither are they random or chaotic. Complex systems tend to display features of both dimensions, sometimes displaying highly-patterned and ordered features while simultaneously being surprising and unpredictable (Morrison, 2008).

Complexity is not always a feature of systems with many interconnected elements. Simple and complicated systems are also composed of multiple components but can be characterized as closed systems capable of decomposing to their individual parts and whose workings follow predictable and precise rules (Cilliers, 2000). In other words, complicated systems may have many component parts, but each component relates to the others in fixed and clearly defined ways. Each component is inert and not dynamic or adaptive. The modern computer is an example of a highly-complicated system that has many interdependent parts that can be taken apart and reassembled. The way it works can be confusing for a novice, but the expert technician can understand the range of parts required and the rules determining the way the parts relate. In this sense, simple and complicated systems are conceptualized as mechanical in the way they function, giving them the ability to behave in predictable ways. This means that something like a computer or car works the same way each time it starts.

By contrast, complex systems are self-organizing and adaptive forms constituted through a large number of nonlinear, dynamic interactions. Complex systems, such as brains, classes of students or economies, are characterized by patterns of relationships that exist within each system as a whole. When the system is taken apart, either physically or theoretically, it is this relational aspect that is destroyed and this subsequently prevents an understanding of the system's dynamics and properties (Byrne, 2005). In complex systems the individual components are self-organizing, adaptive agents in their own right, while interdependent with those with which they are connected. The individual components, while displaying a unity at one level, are themselves complex systems at a different scale (often referred to as the nestedness of self-similar systems).

Davis and Sumara (2006) provide a useful summary of qualities that must be manifest for a system to exhibit complexity:

- Self-organized—complex systems/unities spontaneously arise as the actions of autonomous agents come to be interlinked and co-dependent;
- Bottom-up emergent—complex unities manifest properties that exceed the summed traits and capacities of individual agents, but these transcendent qualities and abilities do not depend on central organizers or overarching governing structures;

- Short-range relationships—most of the information within a complex system is exchanged between close neighbours, meaning that the system's coherence depends mostly on agents' immediate interdependencies, not on centralized control or top-down administration;
- Nested structure (or scale-free networks)—complex unities are often composed of and often comprise other unities that might be properly identified as complex—that is, as giving rise to new patterns and activities and new rules of behaviour;
- Ambiguously-bounded—complex forms are *open* in the sense that they continuously exchange matter and energy with their surroundings (and so judgments about their edges may require certain arbitrary impositions and necessary ignorance);
- Organizationally-closed—complex forms are *closed* in the sense that they are inherently stable—that is, their behavioural patterns or internal organizations endure even while they exchange energy and matter with their dynamic contexts (so judgments about their edges are usually based on perceptible and sufficiently-stable coherences);
- Structure determined—a complex unity can change *its own* structure as it adapts to maintain its viability within dynamic contexts; in other words, complex systems embody their histories—they learn—and are thus better described in terms of Darwinian evolution than Newtonian mechanics;
- Far from equilibrium—complex systems do not operate in balance; indeed, a stable equilibrium implies death for a complex system.

(Davis & Sumara, 2006, pp. 5–6)

Complex systems form when the agents of the system are attracted to a certain activity of a system generating a pattern of behaviour over time. For example, in a physical education setting, such attractors can be:

- singular, where a class of students all focus on a similar solution to a movement task;
- periodic, where certain behaviours are repeated that influence the system such as timed games in tournaments;
- within observable bounds, such as the rules and boundaries in a game of soccer but within those bounds anything is possible; or
- random, where attractors happen but without connection or regard to other parts of the system such as a class of kindergarten children engaged in playground play where suddenly unconnected play becomes united by a common interest for many of the children.

Constraints on a system mediate attractors' power to control the system and, as noted by Ennis (1992), these constraints allow teachers to set up learning conditions in an attempt to shape a system of students' emergent learning.

Emergence

One of the most important ideas central to complexity is the notion of emergence. Emergence can be defined as the appearance of a property or feature not previously observed as a functional characteristic of a system (Cilliers, 1998; Mason, 2008; Richardson & Cilliers, 2001). In other words, new and often unexpected properties, patterns and behaviours can emerge which cannot be predicted from an analysis of the individual system components nor the way these components interact (Mason, 2008). In a very real sense, complex systems become more than the sum of their parts. Examples include the way consciousness emerges from networks of neurons in the brain, teamwork emerges from the activities of players, and meaning emerges from language. Such properties, based on the interaction of the parts, disappear if the parts of the system are disassembled and individually analysed.

Emergence draws attention to three important ideas inherent to an ontology of complex systems. Firstly, the idea of 'supervenience' highlights how the emergent property is dependent on its constituent parts. The emergent property exists only as a function of component interactions occurring at a lower level. Secondly, the emergent properties are more than the sum of the parts and are not just the predictable aggregate of the way the parts interact. Thirdly, the emergent property is not 'epiphenomenal', meaning that the property is more than either an illusion or descriptive metaphor. By its presence, the emergent property exhibits 'downward causation' in that it has causal effects on the components at the lower level. For example, the act of running causes the individual parts of the body to change positions and move (since the 'body system' must remain together in such an act). In this way, emergent properties impose boundary conditions or constraints that restrict the freedom of the component parts.

Emergence also highlights the interdependent relationship that exists between the elements or agents of a complex system and the environment that affords such a system. Once a system reaches a certain critical level of diversity and complexity, a phase transition takes place—what Barab *et al.* (1999) calls an autocatalytic state (self-organize in a continuous activity drawing on available resources) to create a system that sustains itself as its constituent elements interact and, in turn, interconnect with the environment. Therefore, complexity thinking foregrounds a contextual ontology where phenomena such as learning, curriculum and teaching are emergent in response to how contributing agents, as part of a collective, adapt and self-organize in relation to the constraints of a context.

Adaptation and learning

Adaptation is the ability of complex unities to continuously and actively re-orient their structures in order to maintain coherence in relation to their worlds. For example, new neural pathways are created as people learn new skills and teams develop strategies to enhance game play. It is the adaptability and self-organizing processes inherent in complex systems, based on the interest of survival in a changing environment, that create new and emergent possibilities for system-wide understanding and acting (Mason, 2008). Adaptation offers an insight into how complex systems learn and, as such, an analogy for how we can understand human learning.

Critically, for a complex system to reorient itself to maintain coherence with the environment in which it is engaged it must contain enough diversity in its make-up to allow it the ability to adapt to the demands of the environment, but there must also be enough redundancy (commonality) between agents that make up a system so that, if any part of the system fails, the other agents of the system can compensate. In addition, to adapt, the system needs redundancy to facilitate neighbourly interactions as the agents of the system's participation in the environment develop skills in co-mingling roles associated with the intents of the system. As the complex system interacts, it forms a relationship with the environment so that when the conditions are just right, an autocatakinetic process starts where the system, drawing on available resources, develops a self-sustaining exchange with the environment. The conditions in the environment need to offer enabling constraints (affordances) that limit what the system can do, preventing it from being overwhelmed, but, at the same time, offering an openness to possibilities of which the complex system can take advantage. The system must have the capacity to retain the products of previous exchanges, but also the ability to discard elements that are no longer useful. The system forms around nested self-similar structures that emerge from interactions around simple rules that initiated the system's ability to dynamically unfold. This process of unfolding as the system self-organizes to the challenges of the environment represents the critical feature of adaptation in a complex system.

Complexity in physical education

The following section attempts to address the question of what complexity has to offer physical education. In one sense, this is a question about how complexity thinking can facilitate the development of post-enlightenment thought in ways that have the potential to generate new, creative and innovative ways of understanding educational phenomena, which themselves lead to new, creative, innovative forms of engagement. For many, complexity provides a rich source domain of analogies and language which allows them to gain new perspectives on their own work. While we acknowledge this potential, we suggest that complexity also offers a particular philosophical orientation that enables physical educators to gain transphenomenal, transdisciplinary and interdiscursive insights. We demonstrate this in the following section by focusing on the key themes of research, curriculum, learning, teaching and embodiment. In relation to each theme, we summarize the key debates and perspectives represented in the physical education literature and consider how complexity may be taken up by physical educators to generate new insights and ways of working within this theme.

Research

Historically in physical education there has been an active questioning of the appropriateness of those forms of inquiry aligned with the modernist project of uncovering universal truths based on a reductionist natural science approach (for example, Hellison, 1988; Kirk, 1989; Schempp, 1987; Siedentop, 1987, 1989; Sparkes, 1989, 1991, 1993, 2002). More recently, recognizing the growing influence of gender and cultural studies, as well as the contribution from post-structuralism and post-modernism, there has been an increased awareness and discussion of the ways culture, language, subjectivity, politics, ideology, power and narrative all permeate efforts to understand phenomena that elude traditional, analytical methods (for example, Bain, 1995; Faulkner & Finlay, 2002; Fernadez-Balboa, 1997; Kerry & Armour, 2000; Nilges, 2001; Sparkes, 1993, 1995, 2002; Wright, 2004). Complexity thinking offers a way to frame debates around research that embrace postmodern sensibilities whilst offering a sensitivity to educational phenomena that does not become fixed, anchored to a tradition nor blind to the unanticipated (Davis & Sumara, 2006). Complexity thinking accepts post-modern insights about the relational nature of knowledge, truth and identity. However, complexivists argue that such questions are not just a matter of human, intersubjective negotiation—they are also a function of the mutually affective relationships among all phenomena. Complexity thus opens onto the more-than-human world.

Curriculum

Debates around curriculum frequently centre on how changing social beliefs about what is important for the education of young people relate to the work of physical education teachers. Traditional, rationalist notions of curriculum view the relationship between policy and practice as hierarchical and emphasize linearity, control, learner passivity and knowledge transmission (Jess, Atencio, & Thorburn, 2011). In such a view, pedagogical practice becomes the practical articulation of policy and the agency of the teacher is constructed as either conforming or resisting policy (Ovens, 2010). However, such views do not adequately account for the globalization of knowledge and culture, the complexities of power, the influence of networked social relationships or the 'messy' nature of teaching as situated, cultural work. Complexity thinking draws attention to curriculum as a fluid, interactive and unpredictable process emerging within nested, open, interdependent complex systems (Hopper, 2010; Ovens, 2010). It characterizes curricula as nodes, hubs and links in decentralized networks of human-knowing rather than as essential or basic knowledge in discrete disciplines (Barab *et al.*, 1999; Davis & Sumara, 2006); it problematizes the relationship between policy and practice as complex and constantly in a state of flux. Complexity thinking mobilizes the need for sensibilities that foreground the way that key ideas are enabled and constrained by accountability structures interdependent with teachers' workspaces. Seen in the light of the dynamic, self-organizing and adaptive nature of interdependent systems, traditional notions become not only unrealistic but even stifling or suppressing as ways of understanding the changing nature and relevance of physical education as a subject area and set of practices within the contemporary schooling contexts of late modernity (Kirk, 2010; Penney & Chandler, 2000).

Learning

Concerns with the orthodoxy of behaviourist and cognitivist notions of learning have been regularly voiced within physical education literature. For example, Rovegno and Kirk (1995) suggested that there was a need to generate new ways to think about the learning process within their early critique of socially critical work in physical education. They suggested that there needed to be increased attention to how children learn, develop and experience physical education. Such calls are consistent with post-modern sensibilities that challenge dualist thinking and knowledge hierarchies that devalue the embodied forms of learning associated with physical education. Since their call, there has been an increased awareness of how learning is conceptualized and supported within physical education settings, with an interest in holistic, relational understandings of the learner engaged in activity in physical, social, cultural environments. However, as Light (2008) observes, while there has been an increased interest in constructivist theories of learning, little attention has been paid to the assumptions about learning and knowledge about learning inherent in such theories. He suggests that the value in complexity thinking is its ability to focus attention on the key assumptions and discourses clustered under the banner of contemporary theories of learning such as social learning, situated learning, dynamic systems, cultural discourse and ecology, to name but a few (Davis, Sumara, & Luce-Kapler, 2008; Rovegno & Kirk, 1995).

Teaching

Mirroring the constructivist shift in learning has been the increased interest in the teaching role and the ways that teachers should structure the lesson setting. For those working in the sport biosciences, concerns around lesson structure are linked to understanding human movement as a nonlinear dynamical system and the importance of manipulating lesson activities to facilitate the emergence of functional movement patterns and decision-making behaviours (Chow *et al.*, 2007; Davids, Button, & Bennett, 2008). For those working in the education field, concerns with lesson structure are linked to constructivist and situated-learning principles that promote the need for collaborative participation by students in learning communities capable of providing relevant, meaningful and conceptually 'rich' learning opportunities (Macdonald, 2004; Rovegno, 2006). Physical education scholars have taken up complexity thinking as a generative field for furthering such discussions, particularly those working in the area of Teaching Games for Understanding (for example, Butler & Griffin, 2010; Hopper, Butler, & Storey, 2009). More recently, Jess *et al.* (2011) have outlined how complexity thinking underpinned the use of constructivist and ecological models to inform curriculum development in Scottish physical education. They point out that this approach is underpinned by a belief that there is no one correct way to teach. However, they also point out that this belief does not mean that 'anything goes', suggesting that, instead, this implies a need for the teacher to draw on a broad range of pedagogical strategies. By being sensitive to the way learners learn in different ways and at different rates, behaviourist approaches are not rejected, but sometimes employed "as part of developing a richer and more extensive repertoire of pedagogical strategies" (Jess *et al.*, 2011, p. 195).

Embodiment

The body is central to the work of physical education, particularly as it is the object that needs to be physically educated. The evolution of post-enlightenment thought has also increased uncertainty around the nature of the body. Naturalistic perspectives conceptualize the body as a natural, biological entity, different in nature and subservient to the mind. The implication from this perspective is that learning is something only associated with the mind and involves a shift in mental state from one of ignorance to one of knowledge (Beckett & Morris, 2001). Those coming from a post-structuralist position have provided a strong critique of this position, preferring instead to promote the idea that the body is constructed within the languages used to describe it, as well as being shaped by the social practices and contexts in which it is situated (Giblett, 2008). According to this approach, the individual becomes embodied as discourses create particular subjectivities in relation to comportment, muscularity, shape and size (Azzarito & Solman, 2009). Phenomenologists provide yet another perspective and focus on the way that the body provides the basis of participating in and perceiving of the world. For them, the body is a thinking, feeling, moving body, which is not just an entity existing in the world, but is intentionally oriented to constructing the world in which it exists (Hass, 2008).

Complexity thinking has the potential to explore the tensions between the three perspectives in a generative, creative way. As Shilling (2004) notes, there is a need to consider "how the body is not only a physical location on which society inscribes its effects, but a material source of social categories and relations and a sensual means by which people are attached to or dislocated from social forms" (p. xvii). Complexity thinking resists the essentialism inherent in each perspective, replacing it instead with a transphenomenal sensibility that recognizes that the 'fleshiness' of the body is simultaneously resourced with a range of cognitive, affective and movement capabilities that generate both sensual and symbolic meanings as an acculturation process of living in, and inhabiting, the world. In a sense, the body is biologically enabled to connect with other bodies and the worlds they co-habit; it is sensitized for inter-connections and the interactions that arise from such connections.

Concluding thoughts

As many social commentators have highlighted, we are living in 'new times' that are characterized by profound social and cultural changes emerging from increasing globalized connectivity and the flow of information that such social networks allow. The view presented in this chapter is not that complexity thinking (nor science, nor theory) will provide access to more or better truths, but that it may be better suited to the demands of understanding and constructing educational practices within these rapidly changing, ever-more-complicated times. Complexity thinking provides a conceptual framework that has the potential to offer fresh insights into themes central to physical education and to extend the debates in new, generative ways. It addresses the concerns for a sociological perspective that views physical education phenomena as emerging from the networks of relationships that interconnect locally, nationally and globally, and in which physical educators are enmeshed (Green, 2002, 2006). It suggests a significant reworking of social ontology that, 'rejects scientific *objectivity*, relativist *subjectivity* and structuralist or post-structuralist *intersubjectivity*' suggesting instead that

> truth is more about interobjectivity…not about object, not just about the subject, and not just about social agreement. It is about holding all of these in dynamic, co-specifying, conversational relationships while locating these in a grander, more-than-human context…[where] a learner/knower (e.g., individual, social collective, or other complex unity) engages with some aspect of its world in an always-evolving, ever-elaborative structural dance.
>
> (Davis & Sumara, 2006, pp. 15–16)

The use of complexity thinking in physical education is still young and evolving. It is not without its critics, which provides a healthy and necessary constraint on its optimistic claims. However, in 'new times' the capacity to think complexly presents itself as a necessity, in both an analytical sense and political sense, as a practical guide to future action.

References

Alhadeff-Jones, M. (2008). Three generations of complexity theories: Nuances and ambiguities. In M. Mason (Ed.), *Complexity theory and the philosophy of education* (pp. 62–78). Chichester: Wiley-Blackwell.

Azzarito, L., & Solman, M. (2009). An investigation of students' embodied discourses in physical education: A gender project. *Journal of Teaching in Physical Education, 28*, 178–191.

Bain, L. (1995). Mindfulness and subjective knowledge. *Quest, 47*, 238–253.

Barab, S.A., Cherkes-Julkowski, M., Swenson, R., Garrett, S., Shaw, R.E., & Young, M. (1999). Principles of self-organization: Learning as participation in autocatakinetic systems. *Journal of the Learning Sciences, 8*(3–4), 349–390.

Beckett, D., & Morris, G. (2001). Ontological performance: Bodies, identities and learning. *Studies in the Education of Adults, 33*(1), 35–48.

Bernstein, B. (2000). *Pedagogy, symbolic control and identity: Theory, research, critique.* (Revised ed.). Oxford: Rowman & Littlefield.

Butler, J., & Griffin, L. (2010). *More teaching games for understanding: Moving globally.* Champaign, IL: Human Kinetics.

Byrne, D. (2005). Complexity, configurations and cases. *Theory, Culture & Society, 22*(5), 95–111.

Chow, J., Davids, K., Button, C., Shuttleworth, R., Renshaw, I., & Araújo, D. (2007). The role of nonlinear pedagogy in physical education. *Review of Educational Research, 77*(3), 251–278.

Cilliers, P. (1998). *Complexity and postmodernism: Understanding complex systems.* London: Routledge.

Cilliers, P. (2000). Rules and complex systems. *Emergence, 2*(3), 40–50.

Cilliers, P. (2005). Complexity, deconstruction and relativism. *Theory, Culture & Society*, 22(5), 255–267.

Davids, K., Button, C., & Bennett, S. (2008). *Dynamics of skill acquisition: A constraints-led approach*. Champaign, IL: Human Kinetics.

Davis, B. (2008). Complexity and education: Vital simultaneities. *Educational Philosophy and Theory*, 40(1), 46–61.

Davis, B., & Phelps, R. (2005). Exploring the common spaces of education and complexity: Transphenomenality, transdisciplinarity, and interdiscursivity. *Complicity: An International Journal of Complexity and Education*, 2(1), 1–4.

Davis, B., & Sumara, D. (1997). Cognition, complexity and teacher education. *Harvard Educational Review*, 67(1), 105–125.

Davis, B., & Sumara, D. (2006). *Complexity and education: Inquiries into learning, teaching, and research*. Mahwah, NJ: Lawrence Erlbaum Associates.

Davis, B., Sumara, D., & Luce-Kapler, R. (2008). *Engaging minds: Changing teaching in a complex world*. New York: Routledge.

Ennis, C.D. (1992). Reconceptualizing learning as a dynamical system. *Journal of Curriculum and Supervision*, 7(2), 115–130.

Faulkner, G., & Finlay, S. (2002). It's not what you say, it's the way you say it! Conversation analysis: A discursive methodology for sport, exercise and physical education. *Quest*, 54, 49–66.

Fernadez-Balboa, J.-M. (Ed.). (1997). *Critical postmodernism in human movement, physical education, and sport*. Albany: SUNY Press.

Gare, A. (2000). Systems theory and complexity. *Democracy and Nature*, 6, 327–339.

Giblett, R. (2008). *The body of nature and culture*. Basingstoke: Palgrave Macmillan.

Green, K. (2002). Physical education teachers in their figurations: A sociological analysis of everyday 'philosophies'. *Sport, Education and Society*, 7(1), 65–83.

Green, K. (2006). Physical education and figurational sociology: An appreciation of the work of Eric Dunning. *Sport in Society: Cultures, Commerce, Media, Politics*, 9(4), 650–664.

Hass, L. (2008). *Merleu-Ponty's philosophy*. Bloomington, IN: Indiana University Press.

Hellison, D. (1988). Our constructed reality: Some contributions of an alternative view. *Journal of Teaching in Physical Education*, 8, 123–130.

Hopper, T., Butler, J., & Storey, B. (2009). *TGfU…simply good pedagogy: Understanding a complex challenge*. Victoria: Physical and Health Education Canada.

Hopper, T. (2010). Complexity thinking and creative dance: Creating conditions for emergent learning in teacher education. *PHEnex*, 2(1), 1–20.

Jess, M., Atencio, M., & Thorburn, M. (2011). Complexity theory: Supporting curriculum and pedagogy developments in Scottish physical education. *Sport, Education and Society*, 16(2), 179–199.

Kerry, D., & Armour, K. (2000). Sport Sciences and the promise of phenomenology: Philosophy, method and insight. *Journal of Teaching in Physical Education*, 52, 1–17.

Kirk, D. (1989). The orthodoxy in RT-PE and the research/practice gap: A critique and alternative view. *Journal of Teaching in Physical Education*, 8, 123–130.

Kirk, D. (2010). *Physical education futures*. London: Routledge.

Kuhn, L. (2008). Complexity and educational research: A critical reflection. In M. Mason (Ed.), *Complexity theory and the philosophy of education*, 169–180. Chichester: Wiley-Blackwell.

Lawson. (1984). Problem setting for physical education and sport. *Quest*, 36, 46–60.

Light, R. (2008). Complex learning theory. Its epistemology and its assumptions about learning: Implications for Physical Education. *Journal of Teaching in Physical Education*, 27, 21–37.

Macdonald, D. (2004). Rich tasks, rich learning? Working with integration from a physical education perspective. In J. Wright, D. Macdonald, & L. Burrows (Eds.), *Critical inquiry and problem-solving in physical education* (pp. 120–132). London: Routledge.

Mason, M. (2008). What is complexity theory and what are its implications for educational change? *Educational Philosophy and Theory*, 40(1), 35–47.

Morrison, K. (2008). Educational philosophy and the challenge of complexity theory. In M. Mason (Ed.), *Complexity theory and the philosophy of education* (pp. 16–45). Chichester: Wiley-Blackwell.

Nilges, L. (2001). The twice told tale of Alice's physical life in wonderland: Writing qualitative research in the 21st century. *Quest*, 53, 231–259.

Osberg, D., Biesta, G., & Cilliers, P. (2008). From representation to emergence: Complexity's challenge to the epistemology of schooling. *Educational Philosophy & Theory*, 40(1), 213–227.

Ovens, A. (2010). The New Zealand curriculum: Emergent insights and complex renderings. *Asia-Pacific Journal of Health, Sport and Physical Education*, 1(1), 27–32.

Penney, D., & Chandler, T. (2000). Physical education: What future(s)? *Sport, Education and Society*, 5(1), 71–87.

Richardson, K., & Cilliers, P. (2001). What is complexity science? A view from different directions. *Emergence*, 3(1), 5–23.

Rovegno, I. (2006). Situated perspectives on learning. In D. Kirk, D. Macdonald, & M. O'Sullivan (Eds.), *The handbook of physical education* (pp. 262–274). London: Sage.

Rovegno, I., & Kirk, D. (1995). Articulations and silences in socially critical work on physical education: Towards a broader agenda. *Quest*, 47(4), 447–474.

Schempp, A. (1987). Research on teaching in physical education: Beyond the limits of natural science. *Journal of Teaching in Physical Education*, 6, 111–121.

Shilling, C. (2004). Educating bodies: Schooling and the constitution of society. In J. Evans, B. Davies, & J. Wright (Eds.), *Body knowledge and control: Studies in the sociology of physical education and health* (pp. xv–xxii). London: Routledge.

Siedentop, D. (1987). Dialogue or exorcism? A rejoinder to Schempp. *Journal of Teaching in Physical Education*, 6(4), 373–376.

Siedentop, D. (1989). Do the lockers really smell? *Research Quarterly for Exercise and Sport*, 60(1), 36–41.

Sparkes, A. (1989). Paradigmatic confusions and the evasion of critical issues in naturalistic research. *Journal of Teaching in Physical Education*, 8, 131–151.

Sparkes, A. (1991). Towards understanding, dialogue and polyvocality in the research community: Extending the boundaries of the paradigms debate. *Journal of Teaching in Physical Education*, 10(2), 103–133.

Sparkes, A. (1993). The paradigms debate: An extended review and celebration of difference. In A. Sparkes (Ed.), *Research in physical education and sport: Exploring alternative visions* (pp. 9–60). London: Falmer Press.

Sparkes, A. (1995). Writing people: Reflections on the dual crisis of representation and legitimation in qualitative inquiry. *Quest*, 47, 158–195.

Sparkes, A. (2002). *Telling tales in sport and physical activity: A qualitative journey*. Champaign, IL: Human Kinetics.

Stacey, R. (2001). *Complex responsive processes in organisations: Learning and knowledge creation*. London: Routledge.

Wright, J. (2004). Post-structural methodologies: The body, schooling and health. In J. Evans, B. Davies, & J. Wright (Eds.), *Body knowledge and control: Studies in the sociology of physical education and health* (pp. 19–31). London: Routledge.

2 The complexity of intervention

Implementing curricula in the authentic world of schools

Catherine Ennis

Scholars have been attempting to understand the complexity of education and physical education curricula within diverse school environments for many years (Cziko, 1989; Ennis, 1992; Swada & Caley, 1985). As our thinking has evolved from behavioural reductionist to constructivist dynamical, we have gained both clarity and cloudiness (Radford, 2008) in our view of school interactions. We have greater clarity and can attend with greater sensitivity to the social and cultural milieu that influences every aspect of curricular design and implementation (Doll, 2008). Nevertheless, these novel curricular approaches that conceptualize student learning and schools as self-organizing, interactive, open systems jolt our reality, clouding our ability to implement, observe and assess implementations of novel curricula (Mason, 2008; McMurtry, 2008). Complex complexity and supercomplexity (Barnett, 2004; Block & Estes, 2011) are apt terms to describe our evolving understandings of school phenomena. These theories hold great promise to reconceptualize our approaches to large-scale curricular interventions and our attempts to assess outcomes in a manner that is meaningful and that elaborates, rather than reduces, complexity.

Over the last decade, my colleague, Ang Chen, and I have been the designers and principal investigators of two large intervention studies. These projects have expanded our understanding of complex systems, while simultaneously testing our abilities to assess the impact of large-scale curricular implementation within authentic school and physical education environments. We attempt to achieve this process by targeting particular variables for assessment and by employing structural modeling techniques to better understand the multilayered complexity that exists in school–teacher–student interactions. We refine our lens at each level through the use of qualitative methods to better understand the interactive nature of the social milieu in which school-related systems are nested (Haggis, 2008; Horn, 2008).

Analysis of complex, open systems, such as schools, requires an equally complex, multi-layered and interactive research perspective. That said, both the limits of our ability to conceptualize and measure this complexity and the limits of our funding and personnel have necessarily meant that some aspects, influences and variables are identified, but unmeasured, while others admittedly are simply unrecognized. Because complexity theory has been defined and described in Chapter 1, I will focus this chapter on the post-hoc application of theory onto somewhat imperfect practice. I will describe, in part, the complex elementary school environments in which we have implemented physical education curriculum and the middle school environments where we currently are attempting to implement curricula. In the process I will discuss a few of the actions we have taken to interact with the complexity of these open systems and the successes and limitations of our efforts.

Negotiating multiple, complex, open-ended systems

Complexity is the most central and overarching characteristic of the urban and rural school districts in which we conduct our research. I have studied how curricula cascade through a web of complexity within school districts or local education associations (LEAs), never exiting, but continually changing and being changed as long as the elements remain in connection (Ennis, 1992, 2006). Designing large-scale curricular interventions to nest within these complex, open systems permits us to observe how a system is shaped and changed, while simultaneously shaping and changing, at least temporarily, some aspects of the physical education culture. Like adding a coloured dye to a water system, we track a few salient influences and watch as they run the course and dissipate within the system.

Curricular interventions can be both generative and responsive. They permit us to examine 'transphenomenal' interactions and synergies that occur uniquely at different levels of the organization (Davis, 2008; Davis & Phelps, 2005). Our interventions are also transdisciplinary, crossing two or more frames or bodies of knowledge and impacting both physical education and the partner discipline in ways that we hope will increase learning and add meaning and value to physical education (Ennis, 2010). Every stage and level of the research design, methodologies and conclusions involve complexity (Byrne, 2005), as we generate, respond and, when possible, observe a few key variables identified either by our funding agency, our discipline or our unique research focus as central to these stakeholders' diverse definitions of success. Thus, our research designs are multi-faceted and longitudinal and our interventions are detailed, multi-dimensional and redundant (Haggis, 2008).

In this section, I will describe a few of the contextual elements in two large-scale curricular intervention studies funded by the United States National Institutes of Health (NIH) over the last decade (Sun, Chen, Zhu, & Ennis, in press). The first intervention, *Science, PE, & Me!* was conducted from 2003 to 2008 and the second, *The Science of Healthful Living*, our current research initiative, has recently been funded for 2011–2016. I will begin this section with brief descriptions of the context, design and results from our completed research to design and implement the *Science, PE, & Me!* elementary curriculum (children aged 8–11). Then I will attempt to build on this description with an overview of our recently funded middle school curriculum (children aged 11–14) and implementation project, *The Science of Healthful Living*.

Science, PE, & Me!

In 2003, NIH provided five years of support (US$1.5 million) for our proposal to integrate a health-related science emphasis into elementary physical education.

The purpose of the research was to increase students' knowledge and interest in science and science careers. The research design was constructed in two phases. Phase I consisted of a randomized clinical trial (RCT) to design, implement and evaluate a science-based physical education curriculum, while the purpose of Phase II was to disseminate the evidence-based curriculum beyond the schools in the Phase I experimental condition. We conceptualized this study within a rich and long-established partnership with a large urban school district (enrolment = 139,000 students) including a high percentage (84%) of children of colour, primarily African American (77%). The school district represented a range of socio-economic families from predominately middle- to lower-class. Schools ranged from moderately well-performing to low-performing academically with teachers who spanned the continuum from highly-qualified to those not licensed to teach (~15%) in the subject matter to which they were assigned.

We arrived at a partnership agreement with the LEA after extensive negotiations and assistance from administrative and teacher advocates who understood the history, politics and economic realities of the system and helped us negotiate these complexities. Using stratification variables reflecting demographics (e.g., student enrolment demographics including poverty levels, performance on state-wide science tests, instructional time and facilities allocated to physical education, teacher qualifications), we first placed the 150 elementary schools in 15 strata, then randomly selected one school from each strata for the experimental condition and one for the comparison condition. We then worked school by school to engage the 30 selected elementary schools to work with us regardless of whether they were randomly assigned to the RCT experimental or the comparison conditions. We met frequently with each physical educator, encouraging each to embrace his or her assigned condition and work to complete implementation tasks. Comparison school teachers were asked to continue to teach physical education as they had the previous year and to give the fitness knowledge tests and surveys at approximately the same time as the experimental schools.

We could identify numerous attractors that appeared supportive of new curriculum (e.g., the new curriculum, obesity concerns, interdisciplinary focus) and numerous constraints to the implementation of new curriculum (e.g., LEA size, school academic performance, teacher prior knowledge and effectiveness) throughout the entry process. Certainly, the LEA was attracted to a physical activity curriculum that purported to be linked with science education, specifically the scientific inquiry process. Yet, the sheer size of the urban LEA, with five regional offices and the comparatively low student academic performance when compared with suburban LEAs, offered challenges to implementation. Additionally, physical educators expressed concerns both about learning to teach the new curriculum and turning the physical education experience into a science classroom. Likewise, elementary schools most in need of an enhanced physical education curriculum were also those whose students performed at the lowest levels on standardized tests (Ennis, 2006). Over the first years of the project we watched as the instructional time allocated to physical education was gradually diminished in some of these lowest academically-performing experimental and comparison schools. To marshal resources to address academic deficiencies, some principals required physical educators to cancel physical education lessons in order to tutor students in reading and mathematics and to proctor high-stakes standardized tests. These constraints mediated the curriculum attractor's opportunity to shape student learning and physical activity. Nevertheless, these factors occurred at approximately the same rate and in the same magnitude in both the experimental and comparison schools, lending both authenticity and complexity to the process.

Curricular intervention

The physical education curriculum, *Science, PE, & Me!*, represented a multi-dimensional, integrated curriculum with a focus on health-related science (Ennis & Lindsay, in press). The transdisciplinary nature of the curriculum embraced and elaborated some of the many natural connections between life-sciences (e.g., body systems, science as inquiry) and personal fitness-oriented approaches to physical education (see, for example, Kirk, Burgess-Limerick, Kiss, Lahey, & Penney, 2004). Master physical educators, working collaboratively with science educators on the Curriculum Writing Team (CWT), developed the constructivist curriculum, designed student reflective journal entries to match each lesson and wrote cognitive test items to assess each lesson. This unique process required CWT physical educators to consider science strategies such as the 5Es (Engagement, Exploration/Experiment, Explanation, Elaboration, Evaluation) learning cycle strategy used frequently in science education textbooks and lessons (Settlagh, 2000; Trowbridge, Bybee, & Powell, 2000). Similarly, CWT science educators enhanced their conceptualizations of physically active experiments to include student engagement in moderate to vigorous physical activity throughout each lesson as they examined the effects of exercise on their bodies. After discussions and negotiations, observed and facilitated by our project staff, CWT physical educators increasingly acknowledged the value of the internal 5E structure provided by the learning cycle strategy. CWT science educators listened to the CWT physical educators' activity examples, helping them transform their ideas into health-related fitness experiments in which students asked and answered questions, used exercise physiology/fitness concepts and terminology and personally tested the knowledge in student-centred approaches to fitness learning.

After much discussion, the Curriculum Writing Team members divided the *Science, PE, & Me!* curriculum into three: ten lesson units for third, fourth and fifth grade (30 unique lessons for each grade). They designed each unit to focus on one or two of the five fitness components: *Dr. Love's Healthy Heart* (cardiorespiratory) *Mickey's Mighty Muscles* (muscular strength and endurance) and *Flex Coolbody's Fitness Club* (flexibility and nutrition, in lieu of the traditional 'body composition' component). Curricular materials consisted of 90 detailed lessons in three units for three grades; student reflective science journals with reading and writing experiences to match each lesson; teacher resources including posters, charts, vocabulary and encyclopedia; and materials for a family night event in English and Spanish held annually at each school.

The *Science, PE, & Me!* curriculum had many stakeholders. For example, because the funding sponsor was science education, our project and curricular aims were articulated as increasing students' knowledge and interest in health-related science and science careers. Simultaneously, many physical educators also expect fitness curricula to provide a moderate to vigorous physical activity experience for the majority of each lesson, adding an additional criterion of curricular effectiveness and enhancing the complexity of the curriculum writing and implementing processes. The resulting *Science, PE, & Me!* curriculum met the United States National Science Education Standards (National Academy of Sciences, 1996) and the National Association for Sport and Physical Education's Physical Education Content Standards (NASPE, 2004).

Needless to say, *Science, PE, & Me!* looked and felt quite different from the traditional multi-activity, physical education sports-based curriculum (Ennis, 1999) that experimental condition teachers and students had experienced. Asking teachers to implement this curriculum required them to make an abrupt change in their teaching and programming and to teach physical education lessons that they had not developed. Philosophically and instructionally the changes tested their interest and resolve. Accompanying the intervention, experimental school teachers participated in 64 hours of training annually over the first three years of the project to help them understand the curriculum, enhance their student, time and equipment management, and learn to teach physical education within a constructivist teaching and learning format. They practised teaching the 5Es using think, pair, share and simultaneous response strategies, and employing student reading and writing within physically active lessons. This represented a major change for the experienced physical educators, stimulating them to adapt and adjust managerial, instructional and evaluative practices. However, for the 15% of teachers who had yet to earn teaching licenses, some of whom had not completed teacher preparation or had not been prepared to teach physical education, it constituted a new learning opportunity, in which they received formal instruction and follow-up classroom coaching to teach the constructivist physical education curriculum.

Curricular change is not trivial; encouraging statistically significant increases in student learning requires a multi-faceted approach. The pervasive attractor of the status quo, business-as-usual culture is not easily bifurcated. A bifurcation is a change in the structure of a system. Bifurcations can begin as small changes that can unpredictably lead to larger, more pronounced changes as the bifurcation cascades through the system (Ennis, 1992). It is impossible to predict when or how a physical education curriculum will bifurcate at the local school and LEA levels and the uncoordinated nature of this type of self-evolution may never occur. Although interventions do not represent naturally occurring bifurcations, they are buffeted and changed by some of the same factors that facilitate and constrain natural systemic changes. Our research imposed a large-scale, artificial change within a naturally occurring system. Our goal was both to affect changes in the form of enhanced student learning and to examine how the curriculum cascades through the system, shaping and being shaped by agents (e.g., students, teachers, principals) throughout the process.

Monitoring curricular adaptations

Curricularists *expect* curricula to change as they are operationalized. Although there is a minimal requirement of fidelity to the essence of the programme or lesson structure necessary to claim that a particular curriculum was implemented, we always expect many changes to the curriculum throughout the implementation process. One aspect of our research design, therefore, is implemented to identify, track and understand the reasons and nature of these curricular changes. In *Science, PE, & Me!* we expected both large and small changes to the curriculum and to the context at multiple levels. These included varying levels of principal and teacher support, teacher effectiveness, acceptance and adjustments, instructional venue opportunities and constraints, student acceptance and/or resistance, and parental and community support and influence, to name a few. These changes represent self-organizations within the system that impact the extent to which the curriculum functions as a positive attractor consistent with our knowledge, interest and physical activity goals.

At what point, however, do adaptations to the new curricular intervention bifurcate to the point that the stability of the curriculum is disrupted? While most adaptations represent minor changes that often enhance the impact of the curriculum in specific contexts or school environments, there are others that disrupt the process, often returning the system to its previous stability—in other words, returning to the traditional curriculum taught in basically the same manner with the same expectations. This occurs, for example, when a teacher rejects the new curriculum and is no longer willing to continue in the research project. It can also occur incrementally when a teacher feels overwhelmed by the enormity of the change, and implements only the easily managed aspects, while longing to return to the traditional curriculum. Likewise, some teachers do not accept or value the new curriculum, reject it, and return quickly to the previous programme because they are convinced it provided more valued experiences for their students. Certainly, in instances when a curricular intervention does not fulfill expectations, rejecting it to return to the former traditional curriculum is the best option. In these instances, the system returns to previous levels of stability. The intervening curricular attractors no longer draw the system toward the instability necessary to overcome the traditional status quo. Although we can observe and track a few of these internal adjustments in depth using qualitative designs, the sheer scale and complexity of the intervention in 15 schools suggests that other research designs such as randomized clinical trials can provide additional, more comprehensive opportunities to examine student knowledge and interest across multiple contexts.

Attributing system changes to the curricular intervention

Complex systems are multi-faceted with dynamic influences at work at different levels (school, class/teacher, student) and at different times within the instructional process. As the curricular intervention cascades through these levels, the extent to which it impacts student learning is modified, increasing or decreasing student learning, interest and physical activity. Attempting to track these individually would require many researchers, precise instruments and very large amounts of funding. The nature of these projects requires that we use resource-intensive research designs to identify and track the most influential variables. The RCT design permits researchers to monitor multiple factors to examine the extent to which student knowledge growth can be attributed to factors associated with the curriculum. For this reason, RCT is a particularly valuable tool to provide insight into complex system adaptation.

The RCT design for the *Science, PE, & Me!* project consisted of a two-part longitudinal design that permitted us to monitor changes in the system over the five-year funding period. During years 1–3 (Phase I), 6,000 students in 15 experimental schools were taught by 23 teachers using the *Science, PE, & Me!* curriculum while another 6,000 students in 15 schools served as the comparison condition. Student knowledge growth data were collected using pre- and post-tests developed and validated for each unit and grade. Multiple measures at the school, teacher and student levels were collected in experimental and comparison schools and entered into the regression and hierarchical models to examine the impact of the curriculum on each level of the school environment. Instruments were designed and validated to measure student knowledge growth, teacher curriculum ease of use and satisfaction with each curricular unit, the training and implementation process, and family members' interests and satisfaction with Family Activity Night events. During years 4–5 (Phase II) we used a quasi-experimental design to assess the effectiveness of three methods to disseminate the curriculum beyond the original 15 schools in the experimental condition.

Successes

The findings from the hierarchical linear design in Phase I indicated that each cohort of students increased their knowledge of fitness concepts as reflected by their scores on the knowledge tests (Sun *et al.*, in press). The cumulative effects of the curriculum were evident in the statistically significant increases in knowledge scores across unit and grade, and the statistically significant increases in students' interest in science and science careers. Students' ability to solve instructionally-related problems also improved as indicated by students' increased ability to respond to embedded problem-related items in their reflective journals (Zhang, Chen, Chen, & Ennis, 2011). Students' test scores in classes in which their teachers chose to use the reflective science journals to reinforce students' knowledge made statistically significant knowledge gains when compared to those where teachers chose not to use the journals (Zhu *et al.*, 2009; Zhu, Ennis, & Chen, 2011). In general, teachers found the curriculum easy to use and their ability to manage the lessons and the student reflective journals increased over the course of the study (Chen & Sun, 2008). Further, teachers reported in interviews and questionnaires that they were highly satisfied with the training and responded positively by continuing to use the curriculum after the initial Phase I data collection had ended. Thus, we were able to collect five years of data on student knowledge growth during the project.

Accelerometry data indicated that the *Science, PE, & Me!* lessons in the *Dr. Love's Healthy Heart* unit consistently encouraged students to exercise in the moderate, physically-active range with bursts of vigorous physical activity in most lessons (Chen, Martin, Sun, & Ennis, 2007). Further, the science emphasis and the reading and writing associated with the reflective journals did not reduce the amount or intensity of physical activity when compared with traditional physical education programmes in the comparison school condition. Families responded positively to the curriculum as indicated by both their frequent attendance at Family Science Activity Night events and their positive evaluations on satisfaction questionnaires completed at the conclusion of each Family Night event. Results suggested that the curriculum had met the knowledge, interest and activity aims, and was worthy of dissemination during Phase II.

In Phase II (years 4–5), the curriculum was disseminated in four conditions. These were (a) interested Phase I comparison condition schools in the same LEA, (b) other interested elementary schools in the LEA that did not participate in the Phase I research, (c) elementary schools nationally whose physical educators had initiated contact with the project by attending sessions at professional meetings introducing the curriculum, and (d) schools whose teachers had discovered the curriculum via the website. Results of the Phase II dissemination research indicated that students whose teachers initiated contact with the project increased their knowledge at a significantly higher rate than did those who had participated in the urban district. Thus, physical educators who sought the curriculum (conditions (c) & (d)) were able to foster greater knowledge gains in their students than did the teachers in the Phase I research conducted in urban schools. These student knowledge gains occurred without the extensive teacher professional development, consistent coaching or material resources provided to the teachers in the Phase I experimental schools.

The Science of Healthful Living

In the recently funded *Science of Healthful Living* intervention, we leveraged our experience in *Science, PE, & Me!* to compete successfully for a second, five-year grant (US$1.3 million) award. In this proposal we used the same aims and Phase I and II research designs to examine outcomes in a physical education curriculum for the middle school students aged 11–14. This randomized clinical trial will be conducted in 20 middle schools in four different school districts (LEAs). These school districts range in size from small city districts (student enrolment 2,500) to moderately large city/county districts (student enrolment 74,000). Student populations are less diverse (minority 44%) and all physical educators in the four school districts are certified to teach physical education.

Curricular intervention

Currently, the *Science of Healthful Living* curriculum, conceptualized in two 35 lesson modules, cardio-respiratory fitness and body stewardship, is being taught at sixth, seventh and eighth grades. As in *Science, PE, & Me!*, the curriculum was developed by a joint middle school science and physical education Curriculum Writing Team. The content was carefully sequenced to build cumulatively across modules and grades and consists of detailed lesson plans based on the 5E learning cycle strategy, teacher resources, validated online tests and questionnaires, student reflective journals and Family Science Activity Night events. Teachers are participating in a series of professional development workshops to increase their knowledge of the curriculum and their confidence in teaching the lessons within the 5Es, constructivist curricular format. The curriculum will be revised based on physical education teachers' and observers' comments during Phase I of the project. During Phase II (years 4–5) the *Science of Healthful Living* curriculum will be disseminated to (a) interested schools in the comparison condition, (b) other interested schools in the four partner school districts, (c) through teacher hands-on workshops at professional conventions and (d) via the project website. The effectiveness of the dissemination will be examined using a quasi-experimental design.

Purposefully destabilizing systems

Studying the effects of artificial bifurcations such as a curriculum on a complex system requires insight into the context and constraints inherent in the system. This is no easy task as there are always multiple factors that both constrain and stabilize system equilibrium. The size and dynamics of the system make it very difficult for agents inside and outside the system to destabilize the pervasive agents and attractors. Our attempts to destabilize physical education curricula are designed with the purpose of studying the impact of the curriculum as it cascades through the system. In the process we attempt to provide a rigorous, academically-oriented physical education programme with the explicit goal of enhancing students' knowledge of the positive effects of exercise on their bodies within a physically active curriculum (Ennis, 2007, 2010). We approach this challenge using three strategies that appear to temporarily destabilize the physical education system. Specifically, we attempt to (a) maximize the potential destabilizing agents to increase opportunities for change, (b) anticipate, identify and measure the diverse impacts that cascade through varying levels of the system and (c) acknowledge that most attempts developed to date are inadequate to cause permanent bifurcations, resulting in limited sustainability and an eventual return to the status quo.

Maximizing potential destabilizing agents

The complexity inherent in most large-scale systems similar to those that operate within LEAs in the United States involve influential historical, political and economic agents that stabilize the system. Most changes that do occur are regressive, further limiting the impact of physical education as a valued subject area in the academically-oriented school environment (Lounsbery, McKenzie, Trost, & Smith, 2011). Limited and gradually decreasing instructional time and decreases in resources allocated to physical education instruction, for example, have diminished the physical education impacts and lessened its perceived value to students, further diminishing opportunities for destabilization and reform.

To counter this trend, curricular interventions need to address the political, economic and instructional environments that pervade physical education. These stabilizers are powerful and all encompassing. Thus, curricular interventions must be dynamic and pervasive to initiate the destabilization process. For example, curricula need first to address key political touch points in the educational system. The heavy emphasis on high-stakes testing in the United States, for example, suggests that physical education curricula will command LEA administrator and principal attention when they provide evidence of a contribution to the academic mission of schools by increasing students' knowledge in a highly valued tested subject, such as science. Second, they must gain respect within physical education by addressing current standards and highly-valued outcomes, such as increasing physical activity. In other words, they must assist physical educators to effectively reach the goals to which they already aspire. Third, they must purposefully create a web of interconnections among curricular goals and participants (administrators, teachers and students), instructional materials and community stakeholders. By building interdependent and mutually-valued connections, the goals of educational and community stakeholders comingle and thus provide energy to destabilize the traditional multi-activity programmes and invite opportunities that frame possible alternatives.

Anticipating diverse impacts

Complexity theory alerts us to the unpredictable impacts of emerging and adapting systems. The advent of a new curriculum stabilizes and destabilizes multiple factors and agents as it cascades through dynamic, open-ended systems. The adaptations can be novel and unpredictable. Effective attempts to monitor and examine the emerging adaptations begin first with a broadly based monitoring system that scans sites for unpredicted impacts while simultaneously pinpointing particular locations where experience suggests that systems must destabilize (although we cannot predict when or how) for the bifurcation to continue. This involves a wide range of tools and measures both to look *broadly* at the system using comprehensive research designs and *deeply* into possible trigger points using labour-intensive interview and observation methodologies. Because we can never predict with assurance where, when and how the curriculum will evolve, the extensive monitoring system is necessary to alert researchers to bifurcations and unintended restabilizations, facilitating reallocation of research resources to monitor new developments.

These unintended changes can be both positive and negative (Lounsbery *et al.*, 2011). Already in the *Science of Healthful Living* implementation we have been notified by two previously committed teachers that they do not want to give up their current physical education programmes to implement the new student-centered approach because they are concerned that they will lose managerial control of their students. On the same day, an assistant superintendent emailed to say that her teachers were 'raving about the new curriculum' and were optimistic about student learning as a result of the new lessons. In different schools and LEAs we anticipate different constraints and different opportunities, although we cannot predict when, where or what factors will destabilize. Our monitoring system is alerted and we are reallocating resources to increase our understanding of the historical and political contexts that caused these opposite responses to the 'same' curriculum.

System agents will adapt and reorganize

Systems are pervasive and encompass extensive stabilizing agents that dwarf the effects of our best efforts to destabilize and sustain an adaptation. As the curriculum cascades through the various levels of schools and society, it encounters stabilizing agents in other systems that resist adaptations and attempt to return the system to a state of stability. The system may return to the previous status quo or restabilize at a new point that accepts some, but rarely all, of the innovations. This, too, is unpredictable. Our role is to build a dynamic, multi-faceted curricular intervention and provide individuals with the training, equipment and instructional materials that permit them to test the curriculum in their authentic environments. Most will be changed in some way, although the changes may not result in sustainability of the new curriculum (Osberg, Biesta, & Cilliers, 2008). Perhaps some teachers will gain new strategies and techniques associated with constructivist, student-centered teaching and learning, while others will develop a new sense of efficacy to embrace future curricular innovations (Light, 2008).

At the completion of the *Science, PE, & Me!* project, the retirement of our former school district advocate and the hiring of a new administrator led to the restabilization of the elementary curriculum around a behavioural physical activity curriculum. Although the administrator chose not to support the project, physical educators within the LEA continue to speak with pride about their opportunities to contribute to the academic mission of schools through the science-based integrative curriculum. Recently, I received a call that our administrative advocate in one of the *Science of Healthful Living* LEAs had just announced her retirement. Losing a champion of destabilization can be devastating unless a new champion can be found. The process of destabilization/stabilization continues each day with new challenges and opportunities as we monitor the impact of cascading events within our curricular interventions.

References

Barnett, R. (2004). The purposes of higher education and the changing face of academia. *London Review of Education, 2*(1), 61–73.

Block, B.A., & Estes, S. (2011). Supercomplexity in higher education kinesiology. *Quest, 63*(2), 179–196.

Byrne, D. (2005). Complexity, configurations, and cases. *Theory, Culture, & Society, 22*(5), 95–111.

Chen, A., Martin, R., Sun, H., & Ennis, C.D. (2007). Is in-class physical activity at risk in constructivist physical education? *Research Quarterly for Exercise and Sport, 78*(5), 500–509.

Chen, A., & Sun, H. (2008). *Descriptive lab report: Compilation of data from ease of use inventory.* Unpublished lab report from College Park: Curriculum & Instruction Laboratory, Department of Kinesiology, University of Maryland.

Cziko, G. (1989). Unpredictability and indeterminism in human behavior: Arguments and implications for educational research. *Educational Researcher*, 8(4), 18–19.

Davis, B. (2008). Complexity and education: Vital simultaneities. *Educational Philosophy and Theory*, 40(1), 46–61.

Davis, B., & Phelps, R. (2005). Exploring the common spaces of education and complexity: Transphenomenality, transdisciplinarity, and interdiscursivity. *Complexity: An International Journal of Complexity and Education*, 2(1), 1–4.

Doll, W.E. (2008). Complexity and the culture of curriculum. In M. Mason (Ed.), *Complexity theory and the philosophy of education* (pp. 181–203). West Sussex, UK: Wiley-Blackwell.

Ennis, C.D. (1992). Reconceptualizing learning as a dynamical system. *Journal of Curriculum and Supervision*, 7(2), 115–130.

Ennis, C.D. (1999). Creating a culturally relevant curriculum for disengaged girls. *Sport, Education, and Society*, 4(1), 31–49.

Ennis, C.D. (2006). Curriculum: Forming and reshaping the vision of physical education in a high need, low demand world of schools. *Quest*, 58(1), 41–59.

Ennis, C.D. (2007). Charles H. McCloy lecture: Curriculum research to increase student learning. *Research Quarterly for Exercise and Sport*, 78(1), 138–150.

Ennis, C.D. (2010). On their own: Preparing students for a lifetime. *Journal of Health, Physical Education, and Recreation*, 81(5), 17–22.

Ennis, C.D., & Lindsay, E.L. (in press). *Science, PE, & Me!: Science-based elementary curriculum for physical education.* Self-published.

Haggis, T. (2008). Knowledge must be contextual: Some possible implications of complexity and dynamic systems theories for educational research. In M. Mason (Ed.), *Complexity theory and the philosophy of education* (pp. 150–168). West Sussex, UK: Wiley-Blackwell.

Horn, J. (2008). Human research and complexity theory. In M. Mason (Ed.), *Complexity theory and the philosophy of education* (pp. 124–136). West Sussex, UK: Wiley-Blackwell.

Kirk, D., Burgess-Limerick, R., Kiss, M., Lahey, J., & Penney, D. (2004). *Senior physical education: An integrated approach* (2nd ed.). Champaign, IL: Human Kinetics.

Light, R. (2008). Complex learning theory—its epistemology and its assumptions about learning: Implications for physical education. *Journal of Teaching in Physical Education*, 27(1), 21–37.

Lounsbery, M., McKenzie, T.L., Trost, S. G., & Smith, N.J. (2011). Facilitators and barriers to adopting evidence-based physical education in elementary schools. *Journal of Physical Activity and Health*, 8(Suppl. 1), S17–S25.

Mason, M. (2008). What is complexity theory and what are its implications for educational change? *Educational Philosophy and Theory*, 40(1), 35–49.

McMurtry, A. (2008). Complexity theory 101 for educators: A fictional account of a graduate seminar. *McGill Journal of Education*, 43(3), 265–281.

National Academy of Sciences. (1996). *National science education standards.* Washington, DC: National Academies Press.

National Association for Sport and Physical Education. (2004). *Moving into the future: Standards for physical education* (2nd ed.). Reston, VA: NASPE.

Osberg, D., Biesta, G., & Cilliers, P. (2008). From representation to emergence: Complexity's challenge to the epistemology of schools. In M. Mason (Ed.), *Complexity theory and the philosophy of education* (pp. 204–217). West Sussex, UK: Wiley-Blackwell.

Radford, M. (2008). Complexity and truth in educational research. In M. Mason (Ed.), *Complexity theory and the philosophy of education* (pp. 137–149). West Sussex, UK: Wiley-Blackwell.

Settlagh, J. (2000). Understanding the learning cycle: Influences on abilities to embrace the approach by preservice elementary school teachers. *Science Education, 84*(1), 43–50.

Sun, H., Chen, A., Zhu, X., & Ennis, C.D. (in press). Curriculum matters: Learning science-based fitness knowledge in constructivist physical education. *The Elementary School Journal.*

Swada, D., & Caley, M. T. (1985). Dissipative structures: New metaphors for becoming in education. *Educational Researcher, 14*(3), 16–17.

Trowbridge, L.W., Bybee, R.W., & Powell, J. (2000). *Teaching secondary school science: Strategies for developing scientific literacy.* Columbus, OH: Merrill.

Zhang, T., Chen, S., Chen, A., & Ennis, C.D. (2011). *Constructing cardiovascular fitness knowledge in physical education.* Paper presented at 2011 American Educational Research Association Annual Meeting, New Orleans, LA.

Zhu, X., Chen, A., Ennis, C.D., Sun, H., Hopple, C.J., Bonello, M., Bae, M., & Kim, S. (2009). Student situational interest, cognitive engagement, and achievement in physical education. *Contemporary Educational Psychology, 34*(3), 221–229.

Zhu, X., Ennis, C.D., & Chen, A. (2011). Implementation challenges for a constructivist physical education curriculum. *Physical Education and Sport Pedagogy, 16*(1), 83–99.

3 Introducing conditions of complexity in the context of Scottish physical education

Mike Jess, Matthew Atencio and Nicola Carse

Primary physical education has recently been identified as a subject area with the potential to address growing concerns and associated initiatives linked with children's health and wellbeing, sport participation and physical activity levels (Petrie & Hunter, 2011). In Scotland, primary physical education has likewise been placed in a prominent position, structured within the new Curriculum for Excellence (CfE) guidelines aimed at enhancing and promoting children's and young people's health and wellbeing (Thorburn, Jess, & Atencio, 2011). Yet, evidence nationally and internationally suggests a significant variation in the quality of primary physical education, largely in relation to the prevailing use of the multi-activity 'block' curriculum model which provides abstracted elements of sport and physical activities to children in compartmentalized, unrelated and fragmented ways (Rainer, Cropley, Jarvis, & Griffiths, in press). Notably, criticism has been levelled at the ways in which this 'block' model has resulted in the perpetuation of developmentally inappropriate practices (Thorburn, Jess, & Atencio, 2009).

In response to the uneven quality of children's learning experiences within Scottish primary physical education, Jess, Atencio and Thorburn (2011) propose that complexity theory concepts have the potential to promote more developmentally-appropriate, reflective and participative pedagogies. They suggest that complexity concepts such as self-organization, uncertainty, diversity and 'edge of chaos' can underpin curricular practices in primary physical education that allow for children to learn in adaptive and creative ways. Davis and Sumara (2006) support this view that complexity is not simply an appropriate descriptor of postmodern educational conditions; they suggest that complexity-underpinned pedagogy provides a means of affirming and supporting learning experiences that are self-organized and adaptive. This chapter subsequently sets out to consider how one teacher in Scottish primary physical education engaged with complexity theory as part of his evolving professional learning trajectory. We suggest that his efforts were integrally supported by recent curricular policy and professional learning developments in Scotland.

Scottish education: an emerging context for complexity-oriented primary physical education

Scottish education has witnessed significant change in recent years with the introduction of a curricular model, CfE, that moves away from the 'traditional' subject-based curriculum and its associated narrow pedagogy (Bryce & Humes, 1999) to promote learning across the curriculum. Teachers in Scotland are being encouraged to engage with curriculum in innovative ways and to employ more constructivist learning approaches to become "the creative, adaptable professional who can enjoy developing the ideas that arise when children are immersed in their learning" (Scottish Executive, 2004a, p. 19). Within this context, primary physical education has emerged as a topic of particular interest following policy recommendations for two hours of curriculum physical education and continuous staff development for primary teachers (Scottish Executive, 2004b). Additionally, after many years within the expressive arts subject area (Scottish Office Education Department, 1992), primary physical education is now housed within the core curriculum area of health and wellbeing and aligns with new learning outcomes that present a wider vision of physical education linked to health, lifelong learning and sport agendas (Scottish Government, 2009). A national 'active schools' programme has also been introduced and offers children physical activity opportunities outside curriculum time and across the wider community. The aim of these integrated, multi-sector developments is to enhance the role of primary physical education across the education sector and in children's lives. This raised profile has also resulted in the provision of more in-depth physical education professional learning for generalist classroom teachers. For a long-marginalized subject, primary physical education is being offered the opportunity to re-conceptualize itself as a subject sensitive to contemporary educational thinking.

Within this context, the Developmental Physical Education Group (DPEG) at the University of Edinburgh has set out to create a revised conception of primary physical education through the introduction of curriculum, pedagogy and professional learning innovations informed by complexity concepts. The DPEG's initial curriculum attempts focused on Basic Moves for early years children aged 5–7 years (Jess, Dewar, & Fraser, 2004) and aimed to integrate children's core movement learning with the cognitive, social and emotional learning that underpins participation in most physical activities (Bailey et al., 2009). As such, Basic Moves progressed beyond the isolated learning of movement technique by incorporating aspects of adaptability and creativity which resulted in a more nonlinear and interactive constraints-led approach to learning (Chow et al., 2007). The DPEG has now extended its change agenda by creating curriculum experiences covering the 3–14 age range and expanding its theoretical basis to include thinking from ecological (Newell, 1986), dynamical systems (Thelen & Smith, 1994), social constructivist (Vygotsky, 1978), situated learning (Lave & Wenger, 1991) and complexity (Davis & Sumara, 2006) perspectives. Consequently, self-organizing emergence, ambiguous bounding, 'edge of chaos' and connectedness have all made a significant impact on the group's thinking about curriculum, pedagogy and professional learning in primary physical education (Atencio, Jess, & Dewar, 2012; Jess et al., 2011). This has resulted in the emergence of a connected 3–14 physical education curriculum structured around core learning, developmental applications and authentic applications (see Figure 3.1).

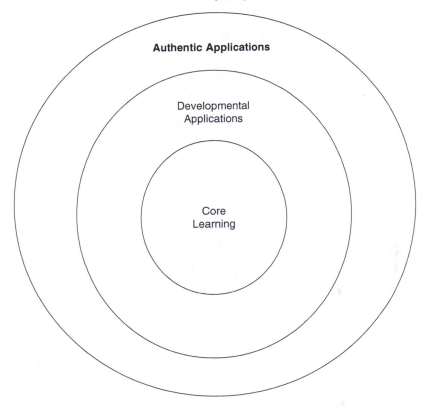

Figure 3.1 The core components of the DPEG's 3–14 physical education curriculum.

Core learning, emerging from Basic Moves, offers children holistic learning experiences focused on the knowledge, skills and understanding that support participation in different physical activities. Developmental applications have similarities with traditional multi-activity 'blocks' as they are taught for short periods of time and are based on activity contexts—for example, games. However, these applications are specifically designed to connect children's core learning with the more extended learning experiences in the authentic applications. Influenced by situated learning theory (Lave & Wenger, 1991), authentic applications take place over many weeks (e.g., a semester) and aspire to enhance children's core learning and developmental applications by contextualizing them across and beyond the school curriculum in situations that have similarities with 'real-life' scenarios (Kirk & Kinchin, 2003). Examples of authentic applications include sport education (Siedentop, 1994), outdoor journeys (Beames & Atencio, 2008) and dance education (Irvine, 2009). Consequently, the DPEG has been encouraging teachers to shift from a narrow 'pedagogy of certainty' to a more open 'pedagogy of emergence' (Jess *et al.*, 2011) that recognizes the importance of engaging children through collaborative learning, problem solving, peer teaching and independent working. This pedagogical shift coincides with the inter-disciplinary and constructivist learning focus of CfE in which teachers are given licence to be more flexible and offer authentic learning experiences (Thorburn *et al.*, 2009).

Theorizing primary physical education through complexity theory

As the DPEG became familiar with complexity theory, it recognized that complexity concepts could be used in line with the other theoretical perspectives influencing its work: social constructivism, situated learning, ecological theory and dynamical systems. A growing affinity with these theoretical perspectives has highlighted a shift in thinking, reflecting the notion that teachers should facilitate children's active exploration and self-organization through reflection, critical thinking and collaboration. This view holds that children's movement knowledge is co-constructed in unpredictable, multi-factored and nonlinear ways. As such, the DPEG is now working to create curriculum, pedagogy and professional learning experiences that are informed by complexity-oriented concepts, namely: self-organizing emergence, ambiguous bounding, 'edge of chaos' and connectedness (Jess & Atencio, 2011). These concepts have informed the DPEG's revised version of primary physical education as follows.

Self-organizing emergence

Complexity theory suggests that humans are self-organizers whose different characteristics (psychomotor, cognitive, social and emotional) interact internally within their own structure and also externally with factors in the environment (Prigogine, 1976). As such, humans are not pre-programmed systems whose parts interact to produce certain outcomes but are instead self-organizers whose multiple interactions result in unpredictable and emergent outcomes that help them adapt and develop in response to ever-changing environmental demands (Morrison, 2003). From a primary physical education perspective, this key complexity concept highlights how children need to develop the self-organizing skills to help them become technically proficient, adaptable and creative movers who can engage with the many different physical activities requiring different and unexpected responses (Jess *et al.*, 2011). Without these self-organizing skills, it is likely that children will lack the adaptability and creativity needed to respond to the many complex situations they meet in physical education contexts.

Ambiguous bounding

This self-organizing process takes place in contexts that have ever-changing and ambiguous boundaries. Consequently, self-organization does not occur in an 'anything goes' manner but is constrained and bound by numerous internal and external factors (Biesta, 2010). Viewing primary physical education from this perspective reveals a more structured phenomenon than may originally be assumed as the notion of ambiguous bounding can be witnessed in many ways. National guidance, school facilities, equipment, children's ages, the amount of curriculum time and the nature of physical education activities create some of the different boundaries influencing children's learning experiences. More specifically, teachers (and children) regularly modify physical education learning experiences by reducing or extending the complexity of tasks being attempted. For example, limiting the possible responses (e.g., throwing in one specific way) reduces the complexity of the task by setting very narrow boundaries. Alternatively, a throwing task with a wide range of possible outcomes will extend the task complexity and offer children opportunities to be adaptable or creative. Consequently, helping children develop technical efficiency, adaptability and creativity in their movement responses requires teachers to constantly be modifying the boundaries of learning tasks.

'Edge of chaos'

Within these different task boundaries children respond in one of three ways. One response is far beyond the boundaries of the task and immediately results in a clear mistake (e.g., in primary physical education, not watching a ball when trying to catch). Conversely, another response may be well within the task boundaries (e.g., repeating the same simple response to a throwing task which offers many possible outcomes). While this simple response may be the safe option and will consolidate this throwing action, it is also likely to lead to limited adaptability or creativity. Between these two responses, the other response can be close to, or near, the task boundary. This may involve the child focusing on the specifications of a narrowly defined movement task or attempting many different responses to a more open-ended task. In both cases, working close to the different task boundaries is working at the "edge of chaos" and results in children being "constantly poised between order and disorder [and] exhibiting the most prolific, complex and continuous change" (Brown & Eisenhard, 1997, p. 29). The more the child moves towards the "edge of chaos", the more likely it is that they will be "creative, open-ended, imaginative" and "demonstrate rich behaviours, ideas and practices" (Morrison, 2003, p. 286). Educationally, this 'edge of chaos' concept arguably challenges existing notions of linear learning curves.

Connectedness

Connectedness is at the heart of self-organizing learning because "new properties and behaviours emerge not only from the elements that constitute a system, but from the myriad connections among them" (Mason, 2008, p. 48). In primary physical education, as discussed earlier, the fragmented traditional 'block' curriculum (Rainer *et al.*, in press) highlights the need for more connected learning experiences that help children and teachers consider physical education as a 'joined-up' experience that integrates across education and lives. Core learning, therefore, not only helps children connect different aspects of their physical education experiences across and beyond the curriculum as a 'lifewide' endeavour (West, 2004), it also engages them in collaborative learning experiences that offer the opportunity to create new knowledge, vision and collective mastery. Connectedness is further developed by the notion of nestedness which, like a Russian doll, highlights how complex systems are "simultaneously a unity, a collection of unities and a component of a greater unity" (Davis & Sumara, 2001, p. 85). Complex systems, therefore, function at many different levels, as smaller, complex systems merge to create larger and more complex systems. The effectiveness of this nesting process is based on the degree of connectedness and communication within and between the different levels of the system. In the educational context, effective nestedness is evident when children, teachers and classes not only interact internally within a school setting but also indirectly with the local, national and global contexts.

In an effort to apply and better understand these complexity concepts, the DPEG now encourages teachers to rethink their physical education practices by exploring the ambiguous nature of task boundaries, helping children self-organize towards and beyond the 'edge of chaos' and seeking out connections within physical education and across and beyond the school curriculum. Consequently, this chapter now describes how these complexity concepts are beginning to influence the pedagogies of class-room teachers in Scotland. In particular, it discusses how one primary teacher, work-ing in a supportive local and national context, has employed notions of self-organizing emergence, ambiguous bounding, 'edge of chaos' and connectedness to change his practice.

The teacher: 'Max'

'Max' is a generalist primary teacher who completed the PgCert in 3–14 physical education[1] in 2008 and subsequently became the physical education specialist teacher in the school in which he had been working for seven years—an urban school with a roll of approximately 400 children. The data discussed below is from Max's participation in a SPPEP-funded PhD study. In the study, Max was one of five primary teachers tracked across an academic year to ascertain how the PgCert had influenced their physical education practice. An interpretive and qualitative approach was adopted; data were collected via semi-structured interviews and unstructured conversations focused on planning and classroom observations. The triangulation of these methods contributed to the validity of the data as it was possible to marry up what the teachers were saying with what they were doing in practice. The data were subsequently analysed in a grounded manner to identify emergent themes and in a top-down theoretical way to identify themes relating to educational change and complexity literature.

A disconnected starting point

A recurring theme for many teachers enrolled in the PgCert is an acknowledge-ment that, prior to their engagement with the programme, they taught physical education through a disconnected 'block' curriculum (Elliott, Atencio, Campbell, & Jess, in press). The following quotes from Max reflect this view:

> She [the PE specialist] did sort of discrete blocks of things .... gymnastics, Scottish country dance, rugby, hockey. I mean very traditional sort of team games.

> If you've got lots of other things to do in your day and somebody's giving you the answer, and if you've seen it working to some extent, and if you've seen the kids developing and progressing, and if there's a structure in place ... it seemed to make sense and seemed to work. I mean there's no way I'd teach like that now looking back after the 3–14 course, you know.

With a 'sporty' background, Max happily followed the physical education specialist because she taught physical education the way he had been taught at school. He consequently commented, "why would I question it?" and it was not until the PgCert that he began to confront his perceptions of physical education and probe his practice. The commentary above suggests that teachers like Max need to reflect upon how they reproduce socialized practices related to their life experiences (Elliott *et al.*, in press), as they reinforce prevailing practices. At the same time, these comments also illustrate the need for teachers to take up a lifelong learner identity, reflecting involvement in sustained and critical professional learning activities that engage with contemporary policy agendas (Atencio, Jess, & Dewar, 2012).

Beginning a complexity-informed professional learning journey

When Max started the PgCert, the DPEG was in the early stages of applying complexity thinking to its curriculum and pedagogy developments. Students read about complexity theory and, in discussions and assignments, attempted to connect this with their practice and national guidance. Max noted how complexity theory, and specifically notions of 'chaos', began to influence his practice:

> I think [the DPEG] was just starting to talk about chaos theory and complexity theory and things towards the end of the course but, for a long time, I've thought of my lessons as being loosely organised chaos which is a term I shouldn't use cause it shouldn't be, but it is. And I think it's this thing of not being too safe and trying new things and trying change and making mistakes and learning from them.

In line with complexity thinking, the PgCert aimed to help teachers develop more open-ended pedagogical practices rather than using direct, outcome-based teaching styles. In the next quote, Max describes how the course was underpinned by complexity theory:

> It's completely open to interpretation, the whole course is ... I really, really enjoyed it because it was a bit shocking and ... chaos theory and it's like [they

say] "well, we're purposefully not going to tell you how to do this stuff, we're just going to tell you kind of why you should be doing it" and "the pedagogy should be like this and shouldn't be so direct."

Max positively identified with the notion of 'chaos', which he felt characterized his ongoing professional learning and the more creative pedagogies he enacted in the classroom. Max later described how he embraced the notion of 'edge of chaos' by innovating and trying new approaches:

> You don't know if you don't try it and I think this year my teaching has been more 'edge of chaos' cause I felt I'd got a bit safe last year. And this year I've tried lots of new things, I've been on lots of CPD and I've tried to do things a bit differently.

The PgCert views teachers as individuals who self-organize and adapt to curriculum guidelines. As Max reflected, "The course was great but I think it kind of dumps you in your job and that's fine. I'm a grown up person, I can fend for myself." Teachers in the course are not provided with prescriptive lesson plans but are encouraged to adapt their knowledge and skills in response to the ever-changing demands of their school environment (Morrison, 2003). Consequently, Max began to modify his physical education lessons in line with the DPEG's ideas of core learning and authentic applications. Bullough (2011) suggests that teacher agency and resilience are vital, involving reflective professional learning as well as enhanced opportunities to control and shape one's own teaching approach despite challenging circum-stances. Max's teaching arguably reflected a high degree of teacher agency, as well as resilience, as he negotiated and instigated curricular change.

Exploring complex pedagogy: self-organizing emergence, connectedness, ambiguous bounding and 'edge of chaos' experiences

Max introduced Basic Moves with younger children before attempting to extend core learning into the upper primary years. His concern, however, was that, while Basic Moves enabled exploration of generic movement patterns, when the children entered Primary 4 (age 8), they were met with the multi-activity 'block' curriculum.

> The PE curriculum that was here beforehand, which I thought was really good … had lots and lots of different things and I kind of tried to force it into six blocks and units so there was an invasion game and a net game and some athletics and some dance—there was six different areas. And over the last year I realised that this didn't really seem to fit with me and this jarred. I'd got all this continuity in the wee [early] years [with Basic Moves] where they were building up and things were rolling and constantly developing and building. And it came to Primary 4 and I would stop that and I would just have these disparate blocks again.

Max went on to describe flaws with the 'block' model pertaining to the lack of coherence and continuity in the children's learning experiences

> having a ball in their hand and being cooperative and competitive in a teaching games for understanding way and then not putting a ball in their hand for two, three, four months of the winter term makes absolutely no sense. And you wouldn't do it in any other part of the school; you wouldn't teach Maths like that or language like that and yet this is kind of what I've been doing in PE.

Max began to experiment with lessons in line with notions of connectedness, ambiguously bounded tasks, 'edge of chaos' and self-emergence. Extending the Basic Moves format, he created lessons focused on core learning experiences for older children. After much experimentation, these core lessons were developed to connect with the discrete application sessions. However, to engage the older children, Max also needed to be creative in how he structured and delivered the core lessons. As such, the core tasks that Max designed not only challenged the physical capabilities of the children but also addressed the social, emotional and cognitive domains:

> [I introduced] this rolling effect in the upper years to try to keep things [developing] so that I dance at the beginning of a net games lesson. I think that's the right idea, and that we can have running and net games as part of a lesson together … And again it was lots of this ['edge of chaos'] cause I tried lots of things and it was horrendous and lots of things didn't work and I haven't got it right now but I think the kids are more [engaged]. Also the kids are not used to this type of lesson. They are used to coming in and having whole class lessons doing 'fitba' or 'baskitba' or 'dance' and I think to get their mindset around the fact that they've got to throw a ball in a team over there and then come and be creative on their own over here and then work cooperatively with somebody over here and then go and be competitive and to use all of this in the space of an hour or whatever, I think they found this quite difficult as well but I think it's the right way.

As just noted, Max adapted his teaching in a way that reflected the 'edge of chaos'; his experimentation encouraged the children to negotiate diverse activities as well as different learning outcomes. In relation to positioning both him and the children at the 'edge of chaos', Max further noted how he struggled and made mistakes, and that the children sometimes failed to negotiate this type of learning context successfully. Despite these initial difficulties, Max regularly created 'edge of chaos' experiences that were bounded in different ways to encourage children's self-organization of their own learning. This ambiguous bounding of tasks is reflected in the following quote describing how Max introduced Basic Moves to the younger children:

the pedagogy to be able to teach that [Basic Moves] is again a bit like this ['edge of chaos'] because it's throwing yourself into chaos. I know the first time … the pedagogy of just putting out some stuff and telling the kids how to be safe on it and then teaching them that there is no starting point and finishing point and just go, is, pedagogy-wise, a bit nerve wracking. And it's more about the learning than the teaching I guess in that way. And again the first time I gave 30 kids some shuttle cocks and told them to throw them in a gym hall into a space and not to stand on lines and throw them but just to throw with them. I think just these first few steps pedagogy wise about not controlling the space but giving it over to the kids and the amount that they can learn and it all makes sense to me now you know.

As Max became more comfortable with complex pedagogy, he further experimented with the bounding of tasks within his upper primary core lessons by encouraging the children to explore and take control of their own learning. The following example is the second in a sequence of core lessons observed by one of the authors over three consecutive weeks with a Primary 7 class (age 11). The lesson highlights how Max was beginning to employ complexity concepts in his practice (see Figure 3.2). The core lessons observed were connected to a series of basketball lessons being taught by the children's generalist class teacher at another time in the week. Collaborating with the class teacher, Max incorporated basketball themes into his core lessons by organizing the gymnasium into different, but conceptually-connected, stations at which the children worked in small groups before moving around each station. A key rationale for structuring core lessons

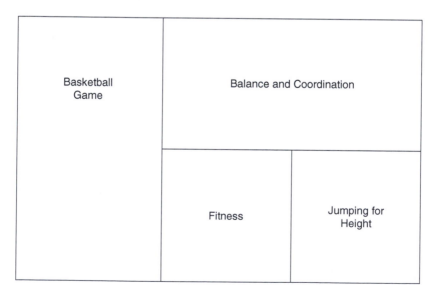

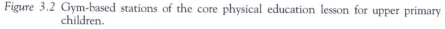

Figure 3.2 Gym-based stations of the core physical education lesson for upper primary children.

with stations around the gym was to help the children experience the connections between different physical education activities so that the children would come to view physical education as a 'joined-up' experience. Max hoped this approach would also encourage the children to understand the cross-curricular nature of learning across all subject areas, including physical education.

Connecting to the other weekly physical education lesson, the basketball station provided an opportunity to apply physical education skills and knowledge in a game situation. In response to the previous week's lesson, when the children did not pass the ball to each other during games, Max set boundaries to encourage collaboration by introducing a conditioned rule that meant the team in possession must make five passes before shooting. He also sought to enhance the children's self-organizing capacities by getting them to work independently by taking on the refereeing duties.

Further, the fitness, jumping and balance and coordination stations were all connected to the basketball theme. At the fitness station the children worked independently in pairs to support and encourage each other. Max had created differentiated fitness cards for tasks such as skipping and speed bounce and the children were expected to choose the tasks that most challenged them. Some children responded positively to working independently, while others found it difficult to remain focused. At the jumping station, Max again bounded the tasks by asking the children to jump for height and, linked to the basketball theme, recreate a tip-off. The group needed to cooperate at this station by taking turns jumping for the ball. This station offered an opportunity to practise jumping for height within an 'authentic' basketball context. As Max pointed out later, the children generally just wanted to play the game; as such, the bounding of this task appealed to their need for exploratory play, whilst offering an opportunity to practise in an 'authentic' context. As suggested by Hopper, Butler and Storey (2009), teaching in this emergent way reflects giving up both 'control' and 'predictability':

> Giving up control of scripted lessons with predictable outcomes takes a belief in learning that moves away from mechanistic and simplistic notions of telling, showing or programming the learner. The shift requires acceptance that learning is nonlinear, subject to individualized constraints, contextualized both physically and socially, and susceptible, but not dependant on teacher or coach guidance.
>
> (p. v)

At these stations, Max bounded the learning experiences by mixing technical movement tasks with more adaptable and creative tasks. By providing conditions whereby the children had enhanced opportunities to make decisions and determine their own actions, Max arguably pushed the children towards the 'edge of chaos' and encouraged them to self-organize in diverse ways.

Max also introduced a balance and coordination station which offered children the opportunity to use apparatus they had only used in discrete gymnastics lessons. Thus, he attempted to link core balance and coordination concepts to other physical education activities. Max based himself at this station to undertake more intensive teaching with individual children. A variety of large apparatus was available and the children were asked to balance on different pieces for an extended period of time. This task emerged from the previous week's core lesson where the children had tried to link rolls and balances and Max had noticed some children lacking control in their balances. Max narrowed the task complexity by preparing balance cards and asking the children to focus solely on controlling their bodies in a balance. Max observed and supported all the children as they looked at the cards, thought about their balances and decided what apparatus they would use. Max then encouraged the children to reflect by initiating discussion during each station rotation. He asked questions about what they were doing at the stations, invited them to share their thoughts on the stations and also asked them to demonstrate what they had been doing. In this one-hour core lesson, Max manipulated the environment to provide a variety of contexts and experiences which enabled the children to self-organize their learning experiences, to apply their knowledge and skills, to reflect on the connections between the different stations and to construct new knowledge and learned skills.

Complex pedagogy and decentralized control

A key feature of Max's core lessons was the observation that the children were being provided with the space to take a self-organizing role in their learning. As noted by Hopper *et al.* (2009), teaching physical education in a way that privileges children's self-organization "is a challenge that requires the teacher or coach to give-up direct control of the learning process. The teacher or coach has to create spaces that shape learning, but that also allow players to actively struggle, ultimately leading to new insights" (p. v). Max's teaching reflected 'decentralized control' (Davis & Sumara, 2006) whereby he focused on facilitating the children's self-emergent learning, rather than delivering predetermined content in a linear, top-down manner. For example, the self-refereeing task at the basketball station highlighted this decentralized control by putting the children in positions of authority. Mason (2008) suggests that this decentralized control is reflected in classroom environments that emphasize distribution of control, so that pupils can engage with interpretive and conceptual possibilities through their own multiple interactions. Haggis (2008) reiterates that decentralized control does not imply 'anything goes', as initial constraints, such as those set up by Max, as well as external influences such as curricular policy and social discourses, still influence the nature of the learning process.

Discussion

Taken together, Max's teaching practices illustrate how complexity concepts were introduced and developed to reorient his teaching practices. Based on his professional learning experiences, Max recognized the self-organizing, nonlinear and emergent nature of the learning process and made efforts to adapt and connect the children's experiences accordingly. His core lessons set ambiguously-bounded tasks by offering children the opportunity to explore the holistic aspects of their learning. His core lessons had a clear purpose in helping the children connect different physical education activities and engage with learning core skills in applied contexts. Rather than teaching in a direct manner, Max took up a more decentralized stance and became the facilitator; he supported the children's ownership of their learning while responding to their learning needs by correspondingly modifying learning tasks. In the context of creative dance, Hopper (2010) suggests that a class of children learning to dance can be viewed as a complex learning system comprised of individual students. Within this complex system individual children react and adapt to the environment and to each other, self-organizing to collectively and individually learn to dance. Similarly, the children Max worked with appeared to operate as a complex system within a core physical education lesson—a lesson that involved individual and collective self-organization as specific tasks were introduced within an integrated environment.

Conclusion

With the PgCert as the catalyst, this chapter has highlighted how the DPEG has reoriented its vision of primary physical education in line with complexity concepts. It has discussed how, in Scotland, a supportive policy context has resulted in increased curriculum time and professional learning to help generalist class teachers create innovative approaches to primary physical education. By considering Max's transition from the traditional 'block' approach towards complexity-informed practices, the chapter demonstrates the self-organizing, nonlinear and emergent nature of children's learning in physical education. In addition, it highlights how Max had the theoretical knowledge and desire to experiment with core learning ideas to create connected and ambiguously-bounded learning experiences that regularly took the children (and himself) towards and beyond the 'edge of chaos'. As such, the evidence presented suggests that complexity concepts have much to offer future developments in primary physical education in terms of curriculum and pedagogical innovation as well as teacher agency.

Note

1 The PgCert in 3–14 physical education is a two-year part-time masters-level programme. It is part of the Scottish Primary Physical Education Project (SPPEP): a government-supported project focused on creating a national primary physical education professional learning pathway.

References

Atencio, M., Jess, M., & Dewar, K. (2012). 'It is a case of changing your thought processes, the way you actually teach': Implementing a complex professional learning agenda in Scottish physical education. *Physical Education & Sport Pedagogy, 17*(2), 127–144.

Bailey, R.P., Armour, K., Kirk, D., Jess, M., Pickup, I., & Sandford, R. (2009). The educational benefits claimed for physical education and school sport: An academic review. *Research Papers in Education, 24*(1), 1–27.

Beames, S., & Atencio, M. (2008). Building social capital through outdoor education. *Journal of Adventure Education and Outdoor Learning, 8,* 99–112.

Biesta, G. (2010). Five theses on complexity reduction and its politics. In D. Osberg & G. Biesta (Eds.), *Complexity theory and the politics of education* (pp. 5–14). Rotterdam: Sense.

Brown, S., & Eisenhard, K. (1997). The art of continuous change: Linking complexity theory and time-paced evolution in relentlessly shifting organisations. *Administrative Science Quarterly, 42,* 1–34.

Bryce, T.G., & Humes, W.M. (1999). *Scottish education.* Edinburgh: Edinburgh University Press.

Bulloughs, Jr., R.V. (2011). Hope, happiness, teaching and learning. In C. Day & J.C.K. Lee (Eds.), *New understandings of teachers' work: Emotions and educational change* (pp. 15–30). London: Springer.

Chow, J.Y., Davids, K., Button, C., Shuttleworth, R., Renshaw, I., & Araújo, D. (2007). The role of nonlinear pedagogy in physical education. *Review of Educational Research, 77*(3), 251–278.

Davis, B., & Sumara, D. (2001). Learning communities: Understanding the workplace as a complex system. *New Directions for Adult and Continuing Education, 92,* 85–95.

Davis, B., & Sumara, D. (2006). *Complexity and education: Inquiries into learning, teaching, and research.* London, UK: Lawrence Erlbaum Associates Publishers.

Elliott, D., Atencio, M., Campbell, T., & Jess, M. (in press). From PE experiences to PE teaching practices? Insights from Scottish primary teachers' experiences of PE, teacher education and professional development. *Sport, Education and Society.* Available iFirst.

Haggis, T. (2008). 'Knowledge must be contextual': Some possible implications of complexity and dynamic systems theories for educational research. In M. Mason (Ed.), *Complexity theory and the philosophy of education* (pp. 150–168). Chichester, UK: Wiley-Blackwell.

Hopper, T. (2010). Complexity thinking and creative dance: Creating conditions for emergent learning in teacher education. *PHEnex, 2*(1), 1–20.

Hopper, T., Butler, J., & Storey, B. (2009). *TGfU … simply good pedagogy: Understanding a complex challenge.* Canada: PHE.

Irvine, W. (2009). *Dance education.* Paper presented at the 3–14 PE Tutor Training Course at the University of Edinburgh, UK.

Jess, M., & Atencio, M. (2011). *Employing a complex ecological approach to inform curriculum innovation efforts in Scottish physical education.* Paper presented at the AIESEP Conference, Limerick, Ireland.

Jess, M., Atencio, M., & Thorburn, M. (2011). Complexity theory: Supporting curriculum and pedagogy developments in Scottish physical education. *Sport Education and Society, 16*(1), 179–199.

Jess, M., Dewar, K., & Fraser, G. (2004). Basic Moves: Developing a foundation for lifelong physical activity. *British Journal of Teaching in Physical Education, 35*(2), 23–27.

Kirk, D., & Kinchin, G. (2003). Situated learning as a theoretical framework for sport education. *European Physical Education Review, 9*(3), 221–236.

Lave, J., & Wenger, E. (1991). *Situated learning: Legitimate peripheral participation.* London: Cambridge University Press.

Mason, M. (2008). Complexity theory and the philosophy of education. In M. Mason (Ed.), *Complexity theory and the philosophy of education* (pp. 1–15). Chichester, UK: Wiley-Blackwell.

Morrison, K. (2003). Complexity theory and curriculum reforms in Hong Kong. *Pedagogy, Culture and Society, 11*(2), 279–302.

Newell, K. (1986). Constraints on the development of coordination. In M. Wade & H.T.A. Whiting (Eds.), *Motor development in children: Aspects of coordination and control* (pp. 295–317). Amsterdam: Elsevier Science.

Petrie, K., & Hunter, L. (2011). Primary teachers, policy, and physical education. *European Physical Education Review, 17*(3), 325–339.

Prigogine, I. (1976). Order through fluctuations: Self organization and social system. In E. Jantsch & C. Waddington (Eds.), *Evolution and consciousness: Human systems in transition* (pp. 93–133). Reading, MA: Addison-Wesley.

Rainer, P., Cropley, B., Jarvis, S., & Griffiths, R. (in press). From policy to practice: The challenges of providing high quality physical education and school sport faced by head teachers within primary schools. *Physical Education & Sport Pedagogy.* Available iFirst.

Scottish Executive. (2004a). *A Curriculum for Excellence. The curriculum review group.* Edinburgh: The Scottish Executive.

Scottish Executive. (2004b). *The report of the review group on physical education.* Edinburgh: HMSO.

Scottish Government. (2009). *Curriculum for Excellence: Experiences and outcomes.* Retrieved June 2, 2011 from http://www.ltscotland.org.uk/curriculumforexcellence/experiences andoutcomes/index.asp.

Scottish Office Education Department (SOED). (1992). *Expressive arts curriculum and assessment in Scotland: National guidelines.* Edinburgh: SOED.

Siedentop, D. (1994). The sport education model. In D. Siedentop (Ed.), *Sport education: Quality PE through positive sport experiences* (pp. 3–16). Champaign, IL: Human Kinetics.

Thelen, E., & Smith, L. (1994). *A dynamic systems approach to the development of cognition and action.* Cambridge, MA: MIT Press.

Thorburn, M., Jess, M., & Atencio, M. (2009). Connecting policy aspirations with principled progress? An analysis of current physical education challenges in Scotland. *Irish Educational Studies, 28*(2), 207–221.

Thorburn, M., Jess, M., & Atencio, M. (2011). Thinking differently about curriculum: Analysing the potential contribution of physical education as part of 'health and wellbeing' during a time of revised curriculum ambitions in Scotland. *Physical Education & Sport Pedagogy, 16*(4), 383–398.

Vygotsky, L.S. (1978). *Mind in society: The development of higher psychological processes.* London: Harvard University Press.

West, L. (2004). The trouble with lifelong learning. In D. Hayes (Ed.), *Key debates in education* (pp. 138–142). London: Routledge Falmer.

4 Complexity, equity and critical approaches to physical education

Katie Fitzpatrick

I begin this chapter with two admissions. First, that I am committed to critical post-structuralist ways of being and writing. Second, and relatedly, that I am sceptical about the potential for complexity thinking to add to what I see as the most pressing issues for physical education: equity and marginality. In order to keep the latter firmly on the agenda, I offer here a tentative dialogue between critical approaches to physical education and the body, and complexity thinking. I use the word tentative as indication that I am unconvinced as to whether, in fact, these ideas can speak to each other at all, and whether such a conversation can be useful. Davis and Sumara (2006) share my concerns about bringing critical views to bear on complexity thinking, but they note that such a dialogue might well be productive:

> We wonder if the respective emphases of complexity and critical theories might be farther apart than is typically imagined—and, perhaps more importantly, that those differences might be brought into productive tension.
>
> (Davis & Sumara, 2006, p. 164)

I am, however, less concerned with productivity for its own sake. I am more interested in ensuring that, when applying new ideas and ways of looking at our field, we do not lose sight of the social justice issues that lie within and are reproduced by that very field. I begin this chapter, therefore, with the reminder that all is not well in the realm of physical education; indeed, marginality and exclusion continue to dominate the field. Second, I bring these concerns to bear on the complexity literature, asking whether it offers something new to the field and whether it can potentially shift physical education practices. In the third part of this chapter, I apply complexity thinking to my own research, adding it to other analytical tools and drawing some conclusions about each in terms of their relative application to the field of physical education.

Physical education, marginality and exclusion

In recent times, physical education scholars have employed various social theories to enable deeper understandings of marginality, exclusion and discrimination. They have tended to reject enlightenment notions that the mind and body are separate, and have argued instead for a more embodied view of the discipline. Post-structuralist ideas are central to this work and many scholars apply the social theories of Pierre Bourdieu, Michel Foucault and Judith Butler, among others, accordingly (see, for example, Evans, Davis, & Wright, 2004; Wright, MacDonald, & Burrows, 2004). In simple terms, these scholars argue that the actions and experiences of individuals in physical education and sport are not limited to individual decisions, psychological processes or biological/physiological selves, but are the manifestation of a dynamic dialectic between the person and embodied social contexts. Such contexts are written into the body in powerful ways at the intersection of, among others, ability, gender, class, sexuality and ethnicity.

Social geographer, David Sibley (1995, p. ix) states that "the human landscape can be read as a landscape of exclusion." He proceeds to argue that some forms of exclusion are obvious while others are more "opaque … [t]hese [latter] exclusionary practices are important because they are less noticed and so the ways in which control is exercised in society are concealed" (p. ix). Opaque forms of exclusion operate in physical education contexts every day. A range of critical scholars have made it their business to expose the subtleties of exclusion, including those at work within physical education settings. In connection with those who do the same in sport and physical activity environments, these writers argue that physical education is a space of complex exclusions and oppressions, articulated along multiple lines (Dagkas & Armour, 2011). Wright (2004), for example, notes that "sport and other forms of institutionalized physical activity (such as dance, aerobics, adventure education) tend to be more conservative institutions where stereotypes are reproduced rather than challenged" (pp. 183–184). Kirk (2004), in turn, critiques what he calls 'decontexualized physical education' which privileges the performance of isolated movement skills and ignores the social and cultural contexts of movement:

> [T]here is a large body of evidence to suggest that this de-contextualised approach to physical education disadvantages girls, particular ethnic groups and alienates motorically less gifted and disabled young people, while reproducing and celebrating hegemonic masculinity.
>
> (Kirk, 2004, p. 203)

These scholars have the overt political agenda of highlighting social marginality, discrimination and exclusion within physical education. While post-structuralist approaches are favoured in this work, does complexity thinking add to this scholarship in ways which may change the field of physical education?

Complexity thinking and social theory

Complexity thinking clearly presents a new way to view and understand our world, possibly a new paradigm (Beinhocker, 2006). It may not be appropriate to call complexity a social theory, as it clearly crosses disciplinary boundaries and is concerned with aspects of the world other than those typically within the reach of social theory. Complexity thinking certainly does provide us with a way of viewing research, a new lens through which to view the world. In this sense, complexity thinking, in a practical sense, can be applied to social worlds and brought to bear on research data in a similar fashion to a social theory. There are, however, some key differences. A strength of complexity scholarship is the commitment in the field to crossing traditional disciplinary boundaries (Blaikie, 2007). Furthermore, complexity advocates insist on viewing social systems as inextricably interconnected, not only within and among social contexts, but also within the natural world. Davis and Sumara (2006) conceptualize complexity along lines of multiple, contingent and, at times, nested, systems. They outline a hierarchy of such systems ranging from human body cells, through to social, species and ecosystems. How research is then approached by complexivists, of course, varies enormously, as is evident in other chapters in this book. Cilliers (2005) argues that the application of complexity thinking ranges from the more fixed and scientific to the more sceptical, cautious and even metaphorical

> On the one hand, there is a more strictly mathematical and computational view … In the cases where such a 'hard' understanding is uncritically appropriated by the human sciences, it can lead to … positivism … On the other hand, there is a more critical understanding of complexity. This view argues that complexity theory does not provide us with exact tools to solve our complex problems, but shows us (in a rigorous way) exactly why these problems are so difficult.
>
> (p. 257)

The diversity of approaches to complexity makes the field interesting and rich but also confusing. The critical approach advocated by Cilliers (2005) above provides a way forward for my purposes here and may help us to understand why the field of physical education, as noted earlier, is wrought with seemingly intractable relations of exclusion. It may help us to see what the questions are and why they are so difficult to solve.

Any theoretical lens proves useful if it enables and deepens analyses of individual circumstances, making them more understandable at a universal level, and allowing comparison between contexts. As Bauman asserts, however, "all theory is selective" and none can be applied universally

> there can't be a theory of everything, just as there can't be a map of everything … As a matter of fact, I suppose that theorising is triggered by the need of selecting …
>
> (Bauman in Gane, 2004, p. 17)

One thing that theory does allow us to do is to focus on the underlying issues, the unseen agendas at play in any context. Theory is a way of applying a deep critique to a setting and exploring the social context with intellectual rigour. It also, crucially, allows us to highlight and interrogate the margins, including the kinds of taken-for-granted and oppressive practices that critical scholars in physical education bring into focus. It is worth noting here that complexity is variably referred to as a theory, a way of thinking and/or as an approach to analysis and intervention. Whether complexity can be thought of as a theory remains contested. It is certainly not a unified and singular theory (Mitchell, 2009) but it does provide us with some theoretical tools and a language for analysis. I proceed on this basis and use the term 'complexity thinking' in alignment with the approach in the rest of this book (see opening chapter).

In the context of this chapter then, two questions follow. First, what does complexity thinking add to our understandings of, and work against, marginality and exclusion in physical education? Second, how does complexity thinking extend the theoretical reach of work on the body and marginality already well-established in physical education scholarship?

To that end, I embark in the next section on a comparison of sorts between complexity and two other theoretical tools. The first is already well-utilized by physical education scholars—Pierre Bourdieu's notion of *field*. The second, Homi Bhabha's notion of *hybrid identities*, is less well known to the discipline.

Working with complexity: a student's story

I recently completed a study of student experiences in school health and physical education. The study was a critical ethnography of one New Zealand high school, within which I spent a year attending classes and talking with the students (aged 16–18). Space here precludes me from discussing the study at length (see Fitzpatrick, 2012) but I draw on some of the data to assess how complexity thinking might further elucidate the research findings. Throughout the study, I used narrative to represent the stories of the young people who were key participants, all of whom were from low socioeconomic and Maori (indigenous) and/or Pasifika (migrants from the Pacific Islands) backgrounds. I take the example here of one young person, Moses, who chose the optional senior high school physical education as one of his subjects. I share Moses' story and then apply the three different theoretical lenses (field, hybridity and complexity).

Moses

The year Moses turned 16, everything in his life changed. Looking back, he wondered if his 15-year-old self would even recognise the young man standing here now. Moses grew up in South Auckland, New Zealand—a sprawling suburban landscape of migrants, indigenous Maori and a general mix of different ethnic groups and cultures. Known for cultural diversity, his home suburb seemed to be a constant topic of discussion in the news. On TV and in the newspaper were stories about gangs, poverty and violence. But Moses saw the place as home and he was proud to be a 'South Aucklander.' Moses knew the gang hype wasn't all that, only some of it was true. He had a gang and would hang with his 'crew' most weekends, get into minor trouble and plan bigger stuff. His boys had his back and would always be there if he needed protection. That was then, as they say, and things are very different now. Now he knows who has his back, but for real.

Moses' family didn't like his gang but they couldn't stop him going out. Like him, they were proud of their Cook Islands' heritage and they weren't afraid to be tough and look out for the little ones. His father wasn't so tough now though, he had kidney failure and might be dying. Moses had to be ready for that, ready to help lead the family. He was worried about money too, his Dad was still working in the factory, packing magazines, but that couldn't go on much longer considering his health.

Moses loved going to school, mostly because his girlfriend Maria was there and he could kid around with his friends, but it helped him to forget about all that other stuff too: the pressure his gang was putting on him to 'man up' and the stuff with his family, his Dad's health. His school friends were mostly 'clean' so there wasn't the pressure to get involved that his gang expected. He liked that, no pressure. And he was hopeful of achievement: he listened in class and physical education was his best subject, second only to playing rugby league which felt a bit like fighting but being able to direct your anger, let it out in a good way.

The summer that year was long and hot; the boys were planning some stuff and Moses only half wanted to get involved. He missed playing league and wanted to hang out with Maria and with his Dad. In the middle of the break and after Christmas, just when Moses was starting to think about the next year at school and being a senior, Maria told him she was pregnant. He felt shock at first and just hugged her, unsure what to do or say. They talked a lot and then it hit him: his Dad was dying, this baby was for the family, was a continuation, was for his Dad. His Dad needed to see the next generation before he passed over to the other side. It just seemed right. Looking back now he remembered how, at the time, they were kind of scared about how the two families would react. And, the worst thing was, Maria's family wanted an abortion. He remembered the arguments and how they had to stand up for the baby. He knew, even then, that the family couldn't stop them. He loved Maria; he didn't want her to go through that. And he wanted the baby, no matter what.

After the birth, Moses knew he'd made the right decision when he saw his own Dad's face. He told Maria, "you know, my Dad was the happiest about Baby because he wants to see my kids before he passes. We've made this family complete."

Things were hard though, right from the start. Everything was so damn expensive and Moses wondered how he could help his family and support his new daughter. It was pretty much impossible to get to school, although he tried. He knew, as well, that to give his daughter a chance, he needed to get qualifications. A constant thought kept going through his head: "I don't want my daughter to see me working in a factory." Looking back on that now, he remembered that each time he tried to work at school and concentrate, the thought of Baby would just pop into his head. And money, wow, that was the big issue. It still is. Moses would work as many hours as possible and had to miss school. He worked night shift too, when he could get it, but he was constantly reminded of his Dad's financial struggles. After bills and shopping, he knew that his Dad only had $40 left. Moses earned $100 so he would give his Dad $60 and spend the remaining $40 on Baby's nappies and other supplies.

Although he missed a lot of school that year trying to sort out the balance, Moses made a break from the gang and he thanked his new daughter for that change. Yip, he thought, being a dad changed my life. I want to be the best dad ever and make her happy. He was thankful too that Maria's parents had come around and they gave them heaps of support, even looking after Baby during the day so Maria and Moses could go to school or work. He smiled to think how happy and smiley they looked as soon as they saw Baby in the hospital; they quickly forgot all about suggesting an abortion.

Without a doubt, the funniest thing that year, despite all the other stuff, was a moment during one of his physical education classes. It was just before Baby was due and the class were all talking about and planning the upcoming outdoor education camp. Moses was pretty quiet during that lesson and then he told his physical education teacher that he couldn't attend camp in case the baby came. The physical education teacher was worried and reminded Moses about the assessments for qualifications that were completed on camp. He suggested that maybe he could attend part of the camp, pointing out that it was worth 15 credits (towards the certificate). At that moment, Moses remembered it so clearly, his friend Tu just burst out laughing in front of the class. He stood up and held his hands out like scales to sarcastically weigh up "Baby: 15 credits. Life: 15 credits." The class dissolved into laughter and yelling and the teacher had to concede; maybe school qualifications needed to be put in perspective. Yip, his school mates and his family sure had his back.

I chose this story about Moses because it disrupts the usual narrative arc of physical education research by de-centring the actual physical education experiences and teaching pedagogies. Indeed, his story highlights the peripheral nature of school within Moses' life and is a reminder of how broader social contexts frame experience.

There are many ways to approach the narrative of this story from a theoretical point of view. I have chosen to apply Pierre Bourdieu's notion of field and Homi Bhabha's notion of hybridity because these highlight, in very different ways, the interrelationships between social context and individual identity (both of which are key theoretical tensions in any analysis). I then apply complexity thinking to enable an evaluation of how it might advance our understandings of Moses' experiences.

Theorizing with Bourdieu

The narrative above ends with an exchange between Moses and his physical education teacher. The teacher is concerned for Moses' achievement and suggests that he attends the upcoming outdoor education camp and complete assessments. These assessments ('credits') carry status and count towards national qualifications under New Zealand's senior school system, the NCEA (National Certificate of Education Achievement).[1] Bourdieu's (1986, 1990) notions of *capital* and *field* can be used to understand how Moses and the teacher are experiencing this moment in different ways.

Bourdieu was particularly concerned with the reproductive effects of power and how educational institutions contribute to social stratification (Bourdieu & Passeron, 1990). Bourdieu defined education as a particular *field*, a context of practice which values and rewards certain knowledges and cultural practices. Fields are formative of what Bourdieu called *habitus*, the embodied ways of being in and viewing the world. Although he acknowledged that every field is a site of both contestation and conformity to a particular logic of practice, Bourdieu noted that fields are held together by an acceptance of the forms of capital by which participants gain status and prestige (Bourdieu, 1990).

Educational qualifications are *the* form of capital in the field of schooling and Moses' teacher is at pains to remind him of this. Moses is, however, moving between the field of education (school) and the broader cultural context of family and community. In that latter field, his capital is earned in his gang associations, in his ability and necessity to earn money, and in his new parental responsibilities.

He draws on that capital to resist calls to abort the baby and he lays claim to a broader cultural value by linking the birth of his daughter with the illness and imminent death of his father. While Moses' teacher was concerned with his accumulation of educational capital, the social family context held more sway. In fact, the birth of his daughter exposed to him, and others in his physical education class, 'the cultural arbitrary' (Bourdieu, 1990) of education—the way rules and protocols operate according to the values at stake. In contrast with the birth of his daughter, educational capital was not as prescient.

Moses' experience is not uncommon in his community which has a comparably high teenage pregnancy rate. The school he attends has a teenage pregnancy unit that provides support to young parents. As Breheny and Stephens (2007) note, however, teenage parenting is "typically framed ... as a social problem through association with psychological dysfunction, poor parenting and socioeconomic disadvantage" (p. 334, see also Statistics New Zealand, 2003, p. 9). Drawing on this particular field, Moses might feel ashamed and regretful. The cultural and family fields, however, inform him (despite some mixed messages) that the birth of a child is a cause for celebration and a reason for Moses' own father to rejoice, even though he is very ill. The birth also compels Moses to leave the gang. Admitting the significant challenges he faces, he is more positive than anything about being a father, which is, for him, a form of capital.

Applying hybridity

Hybridity can also be applied to Moses' situation. Bhabha (1994) theorized that people's identities are not fixed, stable or formed, but rather shift and move, existing 'in between' spaces. He referred to this as 'hybrid' identity and the 'liminal third space'. The implication is that fluid and unfixed identities can change according to context. Individuals can 'take on' new identities, representing themselves according to the conditions they encounter. Bhabha (1994) views identity as existing in the moment of enunciation rather than being deeply fixed and essential. Viewing identities as hybrid highlights individual agency; if identities are unfixed, then individuals have choices and flexibility.

Moses has multiple identity positions. He is a 'tough guy' in relation to his gang, but simultaneously a gentle parent and partner. In the different contexts he inhabits he can alter his enactment of self to reveal or hide aspects of his complex and fluid identity. Among his 'boys' and with the gang he can portray a hyper-masculinity, talk tough and plan petty crime. With his girlfriend and his daughter he can be gentle, loving and relaxed. As a father, he works up to 30 hours a week to provide for his family. His decision to extricate himself from the gang can be viewed as an assertion of his agency, his right to reinvent himself and form a different hybrid self. While he cannot cast off his 'gangsta' identity completely, he can choose a different enunciation—one more compatible with fatherhood and family.

Bhabha (1994, see also Gilroy, 2000) argues that hybrid identities are a form of resistance to power, particularly colonial power relations, which essentialize marginalized, non-white young people like Moses. While Bhabha (1994) argues that individuals do not have a unified singular self that is subject to, or a victim of, outside oppressive forces, he acknowledges that identities are created within particular contexts. Within his community, certain subject positions are, indeed, available to Moses. His hybrid identity, however, is, at once, a result of the power relations of the community *and* a response to it

> Hybridity is the sign of the productivity of colonial power, its shifting forces and fixities; it is the name for the reversal of the process of domination through disavowal (that is, the production of discriminatory identities that secure the 'pure' and original identity of authority).
>
> (Bhabha, 1994, p. 159)

Moses' hybrid identity is a response to the cultural and social class conditions of his community, and a way of enacting identity. On learning that he is to become a father, Moses embraces parenthood. Such a decision is a form of resistance to discourses which position teenage parents in negative ways and teen sexuality as dangerous and risky (Breheny & Stephens, 2007). According to Bhabha, such moment(s) of response disrupt the dominant discourses and "disarticulate the voice of authority"; a hybrid response, then, is a survival strategy—a way to assert agency in situations where others may see no room for agency (Bhabha, interview with Mitchell, 1995, p. 82).

Moses lives through the contradictions of his life, making choices that go against his positioning. Tupuola (2004) argues that Pacific youth in New Zealand (like Moses) actively resist essentialized and homogenized notions of self. She argues that they rather draw on a range of global, youth and local cultures to form complex individual identities. The pregnancy and the birth of his daughter gave Moses an opportunity to re-articulate his life and take up a new parent identity.

Considering complexity

While the different theoretical lenses above focus on the wider social contexts (field) and Moses' own embodied and resistant responses to his situation (hybridity) respectively, I now turn to consider what a complexity reading adds to this analysis. Thinking with complexity, most commonly, compels us to consider the wider social systems of which Moses is a part, and how those systems are interrelated, in turn, with other systems. Mason (2008) reminds us that at the centre of complexity is a concern with "relationships among the elements or agents that constitute a particular and sufficiently complex environment or system" (p. 37). The school Moses attends comprises 1,100 students from Maori (indigenous) and Pasifika (migrants to New Zealand from the Pacific Islands of Samoa, Tonga, Niue and The Cook Islands) cultural backgrounds. The school then tends to operate around the cultural practices of non-white New Zealanders, who share indigeneity and/or migrant status and who are predominantly from low socioeconomic backgrounds. The agents in this system are a mix of high-school students and their teachers and the school is nested within the community. Moses is thus an agent, within a system, which complexity tells us he simultaneously constructs and is constructed by.

There were 17 other students in Moses' core physical education class who spent over 8 hours per week together (physical education had a double timetable slot for this class). The physical education class culture centred around relationships, team-work, care and respect and the class had a close bond. Moses felt his class mates' support in addition to his other networks (family, church, gang). Beinhocker (2006) argues that "individual agent behaviour is only one piece of the puzzle. It is a combination of individual behaviour and institutional structures that create the emergent behaviour of the system" (p. 421).

It might be reasonable to expect Moses to be overwhelmed by the idea of parenting at a time when his father is ill; he might be expected to draw closer to his gang to escape this stress, to follow up gang opportunities to make money, and to even support the idea of an abortion. On closer analysis, his decisions are, indeed, in alignment with the wider culture—the values emerging from the other interconnected systems of which he is a part. The configuration of elements and interrelationships produces an unexpected but understandable outcome. Blaikie (2007) notes that such supposedly unlikely results are in line with complex systems which "have the potential to produce unpredictable and novel outcomes from the interaction between their parts" (p. 208).

Moses' resistance to wider social norms is also enabled by his physical education class relationships. The birth of a baby (as stated by Moses' friend, Tu, in the narrative) cannot even be compared, except in jest, with school achievement. Moses' resolve to take on parenting is strengthened by the interconnectedness of community, self and wider networks (Stacey, 2006). The structures and networks thus enable Moses' actions and produce the emergent behaviour. His resistance to his teacher's suggestion that he attend camp is not an isolated choice but one enabled by the wider context. Tyson (2005) notes that a complexity reading of agency views the very self as self-organizing within the system in line with the principle that systems are in constant flux between equilibrium and disequilibrium:

> A sense of *agency* emerges as a part of this self-correcting, self-organizing, and self-regulating process, for the self is assuming responsibility … To function as an effective agent … the sense of self must include the experience of inner organization, cohesion, and stability over time, and a capacity for self-regulation.
>
> (p. 165)

Moses' decisions then, to leave the gang, support his girlfriend and embrace parenthood, emerge from the system. His lack of schooling achievement, while complex, becomes understandable and not easily remedied.

Peurach (2011) argues that traditional school reforms have not worked for underprivileged and low-achieving students precisely because they ignore the complex interconnections of related parts within the sociocultural system constituting the students' lived world. In short, they fail to understand the complexity of the interrelationships in and beyond schools and so focus on the wrong things. In Moses' case, it is easy to see how this would occur if reformers sought to improve his schooling achievement by common interventions such as refocusing classroom teaching on pedagogical interventions or standards.

So, why complexity, or why not?

The above three theoretical analyses produce quite different readings of Moses' narrative. While each in some way highlights the social context in relation to Moses' personal experience, each focuses on different things. Bourdieu's theoretical tools allow us to see Moses' social conditions and how his dispositions (habitus) are formed within and by that context. This, in turn, focuses us on the marginal positions Moses inhabits in a society which continues to be organized hierarchically along ethnic and class lines.

Hybridity allows us to focus specifically on Moses' forms of resistance to his situation and highlights the potential that a fluid notion of self can provide. He enunciates his resistance in the moment of parenthood by embracing this new identity position and negating social stereotypes about teenage parents and gang members by doing so.

A complexity reading suggests that Moses' actions are a product of the wider interconnected systems of which he is a part and highlights the links between his understandings of family and parenting and those of his class and community. Urry (2003) states that complexity "repudiates the dichotomies of determinism and chance, as well as nature and society, being and becoming, stasis and change" (p. 22). The two other social theories referenced here have both been accused of reinforcing rather than overcoming such dichotomies. While I do not accept this assertion, Bourdieu has been criticized for determinism (Giroux, 1981; Jenkins, 1992; for a response, see Harker & May, 1993). Bhabha, likewise, was critiqued for taking too narrow a focus on the individual at the expense of the social context (Ahmad, 1995). Simplistically then, on the one hand, Moses is subject to the reproductive likelihood of class boundaries while, on the other hand, he is able to assert his agency, choose alternate identity positions and resist. Bourdieu argues, however, that habitus is inscribed in a dynamic relationship within the social context such that the very notion of choice is viewed through the lens of habitus, which is formed in and bounded, though not determined, by the social context (Bourdieu, 1990). Complexity thinking also compels us to consider how we are implicated in the phenomena that we encounter—and, more broadly, to acknowledge that our descriptions of the world exist in complex (i.e., nested, co-implicated, ambiguously-bounded, dynamic, etc.) relationships with our worlds. Davis and Sumara (2006) state that "we are aspects of grander systems, shaped by and contributing to the shapes of the phenomena in ways and to extents that we simply cannot know. Such realizations make education a profoundly ethical undertaking" (p. 174). There are obvious similarities here to Bourdieu's notion of field. While the field inscribes and works in productive tension with habitus, the network (from the complexity point of view) is bound by particular (cultural) practices in intersection with the individual agent in relationship with other agents.

There are, however, key differentiating features which should be of particular interest to critical educators. First, Bourdieu accentuates the embodied and humanist nature of all social contexts. He describes habitus and field in constant production and reproduction of each other, thus challenging more traditional, dichotomous, structure–agency conceptualizations. Complexity thinking also overcomes this dichotomy but in such a way that is profoundly disembodying. My key concern here is twofold. First, the very language of complexity thinking is dehumanizing, mechanistic and technicist. Second, and of most concern, complexity thinking draws our attention away from the body, the human person and the embodied self. The strength of social theorists such as Bourdieu and Bhabha (and others such as Foucault and Butler) is that they highlight in their work how the body is implicated in and inscribed with(in) social contexts in deep ways. Complexity, however, seems to remove the body from the site of study, allowing only for a language of systems, agents and elements. Wherein, I must ask, is there room in such language for emotion, care, cultural understandings? While complexity thinking can be and is applied to a holistic notion of bodies (for example, as pertains to health, see Byrne, 1998), many advocates highlight the complexity of the brain (for example, Cilliers, 1998) and ignore the embodied experiences of individuals within complex systems (and how the body is implicated within such systems). I wonder, as a result, if we can hope to address equity if we dehumanize the subject.

I thus question whether complexity thinking is the best theoretical tool to examine the pressing issues of equity and marginality in physical education. Complexity can clearly act as a complement to other social theories and provide a different level of analysis. I am not convinced that it offers new answers, particularly when applied to questions of equity and opportunity. The already significant body of work discussing these issues in the field remains much more compelling. In applying complexity, or any theoretical lens, we should continue to focus on the key questions or concerns that animate our work and which drive social change—in this instance, the still pressing task of changing the field of physical education toward more equitable outcomes.

Note

1 The NCEA system is both internally and externally assessed. It allows students to accumulate points, in the form of credits, towards a complete certificate.

References

Ahmad, A. (1995). The politics of literary postcoloniality. *Race and Class*, 36(3), 1–20.

Beinhocker, E. D. (2006). *The origin of wealth: Evolution, complexity and the radical remaking of economics*. Boston, MA: Harvard Business School Press.

Bhabha, H. (1994). *The location of culture*. New York: Routledge.

Blaikie, N. (2007). *Approaches to social inquiry*. (2nd ed.). Cambridge, UK: Polity.

Bourdieu, P. (1986). The forms of capital. In J. Richardson (Ed.), *Handbook of theory and research for the sociology of education* (pp. 241–258). Westport, CT: Greenwood.

Bourdieu, P. (1990). *The logic of practice*. Cambridge, MA: Polity Press.

Bourdieu, P., & Passeron, J.-C. (1990). *Reproduction in education, society and culture* (R. Nice, Trans., 2nd ed.). London: Sage.

Breheny, M., & Stephens, C. (2007). Individual responsibility and social constraint: The construction of adolescent motherhood in scientific research. *Culture, Health and Society*, 9(4), 333–346.

Byrne, D. (1998). *Complexity theory and the social sciences: An introduction*. London: Routledge.

Cilliers, P. (1998). *Complexity and postmodernism: Understanding complex systems*. London: Routledge.

Cilliers, P. (2005). Complexity, deconstruction and relativism. *Theory, Culture and Society*, 22, 255–267.

Dagkas, S., & Armour, K. (2011). *Inclusion and exclusion through youth sport*. London: Routledge.

Davis, B., & Sumara, D. J. (2006). *Complexity and education: Inquiries into learning, teaching and research*. Hillsdale, NJ: Lawrence Erlbaum Associates.

Evans, J., Davis, B., & Wright, J. (Eds.). (2004). *Body knowledge and control: Studies in the sociology of PE and health*. London: Routledge.

Fitzpatrick, K. (2013). *Critical pedagogy, physical education and urban schooling*. New York: Peter Lang.

Gane, N. (2004). *The future of social theory*. New York: Continuum.

Gilroy, P. (2000). *Against race: Imagining political culture beyond the colour line*. Cambridge, MA: Bleknap Press of Harvard University Press.

Giroux, H. (1981). Hegemony, resistance and the paradox of educational reform. *Interchange*, 12(3–4), 3–26.

Harker, R., & May, S. (1993). Code and habitus: Comparing the accounts of Bernstein & Bourdieu. *British Journal of Sociology of Education*, 14(2), 169–178.

Jenkins, R. (1992). *Pierre Bourdieu*. London: Routledge.

Kirk, D. (2004). New practices, new subjects and critical inquiry: Possibility and progress. In J. Wright, D. MacDonald, & L. Burrows (Eds.), *Critical inquiry and problem solving in PE* (pp. 199–208). London: Routledge.

Mason, M. (2008). What is complexity theory and what are its implications for educational change? *Education, Philosophy and Theory, 40*(1), 35–49.

Mitchell, M. (2009). *Complexity: A guided tour.* Oxford and New York: Oxford University Press.

Mitchell, W.J.T. (1995). Translator translated: Interview with cultural theorist Homi Bhabha. *Artforum, 33*(7), 80–84.

Peurach, D. (2011). *Seeing complexity in public education: Problems, possibilities and success for all.* Oxford: Oxford University Press.

Sibley, D. (1995). *Geographies of exclusion.* New York: Routledge.

Stacey, R. (2006). Learning as an activity of interdependent people. In R. MacIntosh, D. Maclean, R. Stacey, & D. Griffin (Eds.), *Complexity and organisation: Readings and conversations* (pp. 237–246). Abingdon, Oxon: Routledge.

Statistics New Zealand. (2003). *Teenage fertility in New Zealand.* Wellington: Statistics New Zealand.

Tupuola, A.M. (2004). Pasifika edgewalkers: Complicating the achieved identity status in youth research. *Journal of Intercultural Studies, 25*(1), 187–200.

Tyson, P. (2005). Affects, agency and self-regulation: Complexity theory in the treatment of children with anxiety and disruptive behaviour disorder. *Journal of the American Psychoanalytic Association, 53*(1), 159–187.

Urry, J. (2003). *Global complexity.* Cambridge, UK: Polity.

Wright, J. (2004). Critical inquiry and problem solving in PE. In J. Wright, D. MacDonald, & L. Burrows (Eds.), *Critical inquiry and problem solving in PE* (pp. 3–15). London and New York: Routledge.

Wright, J., MacDonald, D., & Burrows, L. (Eds.). (2004). *Critical inquiry and problem solving in PE.* London and New York: Routledge.

5 Affordance networks and the complexity of learning

Alan Ovens and Kath Godber

It's 5:30am. A well-rehearsed routine is just beginning. Seventeen-year-old Sophie tumbles out of bed, sleepily packs the things she will need for her day and begins the long drive to the gym. As an elite gymnast in New Zealand, her routine includes training for two hours before arriving late to school, catching up on the class she has missed, using any spare time during the day to study and then driving back to the gym for another four hours of training. As she enters the gym on this morning there is a little frisson of nerves, a tingle of excitement that helps to suppress the feelings of stiffness and tiredness of such an early start. It doesn't matter how often she trains, it is never the same twice. Oh, the routine may stay the same, but for Sophie, each day creates some difference. The actual training and performing reflects those subtle nuances in timing, delivery and energy. Each practice is about performing the action over and over again, pushing the body to perfect the movements, but each day has its variation of emphasis, engagement, focus and understanding so that each session is different and progress is unpredictable.

Sophie's coach says being at the elite level is about 'blood, sweat and tears', and while this may well be true, it somehow doesn't completely capture the complex nature of what enables Sophie to develop and compete as a gymnast. Part of being human, of participating competently in human cultural activity, is the realization that "something is always happening to us, in us and between us" (p. 547) (Miller & Saxton, 2009). What may appear to an outsider as mere moments of physical performance are actually moments in which the physical becomes a medium for *making sense of* and *making connections with* a world in which an individual co-participates in creating, and that affords extended opportunities for being (Macintyre Latta & Buck, 2008). Sophie learns by participating in meaningful contexts, which is enabled by her relationships and connections with others, and thus allows her to 'fall into trust' with an aesthetic, sensual engagement with her own body in the learning process (Gottlieb, 2004).

It is the connecting, connectable and connected nature of learning that we investigate in this chapter as we look at the layering of everyday experiences of four elite female athletes through the lens of complexity thinking. The concept of connection invokes an image of joining or linking two or more things together. It is a creative act, enabling a sense of structure and exchange to occur. Humans are social beings with the ability to utilize their social links to create cognitive unities that transcend the summed capabilities of the individuals (Davis & Sumara, 2006). Connections are also relational, meaning that, while they enable a means of exchange (such as the flow of ideas, information or material goods), the nature of the connection is biologically and culturally shaped, evolving and differentiated (Mützel, 2009). Such a relational orientation acknowledges the phenomenal world of the individual as structured within ecological networks of meaning that enable goal-directed actions while simultaneously being constrained within the limitations of the individual's embodied relationship with their world. When the form, nature and content of human connections are in a constant state of change, caught in the rhythms and flows of human interaction over time, what may appear to be a linear and isolated process (the athlete practising and learning under the guidance of the coach), on closer inspection, actually reveals itself to be more complex.

Framing learning in this way recognizes that the world of the learner is always in flux and that the connection between learner and teacher is "not linked by chains of causality, but (by) layers of meaning, recursive dynamics, non-linear effects and chance" (Osberg, 2008, p. viii). From such a perspective, it makes little sense to think about the content, function, setting and acting person as independent of each other. What is needed, we suggest, is an approach that attends to the interconnections, the intricate interrelations, the layering of experiences, events, histories, intentions and biographies that work together to produce emergent effects across a range of embedded and mutually implicated systems. In such an approach learning is not simply perceived as situated *in* social contexts, but as an adaptive characteristic of engaging embedded dynamic networks in a goal-directed way (Barab & Roth, 2006). To evoke such an approach we find it useful to think of the pedagogical environment as consisting of functionally connected networks, or what we refer to as affordance networks. This enables a way to describe the intricate details that formerly have been invisible and provide a language with which they can be spoken.

The concept of affordance networks blends two useful concepts from different disciplinary backgrounds. The concept of affordances is drawn from ecological approaches to psychology and most often associated with the work of James Gibson. Affordances capture the idea that the environment in which an individual is situated is meaningful because it consists of multiple opportunities for action, or affordances (Chemero, 2003). As opposed to mechanistic conceptions of human behaviour that assert that the environment stimulates or causes behaviour, conceptualizing the environment as composed of different possibilities for action allows a space to consider individuals as autonomous and capable of exercising agency (Withagen, Poel, Araújo, & Pepping, 2012). The concept of social networks is drawn from sociology and most often associated with both relational sociology and Actor Network Theory (Mützel, 2009). Networks can be defined as social structures made up of individuals (or organizations) that are tied together (connected) by one or more specific types of interdependency. Social networks exist as a result of friendships, common interest, or through a relationship of beliefs, knowledge or prestige.

Combining these two concepts creates the possibility for focusing on human connectivity as a form of social network that provides particular affordances. An affordance network can be defined as the collection of material, social and human capital, taken with respect to an individual, that is distributed across time and space and is necessary for the satisfaction of a particular goal set (Barab & Roth, 2006). The individual components become enacted as part of an individual's affordance network because they enter an individual's life-world (the world as constructed from the perspective of an individual) either intentionally or because of their being bound up in other aspects of the network. In addition, the agency to engage affordance networks coevolves with the action capabilities of individuals relative to their evolving intentions and goals.

Before we begin our analysis we need to briefly clarify our use of complexity thinking. The word 'complexity' in an educational context brings to mind the sheer diversity of elements interacting in any setting. It resonates strongly with teachers since they recognize that in each pedagogical encounter there is a delicate balancing act between order and chaos that must be achieved to create those moments in which learning can emerge. As an approach to inquiry, complexity thinking offers a way of exploring educational phenomena that is neither reductionist or deterministic, and nor does it attempt to provide complete explanations. On the contrary, it offers the potential for new ways of creative thought rather than closing such thought down.

> Describing things in terms of interaction and emergence, for example, does not attempt to describe *what* will emerge in any given situation; the framing of dynamic systems, the choosing of units of analysis, and decisions about what types of emergent feature may be meaningful, all rest with the researcher.
>
> (Haggis, 2009, p. 54)

In this sense, research framed by complexity thinking can be described in three ways. Firstly, it acknowledges the researcher's own entanglement with the phenomenon being researched. Researchers are themselves shaped by systems that also contribute to shaping the phenomena being studied (Davis & Sumara, 2006). Such an acknowledgement rejects a simple mirroring thesis between reality and empirical facts and shifts attention to the processes of interpretation, identity construction and reflexivity as being central to research activity (Alvesson & Skoldberg, 2009). Secondly, complexity thinking is sensitive to method to ensure that it is disciplined, open minded and evidence based, and is also sensitive to the creativity and insight one brings to the interpretation. Complexity thinking frames research as a craft that is more than technical skill, or patience, or intelligence or accumulation of information. It values alongside these qualities the ability to look with imagination in order to open up more useful interpretive possibilities. The concept of imagination recognizes research as a 'fabrication' (Foucault, 1980) in the sense that the role of the researcher should be construed as a 'producer', rather than 'finder', of knowledge about the world and also as a quality that enables data to spark and generate ideas rather than simply verify and support (Alvesson & Skoldberg, 2009). Thirdly, complexity thinking suggests a temporal epistemology in which the quest is not for more accurate understandings of a finished reality, but about finding ways to initiate a more meaningful interaction with reality of which the researcher is a part. Findings, theories and models are not representations of a universe that exists independently, but are framed as provisional tools by which we negotiate our understanding and being in the world (Osberg, Biesta, & Cilliers, 2008).

In the spirit of framing our inquiry as a form of complexity thinking, we draw on narrative inquiry (Riessman, 2002; Stanley, 2007) to weave in the experiences of four exceptionally talented, young female athletes to illustrate how they access the social resources they need to succeed. In addition to Sophie, the 17-year-old gymnast from our opening story, we also worked with Mary (16, basketballer), Tania (17, rower) and Emily (16, netballer). Our familiarity with the story of each participant was gathered through a series of semi-structured interviews with each athlete, one of their parents and one of their teachers with responsibility for accommodating their needs in the schooling context. Inevitably, our knowledge is incomplete and partial, mediated by the tensions inherent in remembering biography, narrating lives through conversation and interpreting storied lives (Stephenson & Papadopoulos, 2006). Nevertheless, that is part and parcel of our inquiry. What is missing are the voices of the coaches and peers who also co-participated in the discussed events. Our analysis is also constrained by the unfamiliarity of each sporting context (the culture of each sport, the length of the season and its internal organization for supporting talented athletes) and the fact that we only had interviews as reference (as opposed to extended participant observations). However, given that all narrative is messy, partial, ambiguous and tentative (Alvesson & Skoldberg, 2009; Stanley, 2007), the analytic framework of affordance networks provides a useful matrix through which we (and the reader) may make sense of the participants' daily lives and aspirations.

Affordance networks

The concept of affordances suggests that the features inherent in any setting or, more precisely, the patterns these features create, offer opportunities or possibilities for action to the individual in that setting (Withagen & van der Kamp, 2010). Affordances depend upon a person's ability to perceive particular signs as a possibility for action and then be able to act on these possibilities. By focusing on affordance networks, our goal is to extend this concept to provide a language for discussing how social connectivity affords participation in, and extended possibilities for, action that is materially, socially and temporally distributed. That is, particular networks are enlisted because they afford the acting individual the means to pursue their goals and intentions, leading to new connections and possibilities for action. Networks don't just establish contexts for the exchange and acquisition of some content; they also establish the potential to connect the individual to larger networks of possibilities that support richer ways of participating in and making sense of the world (Barab & Roth, 2006).

Sophie had watched her older sister at the local gymnastics club, which led her mum to enrol her also when she turned five. At the club she enjoyed using the apparatus and doing rolls and cartwheels and, later on, flips. The programme at the club provided a good structure for her to learn about gymnastics, progressing her through the different levels so that by the time she was 10 years old she could enter the national championships. It was at this competition that she was noticed for her beam performance (her speciality) and was subsequently identified as someone with the potential to be in the National High Performance Squad. However, her journey into the squad wasn't smooth and, after some difficult months without a coach, she decided to switch clubs where she could now be coached by the New Zealand Head Coach. It also gave her the opportunity to train alongside other elite gymnasts and to learn from seeing their dedication and hard work. The highlight came a couple of years later when she was selected to compete in the Commonwealth Games in India. In preparation, she travelled with her coach to Russia to train and compete in some build-up competitions. At first she felt that she had little chance of success, but winning a bronze medal against the Russians in one competition gave her confidence a huge boost and made all the early starts and long hours worthwhile. On returning, her focus turned to competing in the London Olympics.

Networks develop through the relationships that individuals form with the people and material elements they interact with in their daily lives. Affordance networks are the collection of people, technical knowledge, tools, methods, equipment, concepts and practices that, distributed across time and space, are considered as necessary for enabling an individual to achieve a particular goal (Barab & Roth, 2006). The patterning of the connections between these elements is framed by the communal cultures and discourses that ensure that events and choices are personally and socially meaningful from the perspective of the individual. Whatever the connection, whether it be parent/daughter, coach/athlete, athlete/equipment, student/concept, the network is constituted by the sets of relationships between the elements of the network, rather than by the individual components it contains. The individual contributions of various elements can only be understood in relation to their function in the overall network. These material and cultural relations form the framework of our lives. They enable social interaction and offer the individual a range of possibilities and avenues for future action.

Emily's mum could see her daughter had athletic potential from an early age. Emily was always streaks ahead of the other kids in running at her preschool, so her mum joined her up to the local athletics club. Sport was an important part of family life, with Emily's brother and dad keen rugby players. Saturdays usually involved travelling between sporting venues, watching every family member play. When a coach or supporter was needed, usually dad or mum was there ready to lend a hand. In addition to her athletics, Emily also enjoyed playing netball and her first coach helped by often taking her aside and showing her things to improve her game. Netball is a game where quickness is a distinct advantage and an attribute that is sought after. Young girls with natural speed draw the attention of coaches and enable selection into good teams. At the start of secondary school, Emily moved to a large girls' boarding school in Auckland where she was able to move into the top team as one of the youngest players. She felt the school coach had faith in her and seemed to know how hard to push her to succeed. Her success came in being selected for the New Zealand team to compete in the Pan-Pacific Secondary School Games in Australia. She was also named in the tournament team and identified as one of the best players at the tournament. Emily loved representing her country and in particular those moments where, after being named in the tournament team she caught herself thinking, "I am one of the best players in this tournament." But what gave her special pleasure was knowing how proud her parents were of her.

For Sophie and Emily, affordance networks were manifest in the combination of opportunities available to each athlete within her school, family and sporting environments. One of the most significant factors assisting our student athletes to achieve both sporting and academic success was the extent of support they received from their immediate family. The strength of these connections enabled core material and social and human capital to be mobilized in support of the athletes' goals. Support in the form of transport, finance, nutrition, equipment, day-to-day care, problem-solving and facilitating connections to key people and appropriate opportunities, played a huge part in the ongoing success of the participants in their chosen sport. The recognition of and, in some cases, the facilitation of these opportunities was often initiated by the athlete's parents, then continued through contacts with coaches and organized programmes.

These biographical snapshots help illustrate that learning and development is not a linear process, but is made complex by a curriculum of community (Doll, 2012) in which the distribution of knowledge is shared. Although it is possible to zoom in on any isolated moment and decompose the individual performance into its constituent parts, each performer and performance embodies all previous experiences, including the responses and reactions of those within the performer's affordance network.

Agency and action capabilities

It would be easy to assume that the idea of affordance networks somehow creates structures that determine the activities of those participating in the network. Such a view would suggest that the environment consists of a range of stimuli that initiates a response from the individual. However, suggesting that affordances consist of a diverse range of opportunities that exist in any setting does not mean they cause behaviour; rather they constrain or limit behaviour (Withagen & van der Kamp, 2010). An affordance is a relational concept that emerges between an individual's action capabilities and some feature of a situation (Chemero, 2003). An individual embodies a particular set of capabilities that enables a unique perceptual orientation to the world, including being able to notice certain shapes of networks that are unavailable to others. This view has similarities to Foucault's (1975) notion of gaze,

Bordieu's (1977) notion of habitus and Shaffer's (2004) discussion of epistemic frames. While these similarities are useful, it is important to also stress that affordances are fluid and personal constructs that coevolve along with the capabilities of individuals to perceive and take advantage of them in the service of particular goals.

> As Tania explains, rowing is one of those sports that requires the ability to translate raw power into forward motion, while resisting the temptation to lose effective form because of growing fatigue. This insight shapes her training and also how she thinks of her strengths as a rower. She knows that rowing isn't just about raw physical ability as much as it is about how these abilities are shaped through the training that she does and the attitude she brings to each session. Based on her experience, Tania could see that rowing at the elite level was not so much about having a physical advantage, because at this level there were lots of large and strong girls involved in the sport, as about having mental toughness. Her outlook was "if you can't do it when you train, then you won't be able to do it when you race" and this shaped how she approached each opportunity she had on the water.

The notion of affordance networks raises questions about the nature of individual agency. For example, if individuals mutually construct, and are constructed by, the settings and networks that they participate in, how is it possible for them to mediate or transform their relationships to these contexts? In part, this problem emerges from the way agency has traditionally been conceptualized as a flat and impoverished concept constrained by its inevitable counter-positioning to structure. We suggest that it is more generative to explore the dynamic, relational and temporal interplay between the dimensions of agency and explore how they vary within and between different networked structures. In other words, viewing individuals as embedded in contexts that are both relational and temporal in nature provides for the possibility that they are capable of assuming simultaneously different agentic orientations. For example, at any given moment during a training session an athlete can reflect on their past, dream about the future or be focused on the present. In being sensitive to changes in agentic orientation, we create the opportunity to consider the manoeuvrability, inventiveness, adaptiveness and reflectiveness that individuals demonstrate in relation to how they detect and enlist affordance networks.

> In discussions, Sophie acknowledged that it was her will to win that lifted her from a recreational to a competition gymnast. It wasn't always like that, but when she had joined the levels programme at her club and began to place or win competitions, her approach to training changed. She had been enjoying going along and doing gymnastics, but once she got into the competitions, she enjoyed the challenge of beating her competitors and doing well. As she said, "I like testing myself and I love competing." However, at one point she found herself without a coach and, after six months. She made the difficult decision to switch clubs and was able to link with a new Russian coach. "She believed in me enough because I was at my down point and obviously I wasn't looking too good, but she pulled me back up." Working together they were able to rebuild

Sophie's dream of competing internationally, at first in the 2010 Commonwealth Games in India, and then refocusing on the London Olympics.

Agency does not deny that participation in one context leads to the embodiment of the dispositions, appreciations and actions that characterize skilful engagement in a particular field of action. As Smith (2011) argues, a history of involvement in a particular sport leads to an embodiment of the perceptions, dispositions and actions that enable individuals to understand the logic of the game, have a feel for how it is played and have the practical sense of how to participate skilfully. As our young women reveal through their stories, they embody the attributes necessary for success in their chosen activity, such as mental toughness, drive, competitiveness, dedication, enjoyment of physical activity, resilience, determination and teamwork. They develop their action capabilities as they confront emergent situations that pose increasingly complex problems.

Agency emerges as a temporally-situated process of interaction, simultaneously informed by biography, a teleological capacity to imagine future possibilities and the ability to contextualize these within the contingencies of the moment (Emirbayer & Mische, 1998). In other words, agency is intrinsically social and relational since it is enabled by the connections (and disconnections) of people to the elements that enable intentional activity. Agency simultaneously implies different ways of experiencing the world, as well as the deliberative flow of interactions in context, in much the same manner as an ongoing conversation represents a purposeful flow of communication with an emergent shape (Emirbayer & Mische, 1998).

Life worlds and fields of practice

So far our focus in this chapter has been on the relational nature among individuals and contexts of action, with an appreciation for the manner in which our participants can achieve their intentions and goals by enlisting the necessary resources as affordance networks. It is a relational pragmatist view that argues that individuals are not subjects passively responding to their settings, but embodied participants intentionally oriented to act in the world. However, left unexamined are the questions of how particular intentions and goals are shaped by the ongoing participation of individuals in meaningful settings and how these relate to other, broader aspects of their lives. These are questions that reorient our focus from the relationship between individuals and contexts of action to a focus on how these constitute multiple, overlapping, possibly contradictory and temporal contexts (such as schools, or fields of sport or careers) that constitute the individual's lived world and how this shapes the emergence of intentionality.

Mary's long-term goal was to represent New Zealand in basketball. It was a dream sparked by a conversation when she was ten with her uncle and aunt, both of whom played for New Zealand. She always found it positive spending time with them because they were so knowledgeable and encouraging. They made her believe that playing for New Zealand was an achievable and realistic goal. It was also a goal supported by her parents, who always reinforced the idea that, "if you start something, then you finish it!" For Mary's dad this meant full support by paying for training camps and travel to different competitions. It also meant discussing with Mary possible pathways for her development because a key problem in New Zealand is the quality of the coaching. Ideally he would like her to play in Australia since it may provide a faster stepping stone to getting to the US. Mary could see that Australia had a bigger population of players that would allow more opportunity to push harder and do better.

The most obvious overlapping contexts each athlete had to negotiate was that of their school and their sport. Each context represented different agentic orientations from which the past, present and future each converged to shape agentic activity. From our conversations, it became clear that each athlete positioned their sport as the primary focus of their lives and this needed a flexible approach from their respective schools.

One of the difficulties that made school more of a challenge for Tania was a mild form of dyslexia. She also felt that her strong-willed nature meant that some of the teachers found her hard to get on with. Consequently, she knew that she didn't manage her schoolwork very well, even though she knew how important it was to squeeze as much into each lesson as possible because, once she got home, all she felt like doing was resting before her rowing training. Sometimes she thought she would do schoolwork once she got back from training, but then just found that she would come home tired and want to go to bed. There was a system at her school for helping elite athletes, but she did not know about this. Consequently, she navigated the demands of the schoolwork herself. She found some of her teachers understanding and willing to give her additional help if she asked, while she also found some of her teachers very inflexible and they simply increased her work as some form of penalty. During the year she found that the load just built and built till it got unmanageable and she became unable to do anything because of stress or illness.

Strong enabling influences that made a difference to each athlete and her family hinged on a pattern of factors that existed within each individual's sporting and educational environments. These factors were apparent for all four athletes and included: explicit valuing of the individual's sporting activity; completely supportive immediate and extended family; advanced social and interpersonal skills to cope with the demands of high-level sport; key people and opportunities at various stages of the athlete's development; and appropriate provision from their school to accommodate the disruption and physical demands of the athlete's sporting commitments. Not being able to achieve a balance between the athlete's sporting, educational and social lives created tensions, ill-health and, in some cases, poor academic results. To counteract these obstacles, innovative provision in the form of flexible timetables, tutorials, video-conferencing, sports academies, student/teacher links through intranet technology and advanced planning were implemented by schools which recognized that their individualized provision could make a difference to the elite athletes in their school.

The athletes' understandings and experiences in sport and in their school and social environments are in a constant interaction that creates multiple temporal-relational contexts of action. In other words, each athlete switches between home, school and sport contexts. That process itself provides the individual with different orientations towards their life goals and the educational means to achieve them. The fact that each day unfolds by situating the athletes in these different contexts means they are always adjusting to the exigencies of emerging situations in light of their biography and imagined futures. This interdependence and interaction between these contexts allow for individuals to reflexively transform their orientations to action and provide a means for flexible, inventive and critical responses towards how these contexts structure their actions.

Some final thoughts

As researchers focused on the role of social connectivity in learning, we are drawn to the potential of viewing the world as composed of multiple, nested and open systems. The concept of openness in this view is important, since any dynamic system that is a unit of analysis is simultaneously interacting with, and part of the interactions of, other dynamic systems (Byrne, 2005). In other words, dynamic systems of similar type, such as schools, sports clubs or peer groups, will share in the interactions of other systems with which they are either co-located or embedded (for example, two clubs within a sporting code or young women embedded within a youth culture). Such systems can be thought of as interpenetrative, since they are not only dynamic and continually emergent, but exist in relation to the sets of relationships and wider ecologies in which they are embedded (Haggis, 2009). In this sense, complexity thinking offers more than a view that systems interact with other systems, suggesting instead that interpenetrating systems are both entities and environments for other systems at the same time. Complexity thinking provides a sensitivity to the intricate workings of social connectivity, rendering them available for consideration and reflection.

As we have argued, it makes little sense to think about the content, function, setting and acting person as independent of each other. What is needed is a relational orientation that attends to the interconnections, the intricate interdependencies, the layering of experiences, events, histories, intentions and biographies that work together to produce emergent effects across a range of embedded and mutually-implicated systems. In such a view, learning is not simply perceived as situated *in* social contexts, but as an adaptive characteristic of engaging embedded dynamic networks in a goal-directed way (Barab & Roth, 2006). A framework built around affordance networks provides a more fluid and relational conceptualization of learning.

To return to our opening story, we can recognize that the recursive activity of training, of being in a routine and going back over things again and again, enables Sophie a means to *make* and *take* meaning from connected, situated and embodied experiences. The network she creates, and that evolves along with her, provides the collection of material, social and human capital that fundamentally increases her possibilities for action in the world. When framed in this way, we challenge the educational paradigm that learning is the process of acquisition, that knowledge is ordered and a representation of some external, objective world, that abilities are innate and that physical skills are honed through drill and repetition. Connectivity challenges the belief that content, function, setting and acting person are independent of each other, suggesting instead the need for a sensitivity to the relational nature of what it means to act with embodied competence in complex, discursive movement settings.

References

Alvesson, M., & Skoldberg, K. (2009). *Reflexive methodology: New vistas for qualitative methodology* (2nd ed.). London: SAGE Publications Inc.

Barab, S.A., & Roth, W.-M. (2006). Curriculum-based ecosystems: Supporting knowing from an ecological perspective. *Educational Researcher, 35*(5), 3A–13. doi: 10.3102/0013189x035005003.

Bourdieu, P. (1977). *Outline of a theory of practice*. Cambridge: Cambridge University Press.

Byrne, D. (2005). Complexity, configurations and cases. *Theory, Culture & Society, 22*(5), 95–111.

Chemero, A. (2003). An outline of a theory of affordances. *Ecological Psychology, 15*(2), 181–195.

Davis, B., & Sumara, D. (2006). *Complexity and education: Inquiries into learning, teaching, and research*. Mahwah, NJ: Lawrence Erlbaum Associates.

Doll, W. (2012). Complexity and the culture of curriculum. *Complicity: An International Journal of Complexity and Education, 9*(1), 10–29.

Emirbayer, M., & Mische, A. (1998). What is agency? *American Journal of Sociology, 103*(4), 962–1023.

Foucault, M. (1975). *The birth of the clinic: An archeology of medical perception*. New York: Vintage.

Foucault, M. (1980). *Power/knowledge: Selected interviews and other writings 1972–1977*. London: Harvester Press.

Gottlieb, A. (2004). Foreward: Falling into trust. In L. Bresler (Ed.), *Knowing bodies, moving minds: Towards embodied teaching and learning* (pp. 1–5). Dordrecht: Kluwer Academic.

Haggis, T. (2009). Beyond 'mutual constitution': Looking at learning and context from the perspective of complexity theory. In R. Edwards, G. Biesta, & M. Thorpe (Eds.), *Rethinking contexts for learning and teaching: Communities, activities and networks* (pp. 44–60). London: Routledge.

Macintyre Latta, M., & Buck, G. (2008). Enfleshing embodiment: 'Falling into trust' with the body's role in teaching and learning. *Educational Philosophy and Theory, 20*(2), 315–329.

Miller, C., & Saxton, J. (2009). A complicated tangle of circumstances. *Research in Drama Education: The Journal of Applied Theatre and Performance, 14*(4), 545–560.

Mützel, S. (2009). Networks as culturally constituted processes. *Current Sociology, 57*(6), 871–887. doi: 10.1177/0011392109342223.

Osberg, D. (2008). The politics in complexity. *Journal of the Canadian Association for Curriculum Studies*, 6(1), 3–13.

Osberg, D., Biesta, G., & Cilliers, P. (2008). From representation to emergence: Complexity's challenge to the epistemology of schooling. *Educational Philosophy & Theory*, 40(1), 213–227. doi: 10.1111/j.1469-5812.2007.00407.x.

Riessman, C. (2002). Narrative analysis. In M. Huberman & M. Miles (Eds.), *The qualitative researchers companion*, 217–270. Thousand Oaks, CA: Sage Publications, Inc.

Shaffer, D. (2004). Pedagogical praxis: The professions as models for post-industrial education. *Teachers College Record*, 106(7), 1401–1421.

Smith, W. (2011). Skill acquisition in physical education: A speculative analysis. *Quest*, 63, 265–274.

Stanley, D. (2007). *Complexity and lived-experience: Common ground*. Paper presented at the Complexity Science and Educational Research Conference, Vancouver, BC.

Stephenson, N., & Papadopoulos, D. (2006). *Analyzing everyday experience: Social research and political change*. New York: Palgrave Macmillan.

Withagen, R., Poel, H., Araújo, D., & Pepping, G. (2012). Affordances can invite behaviour: Reconsidering the relationship between affordances and agency. *New Ideas in Psychology*, 30, 250–258.

Withagen, R., & van der Kamp, J. (2010). Towards a new ecological conception of perceptual information: Lessons from a developmental systems perspective. *Human Movement Science*, 29(1), 149–163. doi: 10.1016/j.humov.2009.09.003.

6 Intentionality, coordination dynamics and the complexity of human movement

Wayne Smith

This chapter focuses on skill as goal-directed intentional behaviour. To date, mainstream accounts of goal-directed human movement have privileged particular explanations and ways of thinking about coordinated human movement. This is because the dominant approach has been to favour internal processing models and accept the belief that movement coordination is by homunculus control. Homunculus control of human movement implies 'a little person inside the head' who centrally controls and organizes human actions. In recent times there has been a growing number of challenges to internal hierarchical control models, schema theory and motor representations. Such critiques have been augmented by concerns that there is a lack of recognition given to the performance context. An alternative way of understanding skilful human movement is provided by the work done in coordination dynamics (Kelso & Engstrom, 2006) and ecological psychology (Gibson, 1966, 1979), both of whom argue that intentional human movement involves complex, self-organizing, system integration rather than homunculus control. The basic tenets of this more holistic approach suggest that skill is an emergent behaviour that is dependent on the nonlinear, self-organizing but intentional actions of the performer(s) within discursively rich movement contexts (Davids, Button, & Bennett, 2008). However, many ecological explanations of human movement are confined to the perceptual–action couplings at the individual–environment level without reference to the internal dynamics involved in cognition. In so doing, ecological psychology has been criticized for not offering a plausible account of the role of cognition in goal-directed behaviour (see, for example, Abernathy, 2009; Beek, 2009; Nitsch, 2009). This chapter raises the concern that accounts of human movement should include consideration of conscious goal-seeking behaviours.

Thinking about the complexity of human movement

One of the challenges for physical educators lies in developing skilfulness and we know that this involves the performer demonstrating both clever thinking and coordinated motor actions. The orthodox way of understanding how individuals develop these competencies is that the individual follows a process in which the movement patterns considered key to skilful performance are isolated from the context and are repetitively practised. This approach is most often concerned with mastering particular movement patterns (techniques) in the belief that it is necessary to develop a reasonably stable technique that is stored in the form of an abstract motor schema (Schmidt, 1975, in Wrisberg & Schmidt, 2008) before applying it in contexts as and when required. In such practice situations, teachers focus their attention on the learner's actions and the control of movement, separating the individual from the environment, while positing skill as a property of the body. In contrast, drawing on the work of ecological psychology and coordination dynamics, this chapter views skill as an emergent, relational quality that is the result of the nonlinear self-organization of multivariable and multilevel system components. Being a relational quality, skill does not reside within an individual and, therefore, an individual cannot be skilful but can merely acquire the competencies to enact skilful behaviours, which are context-specific and the outcome of a relationship between individual, task and environmental affordances (Newell, 1986). The acquired competencies I speak of here may include internal coordination dynamics of the integrated body systems, cognitive understanding of the context (in many cases this is termed the 'ability to read the game') and the ability to act appropriately within the temporal constraints of the situation. Skill, then, is determined by the actual act or actions performed in the context of the situation given the goal/s of the task at hand.

As a physical educator, my quest to know more about complexity thinking and what it offers my understanding of human movement and skill development has led me to acknowledge that the phenomenon of skilful movement is complex, to explore ecological and dynamical systems as a way of understanding this complexity and to question the place of intentionality in such theorizing. Subsequently, I have sought answers to the question—what is the place and nature of intentionality in theorizing about skill?

Many contemporary motor control scholars hold the view that the individual–environment coupling is the only important level of analysis. Consequently, in my reading of the literature I have found many helpful explanations of the complex interface between the performer and the environment, but I have not found in this same literature the answer to how a performer integrates conscious decisions with the other self-organizing systems of the body. In contrast, Kelso and Engstrom (2006), two of the most respected scholars in the field of coordination dynamics, have expanded from the individual–environment level of analysis to address thinking and cognition. It is evident in their writing that, while the individual–environment is a most important coupling, it is not the only one that can be addressed when one is interested in skill development. In their text *The Complementary Nature*, Kelso and Engstrom (2006) provide a coordination dynamics explanation of cognition that can be applied to intentional human movement and, as such, explain the place of the neurological system and thinking in skilful movement.

In the first part of this chapter I briefly focus on the nature of skill, then I consider how complexity thinking relates to understanding intentional action in skilful movement. I then move on to provide my interpretation of the place of intentionality in theorizing skill and its implication for skilful human movement.

Reframing the nature of skill

When an appreciative observer recognizes a skilful action he or she often responds with an amazed acknowledgement of, "wow that was skilful! How does she or he do that?" Perhaps the more interesting question is to ask how does the performer know to do that (x) rather than something else (y)? This leads to additional questions such as, how does he or she know when to do it? And how does she or he know in advance that doing that will probably result in the intended outcome? Just as importantly, how do skilled performers 'learn' to do that rather than something else in such situations? This line of questioning leads to our field of practice and we ask how does he or she 'retain' this embodied knowledge? Cognitive theorizing would suggest that a skilled performer sees a particular situation as a stimulus, internally perceives it and then, drawing on an abstract representation in the mind, responds accordingly with a linear, multi-step process and a simplistic notion of skill learning, leading to skilled performance. In contrast, thinking about movement in complexity terms, such as the body moving according to nonlinear dynamics, a skilled performance emerges from a performer demonstrating adaptive behaviours to situational constraints and self-organizing processes in relation to task/environmental demands. So, approaching the topic of the moving body by drawing on complexity thinking, we have to assume that coordinated movement is not a simple step-by-step linear process but rather a dynamic, nonlinear, self-organizing, circulatory perceptual–action coupling that leads to the outcome of doing x rather than y.

Contemporary theorists of skilful movement drawing on ecological psychology (see, for example, Araújo, Davids, & Hristovski, 2006; Davids & Araújo, 2010; Davids *et al.*, 2008; Fajen, Riley, & Turvey, 2008; Passos, Araújo, Davids, & Shuttleworth, 2008; Renshaw, Chow, Davids, & Hammond, 2010; Withagen & van der Kamp, 2010) argue that decision-making is best considered at the level of the performer–environment relationship and view skilful action as emerging from the interactions of individuals within environmental constraints over time towards specific functional goals. They often draw on the initial work of J. J. Gibson (1966, 1979) and his theory of direct perception, which underpins the now widely-accepted field of ecological psychology. Gibson convincingly argued that all neurobiological organisms, including humans, are capable of directly perceiving their environment and therefore do not require internal, abstract representations or hierarchical control mechanisms in the form of a homunculus to direct their actions. The environment and organism, he argued, are directly connected in a meaningful coupling and, as such, the ambient environment is not just something to be observed and interpreted internally but rather it exists as meaningful information to the performer. Importantly, this information is related to what the performer is capable of doing. That is, stairs are climbable, a gap is passable or a ball is catchable for that particular performer, in that particular context, at that particular time. That is why the individual–environment coupling is deemed to be such an important dynamic in human movement. It follows that skilful movement is dependent on both the internal dynamics of the performer and the external dynamics of the environment. In the dynamic situation of initiating and carrying out the movement we have many environmental variables that both enable/deny particular behaviours. Gibson (1966, 1979) called these informational variables 'affordances', arguing that all individual–environment couplings are subject to a whole network of affordances that carry meaningful information for action. For example, in a ball-catching situation the external factors of the ball moving in/as an environment, the internal components such as the skeleto-muscular system moving to catch the ball, and the cortical and sub-cortical regions of the neurological system thinking about the act of catching, as well as the interaction between each of these systems, are in a constant process of change as meaningful task information evolves and the individual doing the catching skilfully self-organizes to the constraints of the task in the environment in order to catch the ball. For this reason performers are seen to be complex interacting systems and our actions are those of agents empowered/governed by our interaction with our physical and social world.

Intentional action as it relates to skilful movement

Ecological perspectives and coordination dynamics begin with the premise that it is not possible for a performer to fully perceive the whole solution to an immediate problem prior to the emergence of the affordances that unfold during the action (Araújo *et al.*, 2006; Davids *et al.*, 2008). Affordances emerge and adaptions unfold throughout the dynamic movement sequence and it is the performer's attunement to these affordances—that is, the process of more skilfully perceiving/acting in accordance with these affordances—which is the basis of skilful human movement. Turvey and Shaw (1999, in Araújo *et al.*, 2006) argued that decision-making includes both the process of perceiving and conceiving in one unitary activity through the direct detection of affordances. This open-systems approach recognizes a greater level of indeterminacy during the decision-making process. As such, complexity theorists argue that skilful action is not characterized by an individual making a decision prior to its behavioural expression (Araújo *et al.*, 2006). Individuals do not need to plan specific actions in advance, nor do they merely react to the environmental constraints. Rather, in this open-system approach, "the decision-making behaviour of successful athletes must be eminently anticipatory and cyclical, based on the perception of key information sources from their actions and the external environment" (Araújo *et al.*, 2006, p. 672). In performance situations, an individual's search for relevant information to achieve specific goals "can induce the occurrence of certain interactions with the environment that facilitate goal achievement" (Araújo *et al.*, p. 672). In this way decision-making involves a cyclical process of searching for information to act and acting to acquire information. The intentional process involves "the coupling of external, environment-based force fields with internal, performer-based force fields, by means of information fields, [and this] forms the basis of a theory of cognition for goal-directed behaviour (e.g., showing an interaction of choosing goals, authoring intentions, using information and controlling actions)" (Araújo *et al.*, 2006, p. 659). Inherent in this argument is the belief that the task goal determines the perceptual–action couplings which emerge through self-organizing system interactions and, as strange as it may seem, the perceptual-action couplings, in turn, set-up or reframe the task goal. This cyclical process is possible because of the ever-present organism–environment coordination dynamics. The actual movements are enabled/constrained by the complex interaction of both conscious and unconscious processes where the affordance networks act in real time to update and modify behaviour. This process creates the information fields where learning, in this sense, is the process of establishing and attuning perceptual–action couplings through practice. The consistent movement pattern of a skilled performer, such as an expert tennis player's forehand stroke, is the embodied attunement of perceptual–action couplings to such a degree that the whole system is capable of attaining attractor tendencies (i.e., coordination patterns that are able to adapt to the specific task demands).

It is at this point that I return to my original question—what is the place and nature of intentionality in this nonlinear, self-organizing process? The cyclical explanation above captures the dynamics of the real-time interaction but does it capture the genesis of intentionality? Surely there has to be some level of conscious intention to move towards this particular outcome—that is, to do x rather than y in the first place. For example, for a player in tennis it could be as simple as deciding to play a forehand topspin rather than a slice drive. While the perceived court position of the opponent will be a determining factor, the player still has a conscious choice to make. Should I drive or slice, cross court or down the line? In this regard, cognitive input is clearly necessary. It could be a global perception of the whole environment and all possible outcomes if certain actions follow; a picture of possibilities, i.e., a holistic 'reading of the game' in the here and now, which emerges through knowledge of the past and a perceived future outcome given the particular individual–environmental affordances of the moment. But a projected, goal-directed outcome requires some form of reference or memory of the probable outcomes, and, unfortunately, too often, memory is left unaddressed in ecological explanations. Within humans (and I think humans are uniquely different from other animals in this regard),[1] memory should be thought of as one of the (highly influential) internal affordance variables that enables/constrains performance. This can be individual or collective memory, meaning it could include the internalized memory of one individual or the collective memory of many—for example, those members of a soccer or volleyball team. Such collective memory often comes into play when set moves are planned and enacted in games. This goal-directed memory carries relational meaning which is afforded by the interaction of both internal and external constraints and is modified in real time by the dynamics of the interacting systems (other team, rules of the game, environmental conditions).

The need to recognize the place of conscious intentionality in nonlinear systems theorizing

As we can see from the previous section, nonlinear dynamic theory clearly articulates the nature of multiple and multilevel system integration, and the interface between the external environment and the individual, but it has not provided the same clarity about the internal dynamics operating to maintain or change our conscious, internal attractor landscape. In our acceptance of perceptual–action couplings we have to be careful not to dismiss the role and enabling influence of our conscious intentional processes.

In their excellent text, *Dynamics of Skill Acquisition: A Constraint-Led Approach*, Davids *et al.* (2008) provide a readily readable account of thinking about skill acquisition in complexity terms for practitioners, but they do not address the matter of individual or collective intentionality. In this text Davids *et al.* argue that "in the theory of direct perception the learner ... is not burdened with the task of developing symbolic memory structures ... rather the perceptual systems become progressively more attuned to the invariant information available in the environments" (p. 64). But they do not go on to explain how one becomes 'more attuned' other than to say through more practice; nor do they state how we retain this attunement. To fully appreciate the implications of this statement, one has to appreciate that the 'perceptual systems' they name do include cognitive processes, but Davids *et al.* do not explain what alternative form this component takes, given that it is not a symbolic memory structure. They add that, by adhering to the theory of direct perception, they do not intentionally eliminate the role of cognitive processes (see p. 65), arguing that "Gibson (1979) did not deny the existence of cognitive processes" and he also "did not suggest that memory played no role in perception" (p. 65) but rather he chose to focus on the performer and environment interaction. Although Davids *et al.* often make reference to conscious control of motor movement or conscious decision-making, they do not address the complexity of this in any way. For example, they argue that a crucial distinction between many biological organisms and human movement is the human ability to "use internal energy sources to intentionally constrain their actions to achieve goals or desired outcomes" (p. 40), but they don't explain how this intentional, presumably conscious, energy source is created and drawn upon to enable meaningful actions. Further to this they state that "during the performance of motor tasks, *'the CNS typically can select'* from a large number of dfs (degrees of freedom) for *'regulating movements'* " (p. 47, italics my emphasis) and later, " *'the CNS has the problem of controlling'* the behaviour of the motor system dfs in dynamic environments, which it achieves through the assembly of functional coordinative structures" (p. 48, italics my emphasis). These statements appear to support a notion of CNS control of movement that involves a selection process. Thus, one could be forgiven for assuming that the ultimate decision of what to do and how to do it appears to still lie in the CNS. At the very least, one can reasonably assume that cognitive decision-making processes still play a significant part in intentional action.

To be fair to Davids *et al.*, in an earlier publication (Davids, Button, & Bennett, 1999) they stated that intentionality is a specific control parameter perturbing the intrinsic dynamics of the movement system. They argued that specific control parameters, such as intentions, can force the system to adopt qualitatively different behaviours (Davids *et al.*, 1999) and added that "a specific control parameter constraining system dynamics could be a memory or an intention of the performer to produce a particular pattern of co-ordination (such as when initiating a specific movement in dance or gymnastics)" (p. 5). They also drew on Kelso (1995, in Davids *et al.*, 1999) stating that intentions are 'specific functional requirements' of a movement system. So, although they have not gone into any depth, they have acknowledged that there is a place for memory and intentional processes in complexity explanations.

Just as Davids *et al.* (2008) had stated in their text, Davids and Araújo (2010) later argued that Gibson (1966) had differentiated between knowledge *about* the environment and knowledge *of* the environment, proposing that knowledge about the environment involves perception, which, they say, is indirect or mediated. As they state:

> There has been a proposed functional division between the pick-up of visual information for perception to identify an object (knowledge about the environment) and visual information for action (knowledge of the environment) by Goodale, Milner, and colleagues ... two dissociated visual pathways with separate functions can be discerned in the cerebral cortex of humans. The dorsal pathway ... picking-up information for action, whereas the ventral pathway ... is involved in detection of visual information to gather knowledge of the environment ... The ventral pathway has only indirect connections with the premotor cortex ... via projections to the ventral prefrontal cortex, which is involved in memory and recognition.
>
> (Davids & Araújo, 2010, p. 130)

In this case, indirect perception is being gathered and stored from direct perception, but we should ask, for what purpose? Possibly to act with intention when called upon. In a sense this offers a background resource of perceptual/action patterns to draw on to form or adapt existing perceptual–action behaviours.

It is fair to assume from this that Gibson did not deny the existence of indirect or mediated conceptual memory in the form of analogical cognition, albeit that this form of knowing is mediated by language, pictures or symbols. But how is perceiving and conceiving through language, symbols or pictures any different in terms of knowing about something than knowing about something from the direct perception of the real environment? Surely, even though we know one is symbolic and the other real, we 'know' both in the same way. Does knowing *of* our environment through direct perception mean that we should not, in addition, accept that we can also call upon and integrate the stored information from our memory during goal-seeking behaviours?

Intentionality implies a purposeful, and, in part, conscious, drive towards a goal. It can involve both a-priori and on-line conscious decision-making integrated with nonlinear, self-organizing movement within a fluid environment. Intentionality also implicitly reflects a future outcome or outcomes which will result from either a change or retention of the current attractor landscape. Such intention implies a knowing, acting agent, which requires the integration of a recognized present, based, in part, on knowledge of the past, with an anticipated future given certain further actions. This conscious, intentional ability to act in a particular way, given the affordances available in the ambient environment, is the uniqueness of skilful human action. As a further example, consider the interceptive movements of catching or hitting a ball—actions that can only be conducted when the performer cognitively intends to undertake this particular task. The cognitive aspect can be highlighted in cricket, for example, when a ball is hit in the air to a close in-fielder such as a slip-fielder. Even in this lightning-fast situation we often hear a simultaneous call of 'catch it' from the keeper as the catcher applies the perceptual–action coupling to catch the ball. It is the keeper's response that tells the story of a cognitive response in this example. The keeper's call of 'catch it' is not so much a movement response but rather a recognition-interpretation response. In this situation the keeper has transformed the physically-perceived into socially-significant speech with the same lightning speed as the catcher has perceived and moved to catch the ball. This indicates that both cognitive–transformative action and perceptual–action responses may be simultaneously possible. We don't know if the catcher also performed an internalized cognitive interpretation but how else would he or she be able to make the decision to either catch the ball or move out of its way. Again, granted, fielders know what to do (i.e., perceive and act) from the early detection of perceptual cues (batter's preparatory hitting actions), but this does not bypass cognition. Therefore, although we can and should readily accept the attunement of perceptual–action couplings, we should not reject the role of cognition in perception. Knowing *about* also plays an important role in prospective and immediate action. As Nitcsh (2009) suggests, "the essential point is not to reject or endorse the role of cognitions and internal representations, but to specify the conditions under which they are or are not necessary and useful" (p. 163).

Similar sentiments are expressed by Beek (2009) and Abernethy (2009) as each separately responded to an article by Fajen *et al.* (2008) on information, affordances and the control of actions in sport. Although Beek supported the theory of affordances, he challenged proponents of Gibson's ecological perspectives to provide a more plausible explanation of the goal-directed behaviours of actors. Beek stated that, "the first question to be addressed is how the athlete knows which actions are most likely to be successful, and how this knowledge comes about. Although the selection of the most successful actions involves awareness of the existing constraints, it will also be based on past experiences and acquired knowledge of situational probabilities and the success rate of particular actions under similar conditions" (p. 148).

Abernethy (2009), drawing from his own research findings, questioned the ecological science view that skill learning involves a progressive (re)attunement from non-informational to informational variables, stating that the transition from novice to expert is not one of a fundamental shift from the reliance on non-informative to informative sources, but rather one in which experts develop the capacity not only to exploit the informational variables used by novices but also to utilize additional, earlier informational sources to which the less-skilled are not attuned.

Nitsch (2009) argued that neither Gibson nor Fajen *et al.* (2008) provide an elaborate process theory of learning with regard to the underlying learning mechanisms. Concepts like attunement and calibration, he says, "emphasise specific tasks and effects of learning; they say nothing about how attunement and calibration are achieved … When a person learns to perceive something, which he or she did not perceive before, why and how does this happen? What processes within the person change as a result in this change?" (p. 161).

Drawing on Ullman (1980, in Nitsch, 2009), Nitsch warned that "rejecting the combination of sensations assumed by classic sensory-based theory of perception did not justify, by itself, the conclusion that other alternatives to direct perception are also refuted, and mediated processes such as categorization, interpretation, inference, etc. have no place in the theory of perception" (p. 162). He continued, stating:

> Concerning the notion of perception without mediating cognitive processes, a fundamental problem has to be solved; if the existence of cognitive processes is not principally denied and if cognitive processes have an evolution-based adaptive function in the interaction of person and environment, and the person acts as a whole, then it is highly questionable maintaining the general assumption in spite of these facts that the environment can be perceived without the process requiring cognitive mediation.
>
> (Nitsch, p. 162–163)

Even if one does not fully accept the arguments presented above, as was the case when Riley, Fajen, and Turvey (2009) responded to these critiques (see Fajen *et al.*, 2008, p. 40), one should acknowledge that there is confusion and on-going questioning about the nature and place of conscious decision-making in theorizing about intentional human movement.

So what is intentional action and how can this be explained within a complexity framework?

In a recent paper, Withangen and van der Kamp (2010) proposed a slight but important modification of Gibson's theory of perception, proposing that "perceptual information does not reside solely in the ambient arrays; rather, perceptual information is in the *relational property* of patterns in the array and the perceptual processes (see also Smith, 2011). What a pattern in the ambient flow informs about depends on the perceiver who uses it" (p. 149) [italics added]. Withangen and van der Kamp (2010) argued that perceptual information is not reified. It does not reside in the environment alone, but rather it emerges and dissipates in the process of interactions. In this way they have re-established the importance of the knowledgeable individual and repositioned skilful movement as a relational property requiring an active perceiver. Such an active perceiver is capable of acquiring and consciously conceiving situation-specific information whilst still recognizing the importance of the nonlinear dynamical relationship between the individual, the task and the environment.

Similarly, Todd and Gigernzer (2003) argued for a place for human rationality or consciousness and that the internal constraints of human consciousness and the external constraints of the environment should be drawn together. They stated that humans exhibit 'ecological rationality', which they described as "making good decisions with mental mechanisms whose internal structure can exploit the external information structures available in the environment" (p. 144). Keijzer (2001, in Davids & Araújo, 2010) added that "the short-time scale dynamics are modulated by *internal control parameters embodied in neural networks*. In their turn these dynamics are coupled to larger-scale dynamics, guiding the formation of behavioural trajectory over longer time scales" (p. 132).

Kelso and Enstrom (2006) provide a most comprehensive explanation of cognition and coordination dynamics. Coordination dynamics, they state, are "a set of context-dependent laws or rules that describe, explain and predict how patterns of coordination form, adapt, persist and change in natural systems" (p. 90). Essentially, they argue that neurological function is just another level of our complex system and that coordination dynamics are central at all levels including cortical and subcortical functioning, where thoughts are created and conscious decisions are made. Patterns of behaviour arise as an emergent consequence of self-organizing interactions among neurons and neuronal populations and this self-organization is a fundamental source of cognitive, affective, behavioural and social function.

Coordination dynamics within our brain and other parts of the CNS, as in all dynamical systems, exhibit metastable tendencies, with metastability being the simultaneous realization of two competing tendencies: the tendency of the components to couple together and the tendency to express their intrinsic independent behaviour (Kelso & Engstrom, 2006). This is an entirely new concept of brain functioning where parts of the brain function autonomously and, at the same time, exhibit coordinated activity. In this way the brain is an informationally-coupled self-organizing dynamical system. A delicate balance between integration (coordination between individual areas) and segregation (expression of individual behaviour) is achieved in the metastable regime and the region between complete integration and complete segregation is the most favourable for cognition (Kelso & Engstrom, 2006). As an analogy we could think of the dynamics involved in a game of rugby where each individual player is doing his or her own thing, playing their own part, whether it be in competition or cooperation with other players, and, at the same time, we have overall pattern dynamics that emerge and dissolve as the game progresses. Equally, the players (parts), although often matched to a particular positional role (attractor), are interchangeable or at least able to adapt to meet the immediate demands of a situation as it arises. In this way thinking as a neurobiological process is no different to the individual–environment couplings. Perceiving triggers a dynamic thought which interacts with action as one constraint in a multilevel dynamic.

Kelso and Engstrom (2006) then draw the link between the dynamic neurological system interactions and thinking, suggesting that

> The creation of information in the mind is a transient non-stationary dynamic process. It corresponds to a flow of converging ... (integrative phase-locking tendencies between brain areas) and diverging ... (segregative decoupling

tendencies and individualisation of brain areas). Both tendencies are crucial, the former to create thoughts, feelings—information in general; the latter to release individual brain areas to participate in other acts of cognition and emotion.

(p. 176)

This self-organizing process is called into action based on engagement in the dynamic relationship of the individual with the task/environmental interactions.

Conclusion

The fields of coordination dynamics and ecological psychology offer plausible theoretical lenses for supporting context-specific skill-learning practices. It has also begun to change the way that physical educators conceptualize the nature of skill and skill-learning (Ovens & Smith, 2006). But how much will it impact on our practice? This will be our on-going challenge.

Some contemporary theorizing, as it relates to skill-learning and associated pedagogical approaches, such as nonlinear pedagogy (Davids *et al.*, 2008), has, at times, also succumbed to the partiality weaknesses of the more traditional cognitive approaches by not being all-encompassing. Unfortunately, in choosing to focus only on the interface between the individual and environment or internal/external constraints, many scholars in the human movement field have failed to adequately theorize the place of cognition and memory in their accounts of coordinated motor action. The place of thinking in strategic planning and tactical responses during games requires cognitive input and this is not something that physical educators can afford to overlook.

In this examination I asked the question—what is the place and nature of cognitive intentionality in nonlinear, self-organizing processes because the answers to this question appeared to be missing in much of the related literature. Fortunately, however, the work of Kelso and Engstrom (2006), who are positioned more in the field of complexity science and cognition do provide answers that help to overcome this question. Neurological coordination dynamics recognizes the place of the past in the present and the relative positioning of the individual and the context. Most importantly, it (re)recognizes the place of intentionality in skilful human behaviour and, as such, enables one to better understand how performers and learners make the often difficult instantaneous decisions that lead to their action to do x rather than y and achieve skilful outcomes.

Note

1 Although other animals are capable of perceiving and acting through instinct and former experiences, humans are capable of conceiving higher order abstract thoughts well beyond that of other animals. As we know, humans are capable of not only holding mental images of events and possibilities, but also of conceiving a complex plan to act. Thus, abstract (holistic) action representation is possible within human consciousness.

References

Abernethy, B. (2009). Some brickbats and bouquets for ecological approaches to cognition in sport. *International Journal of Sport Psychology, 40,* 136–143.

Araújo, D., Davids, K.W., & Hristovski, R. (2006). Dynamics of decision-making in sport. *Psychology of Sport and Exercise, 7*(6), 653–676.

Beek, P.J. (2009). Ecological approaches to sport psychology: Prospects and challenges. *International Journal of Sport Psychology, 40,* 144–151.

Davids, K., & Araújo, D. (2010). Perception of affordances in multi-scale dynamics as an alternative explanation for equivalence of analogical and inferential reasoning in animals and humans. *Theory and Psychology, 20*(1), 125–134.

Davids, K., Button, C., & Bennett, S. (1999). Modeling human motor systems in nonlinear dynamics: Intentionality and discrete movement behaviors. *Nonlinear Dynamics, Psychology and Life Sciences, 3*(1), 3–30.

Davids, K., Button, K., & Bennett, C. (2008). *Dynamics of skill acquisition: A constraints-led approach.* Champaign, IL: Human Kinetics.

Fajen, B.R., Riley, M.A., & Turvey, M.T. (2008). Information, affordances, and the control of action in sport. *International Journal of Sport Psychology, 40,* 79–107.

Gibson, J.J. (1966). *The senses considered as perceptual systems.* London: George Allen & Urwin Ltd.

Gibson, J.J. (1979). *The ecological approach to visual perception.* Boston, MA: Houghton Mifflin.

Kelso, J.A.S. & Engstrom, D.A. (2006). *The complementary nature.* Cambridge, Mass: MIT Press.

Newell, K. (1986). Constraints on the development of coordination. In M.G. Wade & H.T.A. Whiting (Eds.), *Motor development in children: Aspects of coordination and control* (pp. 342–360). Dordrecht, Netherlands: Martinius Nijhoff.

Nitsch, J.R. (2009). Ecological approaches to sport activity: A commentary from an action-theoretical point of view. *International Journal of Sport Psychology, 40,* 152–176.

Ovens, A., & Smith, W. (2006). Skill: Making sense of a complex concept. *Journal of Physical Education New Zealand, 39*(1), 72–86.

Passos, P., Araújo, D., Davids, K., & Shuttleworth, R. (2008). Manipulating constraints to train decision making in rugby union. *International Journal of Sport Science & Coaching, 3*(1), 125–140.

Renshaw, I., Chow, J., Davids, K., & Hammond, J. (2010). A constraints-led perspective to understanding skill acquisition and game play; a basis for integration of motor learning theory and physical praxis? *Physical Education and Sport Pedagogy, 15*(2), 117–137.

Riley, M.R., Fajen, B.R., & Turvey, M.T. (2009). Reply to commentaries on information, affordances, and the control of action in sport. *International Journal of Sport Psychology, 40,* 207–218.

Smith, W. (2011). Skill acquisition in physical education: A speculative perspective. *Quest, 63*(3), 265–274.

Todd, P., & Gigerenzer, G. (2003). Bounding rationality to the world. *Journal of Economic Psychology, 24,* 143–165.

Withagen, R., & van der Kamp, J. (2010). Towards a new ecological conception of perceptual information: Lessons from a developmental systems perspective. *Human Movement Science, 29,* 149–163.

Wrisberg, C., & Schmidt, R. (2008). *Motor learning and performance: A situation-based learning approach* (4th ed.). Champaign, IL: Human Kinetics.

7 Ongoing adaptation as a feature of complexity

Further thoughts and possible ideas for pedagogy in physical activity

Anthony Rossi and Timothy Carroll

It is reasonable to suggest that this is an ambitious chapter. First, we introduce some concepts related to adaptability that might at first seem out of context. This is intentional; we start by discussing theoretical constructs related to human rationality. Through this we introduce Karl Popper's ideas around the notion of propensities and then take this into more familiar ground by discussing the relationship of Popper's ideas with the more familiar concepts of self-organization and affordances. We then change tack and connect these ideas up to a developing, if somewhat contentious, theory referred to as 'optimal feedback control' (OFC). We do this by introducing three empirical studies which, though seemingly counter-intuitive, are representative of the evolving OFC theory. A key feature of this theory is the human capacity for on-line (real time) movement corrections, allowing ultra-fast heuristics that facilitate feed-forward decision-making in movement. It is this capacity that enables adaptation. We commence our discussions with a metaphor drawn from the work of Simon: "Human rational behavior … is shaped by a scissors whose two blades are the structure of the task environments and the computational capabilities of the actor" (Simon, 1990, p. 7).

Notwithstanding the finite limits of this metaphor, in attempting to explain it, Todd and Gigerenzer (2003) sought to demonstrate two things. Firstly, that human rationality cannot be bounded in ways that we have traditionally considered to be the case. In other words, they suggest that to consider ourselves as being 'hemmed in' by two unrelated sets of bounds—the bounds that are external to us or what we might more readily call the environment and all that goes on in it, and internal constraints such as the limits with which we might process information—is entirely untenable. Secondly, in dismantling this edifice of tradition, Todd and Gigerenzer suggest that humans exhibit what they refer to as ecological rationality, which they describe as, "making good decisions with mental mechanisms whose internal structure can exploit the external information structures available in the environment" (p. 144).

It may seem somewhat perverse to start a discussion on complexity by drawing on literature framed by the tenets of bounded rationality seemingly most at home within the field of economics. However, the premise for this is not as strange as it might seem. Bounding rationality has a history of limiting human capacity by either focusing on the world or by consideration of cognitive capability. In other words, human capacity can only be optimized under given constraints. However, Todd and Gigerenzer (2003) regard such constraints as liberating since, as they argue, rationality "emerges" from "the joint effect of two interlocking components: the internal limitations of the (human) mind, and the structure of the external environments in which the mind operates" (p. 148). Notwithstanding that the position we might prefer is of an embodied actor (as simply considering the mind might also be a limiting constraint), in a sense, Todd and Gigerenzer are suggesting that in order to make good decisions we should let the world do some of the work. By this they mean that "by relying on the presence of particular useful information patterns—the decision mechanisms themselves can be simpler; hence our focus on simple, fast and frugal heuristics" (p. 148). We will talk more about this later but, for now, this ecological approach relies on Simon's idea that humans tend to draw on approximate methods to undertake most tasks but also search for more information within ever-changing contexts—hence the frugality of the heuristic. Given the nature of the rate of change within systems, heuristics need also to be fast. Hence heuristics need to be matched to particular environments to facilitate adaptive decisions. We acknowledge that this is a limited discussion of rationality. However, these central ideas have appeal since, at first glance at least, they suggest how the uncertainty within complex systems can be accommodated and how late actions within evolving environments (such as a game) can be facilitated. As we will see later, through processes of recognition, adaptive decision-making or, perhaps better, on-line corrections, changes to action can be made much later than we once thought. The empirical support for this emerging from motor behaviour laboratories suggests that late changes to action can be made within the context of ambiguous and uncertain environments that are prevalent in the world of sport, physical education and physical activity. As Jones (1999) suggests:

> People never make decisions in isolation. They interact with others, who themselves have decision strategies. They must modify their goals in light of the social milieu in which they find themselves. Indeed, some analysts have argued that preferences should be viewed as fluid, not fixed, because of the necessity to be flexible in the face of changing circumstances.
>
> (p. 308)

The idea of 'propensities'

Karl Popper (1990), in seeking to move the evolution debate forward, suggested that the world cannot be considered as closed; rather, he suggested that the world is made up of what he termed 'propensities'—processes or events which may or may not happen. In other words, any organic system is open to a range of potential outcomes dependent on the nature of the interactions between the organisms that make up that system. Propensities, therefore, cannot be seen as the properties of an object. Propensities have to be seen as what Ulanowicz (1997) describes as "inherent in a situation" (p. 219). Propensities then lack certainty as a consequence of the degrees of freedom inherent in the possible interactions within the system itself.

Again we are mindful that there may appear to be serious disconnects between this collection of work and the potential audience of this book. However, beneath the surface there is a familiar message. In the evolution of complex systems either across millennia or nanoseconds, human ecological rationality seems to have a remarkable capacity to adapt. Adaptation is oft-cited as a central tenet in complexity or constructivist science and learning and yet, in the field of physical education, it receives scant attention. However, it just may be that adaptation is what defines 'intelligent performance' rather than the capacity to articulate and justify one's action. We will speak more of this later.

Ulanowicz (1997), again working from Popper, suggests that the idea of propensities cannot be seen either in abstraction of, or distinct from, the surroundings in which they exist. He further suggests that such propensities are then affected by other propensities. It would be wrong to misrepresent Ulanowicz, who, being the biological scientist he is, goes on to develop a calculus of conditional probabilities (rather than absolute probabilities) to ensure that causal relationships can be understood (even if with more caution and in more approximate terms). To dwell on this, however, would miss the point which is that, if 'certainty' can only ever be partial or tentative, then we have no alternative but to accept the presence of uncertainty. If we accept that our lives are guided as much by uncertainty as they are by certainty, then the idea of emergence of phenomena as being bound up in fluctuating propensities of systems seems reasonable. This, in turn, requires us to accept the possibility at least that systems self-organize around the propensities within the system itself. This further suggests that when this principle is applied to learning, linearity in the acquisition of knowledge, skills or both seems unlikely. Consider, for example, the world of sport, which tends to be a central component of school physical education. Sport (regardless of what sport) is a dynamic structure where environmental stability is unlikely—in other words, it is structured by uncertainty rather than certainty. This means that there is a large number of propensities within the system, some of which will happen and some of which will not. A linear (predictable) response to a movement problem is unlikely to be successful. However, being able to adapt by self-organizing around the most likely events allows a greater possibility of success. The key then is being able to self-organize by drawing on fast-feedback systems and frames of reference that allow an image of possible outcomes.

Getting self-organized

Haken (1996) points out that there is plenty in the field of physics that describes how the behaviour of a system changes almost imperceptibly but does so in a way that is controlled by the system itself. In other words, the propensities of a system are aligned, recruited and organized in ways that best suit the evolution of that system. What this means is that the system itself 'self-organizes', often from one that had microscopic properties to one that has macroscopic properties (Haken, 1996). Physicists have shown that this happens even at the sub-atomic level.

In motor behaviour, some of Kelso and Schöner's (1988) work done in phase transitions in finger movements has also demonstrated the human movement system's capacity for self-organization. Remember, these experiments showed the involuntary change from out-of-phase finger movements to in-phase movements. Haken (1996), when describing these types of changes said, "what happens here is a qualitative change of a system on a macroscopic level" (p. 239). Haken emphasizes that most complex systems (including human beings) have degrees of freedom in vast numbers and is sceptical about the predictions within complex systems. However, predictability is of less interest and ideas around 'emergence' drawn from complexity theory are probably more useful within the context of self-organization and adaptability.

It remains ambitious, however, to suggest that complexity and its connections to constructivism offer a better explanatory account for how motor skills are learned, remembered, adapted and applied to evolving situations. In light of this we tread lightly here with some reluctance to point to causal relationships between grand ideas. As we have suggested, our preference is to focus on aspects of complexity seldom considered in depth.

It is not too long ago that Williams, Davids, and Williams (1999), presented their work with similar caution. Positioned in the field of motor control, their view of learners, based on large data sets and comprehensive statistical analyses, was that they were explorers of what they called a perceptuo-motor space. In doing this, the authors suggested that learners can be regarded as novelists, constructing an ever-evolving story within the motor domain which itself was ever evolving. There is something attractive, and even romantic, about this idea. It frees the learner from the confines of linear modes of learning and opens up a myriad of possibilities in terms of responses to environmental demands. More than this, however, it begins to connect the field of learning and performance in sport and physical activity to the literature on adaptation and we will pursue this further towards the end of the chapter.

Connecting self-organization and emergence

These words have become commonplace in physical education probably over the last 20 years as research in dynamical systems and constraints-based pedagogy has gained purchase (see Davids, Button, & Bennett, 2008). As we press further into the linguistic and conceptual nuances of the fields traditionally associated with physical education such as motor control and learning and social and cognitive psychologies, as more obvious examples (see Rovengo & Kirk, 1995), we ambitiously seek increasingly sophisticated answers to the mysteries of learning. Nonlinearity, complexity and emergence are codes of language that have been recruited into the world of physical education as part of that increasing sophistication. However, it is perhaps timely to look at some of this more closely before we invest time considering the ideas of adaptation—the challenge we have set ourselves in this paper.

A chronology of 'self-organization' as a concept is not necessary; the principle is recognized by biologists and has been for some time. However, it serves us, perhaps, to draw upon Ashby's classic paper from 1962 (Ashby, 2004). In a contemporary presentation of this paper (downloaded March 30, 2010), Jeffrey Goldstein (2004) indicates that one of Ashby's purposes was to move away from the rather casual use of the term self-organization that can sometimes infer that organisms (or indeed machines) can independently change their own organization. In other words, according to Ashby, organisms have no innate property for autonomous change. Perhaps, rather like Popper after him, Ashby could not accept such certainty and, in a similar vein to Popper who chose to frame his analysis around 'propensities', Ashby drew on the principle of 'conditionality'. At the time this was not a familiar term and, indeed, the original paper goes into some depth about the converse of all of the terms that he chose to use; it is an extremely thorough analysis and we have only limited space here to draw on some of it. We acknowledge that this may fail to represent the magnitude of Ashby's contribution more fully. Nonetheless, his analysis is helpful. His first principle was that, regardless of how 'conditionality' is treated, at the core of this idea is that there exists what he called a 'product space' or a space of possibilities. Within this space are the 'actualities' (or realities) of the organism or better, of the 'system'. As a consequence, he argued, it is the communication between the actualities of the system that leads to self-organization. This is a gross oversimplification so we are charged with pursuing this a little further. Ashby suggested that organization theory has a peculiarity not found in the so-called "objective" sciences (he listed physics and chemistry) and that peculiarity is that the "product space … *contains more than actually exists in the real physical world*" (p. 105; p. 257 in original, italics in the original). It is the physical world, he suggested, that contains all of the constraints of a system; it is the communication or interplay between the constraints that creates the emergences in the 'product space'. As he said, a theory of organization is concerned with "*properties that are not intrinsic to the thing but are relational between observer and thing*" (p. 106; p. 258 in original, italics in the original). Ashby highlighted that, at the time, there was an increasing research effort in dynamics that did not observe parts of a system but observed the whole. We would consider this commonplace now. However, as Ashby describes, how one views the connectedness of parts of a whole (and therefore the start of organization within the system) is contingent upon the observer (in other words, the actor and their subjectivity). This is eminently relevant in our case since, for the most part, we invest in complexity theory (or otherwise) to explain what we think we see happening in learning—we have no real way of knowing how the degrees of freedom within a system interact to have cause within the 'product space'—all we are able to witness is what 'emerges', in other words, the behaviour. We *assume* this to have happened through the capacity of the 'whole' of the system to self-organize.

A few words about affordances

We will not talk at length here about affordances, as others in this volume will undertake such a task. However, suffice to say that in ecological psychology the idea of affordances is used to describe all of the possible behaviours within a given context or environment or, again, to use the words of Popper, the propensities.

Affordances are the properties of both the environment and the organism. They act both as opportunities but also as constraints. Therefore, the movement possibilities within any given environment are not limitless. We have already visited this; there are only so many degrees of freedom within any given context. However, Riccio and Stoffrengren (1988) suggest that these limits or constraints—the properties of the environment and of the organism—actually determine the possible behaviours. Remember, we are not just referring here to the biological assets of the organism but the experience of the organism also. This makes intuitive sense; even Sir Fred Bartlett[1] talked about how, when he played a tennis stroke, it was neither exactly the same as he once played it, nor was it entirely new. Affordances, then, have consequences and this follows given that affordances represent the limits of possible behaviour. If there are possibilities, there must be consequences or, to use contemporary vernacular, 'outcomes'. In physical education and sport, however, we can really only observe this as outward behaviour, and that behaviour is not random but goal-directed. In other words, there is a motivation factor (which includes zero motivation). Given the dynamic space represented by sport (as subject matter for physical education and coaching), one could reasonably argue that the environment is constantly shifting and therefore the affordances similarly change leading to, if we follow the logic, a renewed set of possibilities for behaviour. However, there are not endless possibilities in any given situation. In addition, we know that the rate of change in an environment would be too fast for constant adaptation to occur—the science of reaction time and movement time tell us that. Indeed, periods of consolidation, either through repeated movement success *or* periodic failure, are probably advantageous. However, the capacity to manage changing environments, in other words, to adapt to constantly changing conditions, is tolerable by increased experience (part of the process of consolidation) and feedback systems that are able to minimize the 'costs' associated with movement. We take this up in the next section where we consider the role of adaptation in terms of some current research in motor control.

The role of adaptation

With the reader's indulgence, we will start this section with a short narrative.

> In the perceptual motor lab a subject sits in a strange configuration at a computer. Using only isometric contraction of the forefinger, the subject guides a cursor on the monitor from a starting point to where a marker appears on the screen. Being the able person that he is, he accomplishes this task with ease on most of the 80 trials. The seating arrangements are re-configured, the task recommences, however, success is not immediate. It seems there is a distortion in the movement (a perturbation). However, well within the 160 trials, success returns. It turns out that there was a 45-degree distortion of the visual feedback. This was unknown to the subject, however, this was overcome through the trials and accuracy returned. When asked by the research team, "How did you do that?" the subject answers, "I have no idea."

We tell this story for two reasons: first, it is a real story that involved the two authors—Timothy as researcher and Anthony as the subject. Secondly, the phenomenon that occurred led to the co-joined interest in what this might mean for pedagogy. The adaptation occurred at a level that was inexplicable by the subject but clearly involved adaptation strategies that enabled responses to be constantly modified even though the subject had no idea what was going on in terms of the perturbation. We acknowledge that experiments like these attract criticism from practitioners in the field as being inauthentic and the data generated from impoverished environments. However, it was the principle that intrigued us both. To that end, some of the current work being undertaken in motor behaviour laboratories is worth exploring and to do this we draw on three key studies from the field as being not only informative but also representative of one of the current directions within the field of motor control.

Three key studies

Mazzoni and Krakauer (2006) conducted a visuomotor adaptation experiment that is potentially provocative for pedagogy practice, in that the results are counter-intuitive and raise questions about some of the core assumptions underlying some aspects of the popular conventions of physical education pedagogy. As was the case in the experiment that provided the context for our anecdote above, the paradigm was one of visuomotor rotation.[2] That is, participants make reaching movements to targets with visual feedback of a cursor that represents the position of the hand. The feedback is then experimentally manipulated to cause errors; in many cases the visual information is rotated by around 30–60 degrees. People initially make large reaching errors as specified by the perturbation, but gradually adapt (or learn) to move accurately to targets with the new feedback. In this particular paper, the authors asked participants to use a cognitive strategy to counter the early errors caused by the perturbation (i.e., "there is a 45 degree rotation; aim to the target 45 degrees away from the one that is specified"). As expected, the strategy was initially effective at cancelling the aiming errors. Surprisingly, however, the participants subsequently made incrementally larger aiming errors in the opposite direction with practice. Indeed, the rate of adaptation was no different to a group that aimed at the primary target and gradually improved performance via implicit learning. This indicates that the 'reaching control system' automatically adapted to the mismatch between motor commands and visual feedback (i.e., aiming to the adjacent target, even though visual feedback reported that the motion was toward the primary target). So, irrespective of explicit strategies and whether or not the task goal was achieved, individuals are unable to prevent their sensorimotor control systems from implicit modulation. The implication is that explicit instructions or reflections may not be relevant for some aspects of motor skill acquisition. Indeed, despite the fact that the paper was published in the field of neuroscience, the authors were prepared to discuss the practical implications of their findings. The final sentence reads: "Sports coaches should take note that, when it comes to motor learning, the brain has a mind of its own" (p. 3645).

Hinder, Riek, Tresilian, de Rugy, and Carson (2010) also used a visuomotor rotation task to explore the importance of feedback on the acquisition of motor skill, but used isometric force production of arm muscles to drive a visual cursor towards targets. The aim was to determine the relative importance for motor adaptation of: (1) having 'real-time' feedback available during a movement; (2) making on-line corrections to any errors that occur during movement; (3) having delayed (i.e., post-trial) feedback of the movement trajectory (knowledge of performance, KP); and (4) having post-trial feedback only of task outcome (knowledge of results, KR). The results showed that both conditions in which on-line feedback was available resulted in motor adaptation *and* persistent errors in the opposite direction once the rotation was removed and feedback was veridical (coinciding with what would be expected). In contrast, in the two conditions in which only post-trial feedback (KP and KR) was available, performance increased but no 'after-effect' errors occurred when the rotation was removed. Since after-effects are viewed as evidence that the control system has stored a representation of the new sensorimotor conditions, the data suggest that continuous sensory feedback is required for motor learning via implicit processes, but that post-trial feedback might be useful to facilitate the acquisition of cognitive movement 'strategies'. The discursive exchange between teacher/coach and learner might provide a useful mechanism for developing broad strategic understanding of a particular game, for example. However, such an exchange is unlikely to affect the performance of tasks requiring continuous sensory feedback within the changing condition of that game. For example, discussing action/decisions taken during a sequence of play may be useful at a strategic level and, indeed, can provide insight into the particular configurations of games such as common shapes and patterns of offensive and defensive plays. However, the effectiveness of such discussions may be tempered by task performance or technique, which appears to rely on continuous updating from the sensory system.

Finally, a paper by Huang, Shademehr, and Diedrichsen (2008) also used a sensory–motor adaptation paradigm, but in this case, a computer-controlled robot was used to perturb reaching movements. The participants were required to "become as proficient as possible at hitting a small target in one of four directions with a rapid center-out strike using a robotic manipulandum" (Huang *et al.*, 2008, p. 880). Participants learned to make accurate aiming movements in a velocity-dependent force field (i.e., the amount of force the robot applies to push a participant's limb off target is proportional to the instantaneous velocity of the movement). The purpose was to compare the effectiveness of learning when subjects chose the order of targets (from four available) versus when a computer specified the training order on the basis of optimal 'machine learning' algorithms. The results indicate that people tend to use inefficient training sequences intuitively, and learning can be enhanced if an external agent (e.g., coach or teacher) guides the training on the basis of principles to optimize performance. More specifically, when the training sequence was self-selected, people tended to repeat both accurate and inaccurate reaches at probabilities above chance. It turns out that repeating movements to targets where an error occurs is a strategy favoured by machine-learning principles, while repeating successful reaches is not. The results confirmed that these principles are also relevant for human motor learning. For example, repeating successful trials is inefficient for motor learning, as shown by the superior performance of a group of subjects who practised according to the schedule selected by the computer, and a negative correlation between the strength of the tendency to repeat successes and the rate of learning.

The results from this study have very clear and obvious implications about how we can begin to think about physical education pedagogy and, as a teacher or coach, experiment with these ideas drawn from basic science. We acknowledge that sometimes it seems like a long stretch from the laboratory to the sports field or gym. However, what these studies illustrate is that engagement with the most recent motor control literature has attractive potential benefits for encouraging teacher/coach-based 'experiments' in live physical activity settings within coaching or physical education environments. It seems to us that the fast heuristics available to humans may serve a 'search and execute' strategy well in that it might lead to enhanced learning. However, we suggest that the teacher or coach is not redundant in this process. What seems to be the key is the degree of intervention by the teacher that enables adaptation to changing environments.

We have spent time reviewing three influential papers that can shed some light on what laboratory-based studies are tending to demonstrate about learning. The reason for this is that these studies tend to show that adaptation, via constant update mechanisms available through the senses, facilitate a learner in 'managing' the propensities of an environment in the pursuit of an intended outcome. To return to Simon (1990), this is how the blades of his metaphorical scissors work. However, current theory in motor control also illustrates how adaptive responses can occur, not only from one movement or performance to the next, but also rapidly *during* a given task. Indeed, in order to generate the best possible motor performance, we should assess sensory information about our bodies and the world continuously, and the details of our actions should be specified at the last possible moment. For example, if asking students to learn how to serve a tennis ball, the teacher could ask learners to make a conscious effort to 'gather information' at a range of points during the movement (posture, limb position, head, ball in space, etc.) such that this becomes the information used to ultimately execute the task. The difficulty of this should not be understated; however, understanding how conditions could change (Popper's propensities) is as important as developing the movement pattern itself. This allows movements to be based on the maximum amount of information. It is this principle that led Todorov and Jordan (2002) to suggest the computational framework of OFC as a general theory of how motor coordination might be achieved. Although some aspects of the theory have been called into question (see de Rugy, Loeb, & Carroll, 2012) it is a reasonable generalization to say that OFC remains one of the dominant current frameworks for understanding movement control.

The core idea that underlies the framework of OFC is that motor coordination can be considered as the solution to an optimization problem. The learning environment in physical education has never been conceptualized as an optimization problem—but, of course, this is exactly what it is; it is an unpredictable environment with only limited certainty of outcome. What OFC really means is that our motor system has evolved, developed or learned to perform movements that achieve task goals in a way that minimizes the 'cost' of the movement. Precisely how the nervous system defines the cost of the movement is debatable, but terms associated with task success variability and effort of movement are common in computational models that have been shown to capture behaviour well. OFC theory extends the core idea of cost minimization to include the use of *feedback systems* in coordination of movement. Thus, the control system specifies feedback gains for sensory–motor loops in order to minimize the cost of movement based on *estimates* of the current state of the body and environment. The advantage of this type of system is that it allows the details of motor coordination to be specified at the last possible moment—an important factor when one considers that the environment–actor system is nonstationary and that 'noise' contaminates both our motor and sensory systems (leading to errors). In this framework there is no formal distinction between open- and closed-loop control— all movements are closed loop and based on the 'optimal' way to go from the current state of the system to the desired state. One critical element of an optimal feedback controller that is required to avoid the problems of delays in sensory–motor loops that made previous servo-control theories intractable is a method to obtain accurate estimates of the *current* state of the system (body and world). Accurate state estimation relies on predictions about one's future effect on the world from knowledge of the consequences of motor commands, which are provided by a processing network termed a 'forward internal model'. These predictions are integrated with sensory information, which is a delayed and noisy approximation of reality. The result is a type of 'internal feedback' that produces a moment-by-moment estimate of the actual current state of the system. Hence, as environment–actor systems evolve and change, there is great, but not endless, capacity to adapt; the limits of adaptation are defined by the shortest possible sensorimotor delays. The 'quality' of the predictions made by forward internal models might be an important factor that determines motor skill. Indeed, Yarrow, Brown, and Krakauer (2009) speculated that the development of a rich and accurate forward model might underlie not only motor expertise, but also perceptual skills of expert performers. For example, a tennis player who can anticipate the response of an opponent to placement of a particular serve will be able to execute the next shot with time and space to set up a winning point.

There are potential implications for physical education pedagogy of the principles suggested by optimal feedback control theory and some of the experimental work we have identified. Our purpose is to raise awareness regarding some of the more recent ideas from motor control that might be of use. First, the evidence suggests that motor adaptation occurs automatically, based on observed discrepancies between motor commands and on-line feedback of their outcomes, and that there is a fundamental disconnect between this adaptation process and conscious intensions and delayed feedback or reflection about movements 'after the fact'. This suggests that being able to articulate the principles of skilful motor performance is, at best, inadequate, and, at worst, irrelevant as an index of the underlying capability. Secondly, results showing that people tend to adopt suboptimal training schedules (in teaching this might be better described as non-challenging) illustrate that, although the process of skill acquisition appears to follow something like lawful principles, these are not always intuitive. Thus, it would appear, at least, that the set of experiences required to improve motor skill most effectively may only emerge naturally within limits. 'External' intervention by way of a teacher or coach still seems to be a viable idea. Finally, internal feedback systems allow 'intelligent', adaptive responses at very short latency (delay between stimulus and response). In this case, players are intelligent in the sense that they effectively make use of information to generate responses that assist the realization of goals, not in the sense that they involve cognitive processes to figure out what to do in the situation. It may be that assessing 'automatic' responses in highly time-constrained contexts, rather than 'after-the-fact' question and answer sessions, might provide more robust measures of expertise. In a physical education lesson this might require teachers to consider (and record) how learners are developing the capacity to adapt to ever-changing environments, rather than simply relying on learners to articulate what it was they either did or were trying to do.

Inconvenient challenges

We have avoided parodying Al Gore's catchphrase on the basis that truth is something of an elusive entity. However, the findings we have marshalled here through three papers (that, though seemingly counter-intuitive in what they suggest, are representative of a particular line of feedback research), create some challenges for physical education pedagogy. For instance, it may be prudent to reassess what we mean when we use the words 'intelligent performance'. As we indicate above, the cognitive process of being able to rationalize one's action after-the-fact may not make much sense for fast-action, adaptive aspects of motor performance. The direction of the work to which we have alluded here suggests that human action that seems to demonstrate adaptation to change is as likely as anything else to be attributable to on-line corrections with very short latencies. This suggests that much of this action must be below the level of consciousness. The failure of this system, which in overt behaviour terms might look like a bad decision, may be more to do with the evolving system being unable to use all of the information in the system. In other words, the human 'blade' of Simon's metaphorical scissors may be limited by the actor's computational assets from taking advantage of all of the propensities within a movement 'product space'. Lack of multiple experiences in similar (but not identical) product spaces will limit the referent upon which the actor within the system can draw. At a practical day-to-day level this may not be that unfamiliar; the need for rich and varied experiences (rather than blocked repetitive practice) has been a principle of advocacy in the motor learning literature for some time (see Schmidt, 1975) and has been advocated as a principle of pedagogy for about as long (see Pigott, 1983, but also Davids, Button, & Bennett, 2008, for a broader overview).

It is also apparent that, in spite of motor skill acquisition following law-like principles, the experiences required to bring optimal skill development about may not occur naturally or 'by discovery'. This seems to be the case because, when left to their own devices, actors seem to select suboptimal training regimes or, to put it another way, they make attempts at tasks by limiting the degrees of freedom they bring to the system. External feedback (by way of teachers, coaches or others), then, appears to be crucial. Interestingly (and perhaps ironically), this claim could be used as a point of advocacy for any number of approaches to physical education pedagogy. However, at a level of common understanding, this does suggest that the role of the teacher remains important. It also suggests that doing 'technique' work (which probably sounds entirely unappealing) can be achieved through manipulation of the degrees of freedom. Whilst the isolation of technique as a pedagogical process probably goes against the philosophical grain, it can provide an opportunity for mastery within very few degrees of freedom—in other words, where the affordances (the propensities within a system) are greatly reduced. This may have the appearance of reducing the teaching and learning process to a linear mechanism. Yet this is only the case where blocked practice is used in some kind of pure form for the entire learning session. Most teachers and coaches modify the environment (most commonly by adding layers of difficulty) and have the learners 'adapt' their technique to overcome a new and evolving set of challenges. How this is different to setting up a learning environment (a modified game, say) with some inbuilt target behaviours which we sometimes call problem-setting or task-setting (keep the ball away, score a basket, get the ball to the line, etc.) and have the learners 'solve' the movement 'product space' problems based on previous experience and previous exposure to similar problems is probably not even discernible (see Butler & Hopper, 2011; Thorpe, 1990).

Some final thoughts and questions

We would argue that an important question to ask is, though ongoing adaptation is generally regarded as central to complexity, can we attribute motor skill learning to pedagogy informed by complexity thinking? The case we have built here suggests that it is feasible; however, how we label this may not be *as* crucial as understanding just what is going on. If we know *what happens*, we can use those principles to build a pedagogical repertoire. There is evidence from other areas of the school curriculum that those characterized as good teachers weave in and out of pedagogical approaches as they seek to bring about ongoing adaptation to ever-evolving challenges and systems, and, in some cases, teachers decide to simplify the systems as far as possible (see Newman & Associates, 1996; Queensland Government, 2004). Our view is that, in physical education, this approach is probably not yet prevalent enough. However, we suggest that this can be done by manipulating the degrees of freedom within a product space and, in doing so, bring about stable to unstable conditions for learners to experience, be challenged by and then manage. Intelligent performance can be more readily understood by the evolving capacity to manage unstable conditions through ongoing adaptation supported by on-line corrections with ultra-fast heuristics.

Notes

1 Sir Fred Bartlett was known for his groundbreaking studies of *memory* and social psychology in the 1930s.

2 Visuomotor rotation is a screen-cursor transformation that introduces a systematic directional bias around the hand and thus can be used to probe the adaptive processes underlying planning of reaching direction.

References

Ashby, W.R. (2004). Principles of the self-organizing system. *Classical Papers—Principles of the Self-Organizing System*, 6(Special Double Issue (1–2)), 103–126.

Butler, J., & Hopper, T. (2011). Inventing net/wall games for all students. *Active and Healthy Magazine*, 18(3/4).

Davids, K., Button, C., & Bennett, S. (2008). *Dynamics of skill acquisition*. Champaign, IL: Human Kinetics.

de Rugy, A., Loeb, G.E., & Carroll, T.J. (2012). Muscle coordination is habitual rather than optimal. *The Journal of Neuroscience*, 32(21), 7384–7391.

Goldstein, J. (2004). Introduction to principles of the self-organizing system by Ross Ashby. *Classical Papers—Principles of the Self-Organizing System*, 6(Special Double Issue (1–2)), 102.

Haken, H. (1996). *Chaos and order in nature* (2nd ed.). New York: Springer.

Hinder, M.R., Riek, S., Tresilian, J., de Rugy, A., & Carson, R.G. (2010). Real-time error detection but not error correction drives automatic visuomotor adaptation. *Experimental Brain Research*, 201(2), 191–207.

Huang, V.S., Shademehr, R., & Diedrichsen, J. (2008). Active learning: Learning a motor skill without a coach. *Journal of Neurophysiology*, 100, 879–887.

Jones, B.D. (1999). Bounded rationality. *Annual Review of Political Science*, 2, 297–321.

Kelso, J.A.S., & Schöner, G. (1988). Self-organization of coordinative movement patterns. *Human Movement Science*, 7(1), 27–46.

Mazzoni, P., & Krakauer, J. (2006). An implicit plan overrides an explicit strategy during visuomotor adaptation. *The Journal of Neuroscience*, 26, 3642–3645.

Newmann, F.W., & Associates (1996). *Authentic achievement: Restructuring schools for intellectual quality*. San Francisco: Jossey-Bass.

Popper, K. (1990). *A world of propensities*. Bristol: Thoemmes.

Queensland Government. (2004). *The new basics research report*. Brisbane, Australia: The State of Queensland.

Riccio, G.E., & Stoffregen, T.A. (1988). Affordances as constraints on the control of stance. *Human Movement Science*, 7, 265–300.

Rovengo, I., & Kirk, D. (1995). Articulations and silences in socially critical work on physical education: Toward a broader agenda. *Quest*, 47(4), 447–474.

Schmidt, R.A. (1975). A schema theory of discrete motor skill learning. *Psychological Review*, 82(4), 225–260.

Simon, H.A. (1990). Invariants of human behavior. *Annual Review of Psychology*, 41, 1–19.

Thorpe, R. (1990). New directions in games teaching. In N. Armstrong (Ed.), *New directions in physical education* (pp. 79–100). Champaign, IL: Human Kinetics.

Todd, P.M., & Gigerenzer, G. (2003). Bounding rationality to the world. *Journal of Economic Psychology*, 24, 143–165.

Todorov, E., & Jordan, M.I. (2002). Optimal feedback control as a theory of motor coordination. *Nature Neuroscience*, 5(11), 1226–1235.

Ulanowicz, R.E. (1997). *Ecology, the ascendent perspective*. New York: Columbia University Press.

Williams, A.M., Davids, K., & Williams, J.G. (1999). *Visual perception and action in sport.* London: E & FN Spon.

Yarrow, K., Brown, P., & Krakauer, J.W. (2009). Inside the brain of an elite athlete: The neural processes that support high achievement in sports. *National Review of Neuroscience, 10*(8), 585–596.

8 "Another damned, thick, square book!"

Tracing learning theory in physical education textbooks, 1900–2010

Ellen Singleton

The purpose of this chapter is to trace the progression, over time, of theoretical pedagogical thinking found in textbooks produced for physical educators.[1] As a means of providing a framework for identifying and assessing various theories, Richard Light's (2008) comments on behaviourism, constructivism and complicated and complex learning theories will provide a basis for this search. The nature of learning theories as they have been circulated in textbooks designated for physical education professionals, students and the general public from selected decades over the last 100 years will be examined.[2] Although recommended physical activities and exercises are an important part of many physical education textbooks, it is not within the scope of this chapter to examine these, nor to determine if the theories advanced by the authors are, in fact, applied in the practical activities that they suggest. Three questions will be discussed as a conclusion to this chapter: Is there evidence that theoretical thinking in physical education textbooks has changed over time? Does complex learning theory appear as an aspect of theoretical thinking in physical education textbooks? Is there a future for physical education textbooks?

It is surprisingly difficult to define the term 'textbook'. Notwithstanding the opinion of the Duke of Gloucester cited in the title above (Bartlett, 1980, p. 387), and one shared I am sure by many students (who would probably add 'expensive' to their complaint), textbooks cannot be defined by size, by cost, nor, as some have argued, by the fact that they are used in schools (Rosenberg, 1995). Ian Michael (1990) notes that "there is a large class of 18th and 19th century books written especially for home use" (p. 1). Furthermore, in addition to books published for use in social institutions such as the home and the school, texts, manuals and other 'companion' volumes traditionally have been produced for young apprentices and working men (Michael, 1990).

The focus on learning may be the key to the definition of 'textbook'. Hoskin (1990) states that "the invention of 'the textbook' is a sign, and a central part, of a historically new way of learning, or more properly of 'learning how to learn' " (p. 1). As a means of providing depth to this useful description, Hamilton (1990) notes textbooks visibly reflect pedagogic considerations. That is, a textbook is not just a book used in schools. Rather, it is a book that has been consciously designed and organized to serve the ends of schooling.

(p. 1)

A quick conclusion might be, then, that textbooks are books used explicitly for learning. However, Hoskin (1990), Michael (1990) and others (Issitt, 2004; Nichols, 2005) qualify this summary by adding that the decision to treat a publication as a 'textbook' depends, in Michael's words, upon the

> author's explicit or implied intentions; publisher's advertisements; publishing history; use made of the book; price; tone of the book (instructional, explanatory, moralistic).

(Michael, 1990, p. 3)

Another element of importance is the question of epistemology or of the knowledge contained in the textbook. This is particularly important in light of the observation that "textbooks themselves lay a definitional claim to the knowledge they contain—they claim that 'this is certain knowledge and this is the knowledge you need' " (Issitt, 2004, p. 685). Textbooks, in other words, are presented by authors, by publishers, and often by educators as authoritative 'voices' encapsulating the knowledge necessary for learners at particular and specific stages of their educational process. Issitt (2004) sums this up by observing:

> In their creation they take their impulses from a mix of sources including the configuration of dominant ideas and social values, the commercial impulses of the publishing industry, particular academic disciplines and conventions of authorship, and from the progressive technologies of media production.

(p. 685)

But the knowledge in textbooks cannot be considered to be simply assemblages of the concepts or ideas of the moment. Competing definitions of what constitutes knowledge and purposeful choices about which knowledge is included or excluded affects the content and the perspectives of the 'certain knowledge' in textbooks (Nicholls, 2005). Underlying textbook knowledge are serious questions about the construction, reproduction and manipulation of power and ideology. All knowledge appearing in textbooks is bracketed by questions—why was *this* knowledge included? Is there *other* knowledge? *Whose perspective* does this knowledge serve?

The assumption of political neutrality characterizing textbooks is supported and sustained by an "authorial monotone" (Issitt, 2004, p. 688) that focuses the reader's attention on the description and explanation of the theory (or practice) rather than on the origin of the explanation. Furthermore, when the bland, authoritative voice of the author is legitimized by descriptions of academic accomplishment and/or workplace experience, a powerful combination of objective knowledge and cultural support is created and maintained. This is, for example, particularly evident in early physical education textbooks which leaned heavily on the expertise of medical doctors and experienced school and city (playground) administrators for the development of their pedagogical perspectives.

Issitt (2004) argues that "Textbooks function to some extent as the voices of the disciplines—as such they have a key function as building blocks in the architecture of knowledge" (p. 688). As physical education slowly came to be viewed as a discipline in the later stages of the nineteenth century, physicians and educators led the way with textbooks for the home and the school that extolled the correct methods of instruction for learning how to live a fit, productive and therefore happy life.

Textbooks in physical education: some 'light' discussion

Who uses textbooks in physical education? In school subjects such as Mathematics, English or History, it is common practice for students to be assigned textbooks to augment part of their learning. For physical education, the pedagogical thrust is on experiential learning. That is, students are expected to participate actively throughout the majority of their classes and book work is not considered a regular aspect of the class programme.[3] But textbooks are used in physical education and have been in use for well over 100 years. Professional physical educators at all levels of schooling and in a variety of institutions such as the church, the armed forces, playgrounds, the YMCA and Scouts (Boy and Girl), as well as the general public, have and have had for many years, a montage of textbooks from which to learn the fundamental elements of their discipline. Physical education textbooks traditionally have included a firm grounding in anatomical, physiological and health-related science, principles of programme administration suitable for various institutions, and recommended pedagogical practices and principles that often reflect the common social and/or cultural mores of the era. It is this last element to which most attention will be paid in this chapter.

Pedagogical theories are inextricably bound up with the social and cultural practices of the time. According to Issitt (2004):

> Study of the textbook can therefore illuminate the history of ideas and the evolution of dominant ideologies as well as the effects of government rhetoric, cultural mythology, pedagogic design, authorial intent and many other areas. At the level of the evolution of ideas, textbooks offer a way of tracing the changing pattern of socially legitimized ideas and the way the learner, teacher and text are positioned.
>
> (p. 696)

Beliefs about learning in physical education have been profoundly influenced by historical and long-standing associations with medicine and science, and through the continual efforts of educators to legitimize physical education knowledge claims within Western culture (Light, 2008; Tinning, 1991). Educational theorist Richard Light (2008) unequivocally asserts that the traditional beliefs and practices still observed in most physical education programmes are representative of the behaviourist views that have dominated learning theory for much of the twentieth century.[4] Behaviourism is characterized by a dualism in thinking that separates mental activities from physical experiences and

> the separation of thought from action, self from other, knower from known, and subjective from objective ... behaviorism requires a highly structured and technical pedagogical approach. Behaviorists conceive of cognition and learning as being mechanical processes and strive to understand learning by reducing it to its simplest components.
>
> (Light, 2008, pp. 22–23)

Light (2008) contrasts behaviourism with constructivism, a teaching and learning approach that has gained popularity with educators over the past two or three decades, in part because constructivist approaches focus on learning as "a process of adapting to and fitting into a constantly changing world" (p. 23). He points out that these beliefs about learning are quite unlike behaviourism in that constructivism

> rests upon very different epistemology, or conception of knowledge, to adopt a more ecological view of learning that challenges the dualistic division of mind from body, learner from learned, and subject from object. Implicit within this rejection of the division between mind and body is the importance of the body and its sensations in learning.
>
> (Light, 2008, p. 22)

Like many proponents who wish to move away from traditional, dualistic physical education teaching approaches to more holistic approaches, Light (2008) believes that embedded commonsense assumptions about learning in physical education, a lack of research in constructivist epistemology as it relates to physical education and the availability of more than one form of constructivism all contribute to continuing difficulties in implementing pedagogical change in physical education.

'Lighting' the way: distinguishing between complicated and complex learning theory

How can these challenges be addressed? Light draws upon the seminal research of Davis and Sumara (2005), Griffin and Butler (2005), Kinchloe (2005), Kirk and MacDonald (1998), Lave and Wenger (1991), Rink (2001) and Rovegno (1998) to support Davis, Sumara, and Luce-Kapler's (2000) contention that their notion of a complex learning theory is useful in integrating some of the common properties of various constructivist approaches, particularly in their application to physical education pedagogy. Kinchloe (2005) notes that, when we begin to examine "the contexts and relationships connecting learner, culture, teaching, knowledge production and curriculum" we are "moving into a more complex paradigm" (p. 28). That is, Davis *et al.* identify *complex learning theory* as a focus on learning that emphasizes an on-going process of adaptation, on learning that is inextricably linked to social interaction and on 'knowing' that is inseparable from 'experiencing'. Kinchloe (2005) concludes that in complex systems, "learning is viewed … as a dynamic and unpredictable process" (p. 28).

'Complex learning theory' is the term developed by Davis *et al.* (2000) to identify common elements shared by different formulations of constructivism. They have also developed the term 'complicated learning theory' to reference common characteristics of traditional 'commonsense' or behavioural views of learning and to compare and contrast these modes of thought in education. These commonsense views include the assumptions that learning is linear—for example, that skills are built through a series of carefully planned progressions. Learning is objective and requires highly technical, structured and controlled approaches to instruction. All students begin from the same state of 'not knowing'. Personal circumstances should not be allowed to infringe on the homogeneity of instruction. Given that each student has the same chance to succeed, it is up to the individual student to take responsibility for his/her own success.

Is complicated and complex learning not simply a form of thinly disguised dualism?

The comparison is, I believe, more 'complicated' than that. Dualistic comparisons are usually most easily made between the polar opposites of a single concept: mind/body focuses on ranges of human experience; learner/learned on the act of knowing; subject/object on poles of human perception, and so on. Although dualistic comparisons can be illustrative, they are often also simplistic and superficial. Complex and complicated learning theories, on the other hand, seem to me to be more complementary than contrasting. *Complicated* learning theory has been how educators have understood the world of teaching and learning for many years. This is the theory that has been applied in physical education class since marching, drill, group calisthenics, playground games and 'girls' rules were taken-for-granted necessities in any physical educator's teaching preparation. And while the practice might have changed, it is still the theory many physical educators espouse. But it is from these linear and dualistic practices and theories that the contemporary interest in more holistic approaches to teaching and learning in physical education have arisen.

Recognizing complex forms in early textbooks

Although Davis and Sumara (2005) note that some qualities are common to all complex forms, how can we recognize if these qualities are present in textbooks that were written long before educational specialists began to theorize about 'complexity learning theory'? Davis and Sumara (2005) describe all complex forms as emergent, transcendent and adaptable (p. 456). Complex systems have the potential to emerge in physical education when the rules for engaging in activity are seen to be 'enabling constraints'. They provide structure for students, but are not prescriptive. Instead, rules are established that delimit possibilities and allow choice (p. 193). In physical education this may mean that game-like activities are introduced with only a minimum of constraining rules to guide them. As expertise increases, players determine whether additional constraints are needed to ensure fairness and safety while enhancing the game experience.

Through a process of sharing and juxtaposing ideas, learning moves away from traditional teacher-centred or even student-centred classrooms to where action is driven by emerging possibilities. Through self-organization individuals are able to move into coherent collective behaviours with others and, because a collective is more than the sum of its parts, complex systems transcend the potential of one by harnessing the power of many. In physical education these experiences may best be associated with the networks of creative group work that students and teachers engage in together as fitness, dance or gymnastic routines are prepared, or as game strategies are discovered in a Teaching Games for Understanding lesson.

As complexity theorists understand it, learning is not linear; it is recursive. Learning is not conceived of as a straight line nor even as a spiral slowly spinning ever upwards, but rather as a process that folds back onto itself as learners move back and forth between what they know and what they are learning. Learners make sense of their experiences and then use this 'sense' to understand further experiences. For example, students who begin aquatics as non-swimmers should have many opportunities to experience and come to understand the limitations and possibilities of buoyancy. More advanced swimming skills are introduced as students develop confidence in their capacity to safely control their body in the water. It is understood that learners may have to return to earlier notions of buoyancy in order to develop a better understanding of more challenging skills.

Finally, complex class systems made up of diverse collectives of largely self-directed students capable of altering and adjusting to a variety of learning conditions are adaptable. While they are able to maintain coherence in the face of changing circumstances, their adaptability also makes them highly unpredictable.

Is there evidence that theoretical thinking in physical education has changed over time? In the following section, selected textbooks representing more than 100 years of pedagogy in physical education will be analysed for evidence of the learning theories that may have influenced the recommended practice of the era. It may be expected that earlier textbooks will display, for the most part, *complicated* learning theories that include clear expectations for the training of a corporeal 'machine' guided by step-by-step linear physical rehearsal and repetition. But will there also be evidence of interest in the more holistic qualities identified with contemporary *complex* learning theories? In order to maintain a consistent standard of comparison while examining textbooks that were published in different eras of the past and present century, the common qualities of complicated (linearity, objectivity, homogeneity and individuality) and complex (emergence, transcendence and adaptability) systems will be sought in the representative samples of physical education textbooks that follow.

"...more or less dull Text-books": constructing the discipline of physical education

In 1901 Eustace H. Miles observed, "There are many excellent Papers on the subject of health. In America alone there are three..." (Schmidt & Miles, 1901, p. ix). Clearly, the discipline of physical education, represented in this early textbook by terms such as "Health, Training, and Athletics" (p. x) is a subject in its infancy. At first, physical education content and methodology was influenced by rigid systems of exercise called European gymnastics and British systems of calisthenics. physical education was later affected by play theory that grew out of the playground move-ment in the United States. The fledgling physical education curriculum for Canadian schools adopted ideas from a variety of sources (Houghton, 1891; Kidd, 1996; Morrow & Wamsley, 2005). Strong support from most political and social leaders kept the military in the public eye and gymnastics, which resembled rigid military drill, as well as marching and calisthenics, were often taught by ex-military personnel (Kidd, 1996; Morrow & Wamsley, 2005). Early physical educators enthu-siastically embraced Descartes's notion of a separate mind and body and supported their practice with learning theory that postulated that a body was well educated when it was trained to respond to the dictates of the mind. Baron Nils Posse advised in *The Swedish System of Educational Gymnastics* (1890) that "there should exist an equilibrium between all parts of the body, so that they form a well-balanced whole under the perfect control of the will" (p. 3). Each student was drilled with a series of scientific exercises designed to help attain the ideal of physical development suitable for that particular person "according to the laws of nature" (Posse, 1890, p. 3).

Gymnastics was particularly popular in schools, where systems of exercise that were rigidly organized and even more rigidly followed were welcomed by teachers burdened with large classes (Houghton, 1891).

Some physical educators, however, advocated for opportunities for more chal-lenging and engaging activities such as competitive team games for boys (Schmidt & Miles, 1901) and, occasionally, for girls (Hill, 1903). In addition to their enjoyment value, the inclusion of games in the curriculum was justified on moral, patriotic and developmental grounds. Games helped boys to develop into masculine, heterosexual men by instilling a code of conduct that emphasized honour, justice and responsibility. In an impassioned plea for the inclusion of games into schools, Schmidt and Miles (1901) wrote:

> All those lessons which *are* taught from more or less dull Text-books and which *can* be taught from Games should be taught from Games...What need is there to go to a dull statistic-book to get such ideas as Co-operation, Division of Labour, Independent Activity and Originality, Honour, Discipline, and so on, into a boy's mind, when there is a special field of study in every school worthy of the name, and a field of study in which a boy is *bound* to be interested, if he *is* a boy (italics in original).
>
> (Schmidt & Miles, 1901, p. 61)

Games instruction for girls had somewhat different aims. Moderate games participation was believed to contribute to strength development for successful childbearing (Hill, 1903; Schmidt & Miles, 1901). Furthermore, team-oriented experiences helped women learn the virtues of self-sacrifice and the importance of supporting others to ensure success (Hill, 1903; Sumption, 1927).

Regardless of the activity, physical education learning theory around 1900 was complicated in nature—linear (strict progressions were followed for skill acquisition), objective (the body was considered to be under the control of the mind), homogeneous (every participant moved in unison with others) and individualistic (every participant was responsible for his/her own success).

Just over two decades later, Europe and North America had experienced a World War, a new European political landscape, increased immigration, increased migration of workers from rural to urban centres, female suffrage and Prohibition. Many people were ready for a change from regimented schools, lockstep gymnastic exercises and rule-bound skill progressions as the introduction to game play. Educational theorist John Dewey (1899, 1908, 1916), greatly influenced by research in the new science of psychology—particularly in the areas of child development and learning—advocated a move away from rigid approaches to schooling where children were expected to sit still for long periods of time, exercise in static rows, progress through course content in identical lockstep formation, and memorize lessons for class 'recitations'. The Progressive movement that grew out of Dewey's theories emphasized a child-centred approach that fostered personal learning based on individual readiness, interest and motivation. 'Play' took on new meaning in both elementary and secondary school and physical education textbooks came to include such passages as

> ...play is a genuine factor in the promotion of good citizenship in the home, in the school and in the community. Emphasis [should be] placed on pleasurable activity, on pupil initiative and on the transfer of play achievement to life situations that are bound to arise outside of ... school management or teacher control. By playing suitable games in this way, the whole life of the individual child is influenced and those personal qualities, but imperfectly expressed by the terms courage, initiative, self-control, honesty, courtesy and co-operation, developed.
>
> (Brandreth, 1931, p. 3)

Reading this, it is easy to assume that elements of complex learning theory appeared as aspects of theoretical thinking in physical education textbooks at a fairly early date. The rigid formations and strictly-controlled activities of earlier times are dismissed, and in their place is the freedom to move, to cooperate with others and to make decisions 'on the fly'. However, the "authorial monotone" (Issitt, p. 688) emphasized teacher-centred pedagogy that held emergent notions of student-centred learning firmly in check. Teachers are cautioned that

> It would be a mistake to think that merely providing an opportunity for children's play is sufficient ... games must be learned in an orderly way ... the

teacher must be in control of the situation, but without domineering or suppression of individual enthusiasm.

(Brandreth, 1931, p. 5)

While elementary physical educators used play to engage young learners, secondary physical education teachers used the concept of play to justify the introduction of more intense forms of competition into their classes, particularly into classes for male students (Mitchell & Mason, 1934; Nixon & Cozens, 1935; Singleton, 2010). Female physical educators, however, intent on maintaining their hard-won positions in school physical education departments, interpreted the notions of play and competitive team sport quite differently, and resisted the trend to increase the amount and intensity of competitive team sport in the curriculum (Hall, 2002; Lenskyj, 1986).

Female physical educators soon found it necessary to publish their own textbooks if they wished to promote their subject area (Cassidy & Kozman, 1943; Hill, 1903; Sumption, 1927). These textbooks concentrated on the proper methods of teaching fitness, calisthenics, gymnastics, dance and individual or paired sports.

Authors advocated mild, competitive experiences and advanced a 'complicated' learning theory that supported belief in the dual nature of male and female, mind and body, and learning and the learner (Cassidy & Kozman, 1943). As recently as 1969, American textbook authors Margaret Meyer and Marguerite Schwartz noted that female physical educators were reluctant to include more team sports in their programmes—"Concentration on individual and dual sports because of their greater 'carry-over' value (and preoccupation with the dangers of team competition[5]) generally characterize the programs of physical education and recreation for girls and women" (p. 1).

In fact, for more than 70 years, most physical education textbooks were written with a male audience in mind. Supported by the bland yet authoritative voice of the author, little attempt was made to explore learning theory that might move the profession of physical education into new ways of thinking about learning and teaching. It was not until the latter half of the twentieth century that new learning theories in physical education began to appear and the pedagogical emphasis in physical education began to shift from the question of which activities should be included in the curriculum to questions about how activity should be taught.

Complicated problems in a complex world

Does complex learning theory appear as an aspect of theoretical thinking in physical education textbooks? As the twentieth century advanced, changing perceptions of work, play, sport and gender affected the pedagogical theory and practice appearing in texts. Although a variety of new approaches for teaching physical education were identified in the 1960s and 1970s (Mosston, 1966), two learning theories popular at the time were particularly noteworthy in that one appeared to demonstrate a shift from traditional, complicated learning theory to more complex responses, and the other did not. The latter was Metzler's (1982) ALT-PE model and the former was commonly referred to as 'movement education'.

From the 1960s into the 1980s some theorists continued to refine the traditional behaviourist, pedagogical model as they concentrated on teacher preparation (Metzler, 1982; Siedentop, 1983). It was their belief that teachers should be adequately prepared to maximize the skill development of students through the efficient use of specific teaching "tools of the trade" (Siedentop, 1983, p. x). In their textbooks they emphasized the importance of planning, of establishing clear objectives, of well-thought-out class organization, of management and discipline, and of assessment and evaluation of step-by-step skill development. Metzler's (1982) ALT-PE (Academic Learning Time—Physical Education) teaching model[6] provides a clear example of the direction in which 'complicated' learning theory was travelling:

> The Presentation Function (in the ALT-PE learning process) includes several decisions for teachers ... The process involves the selection and presentation of stimuli to students in order to facilitate both frequency and mode of responding. For physical education the goal is to select stimuli that allow students to experience the fewest errors possible when making motor responses ... [teachers] must accurately describe what the exact behaviours are for a given learning task ... they must give the students pertinent, detailed cues about how to perform the task correctly.
>
> (p. 50)

Teacher-centred instruction, homogeneous, segregated female or male classes, universal instruction with minimal accommodation for difference, and individual responsibility for skill acquisition were the foci of complicated learning approaches at this time. Science provided the structure for knowledge as physical education embraced the advancing notions of measurement, motor development and behavioural psychology.

At the same time, shifts in the perspectives on the diversity of learners, as well as more politicized theorizing about learning and learners (Apple, 1989), resulted in textbooks that did not discard former practices so much as highlight new ways of teaching and learning that emerged from elements of previous approaches. Since the 1960s teaching approaches variously identified as movement education, Teaching Games for Understanding, reflective practice and sport concept education have appeared. Student activity choice has also been featured in some programmes, particularly in the upper grades, while others have focused on group problem-solving and decision-making. Although they were not named as such, complexity-oriented learning elements may be identified in these textbooks. In particular, the recursive nature of complexity-oriented teaching and learning is highlighted in that many of the elements found in these approaches grew out of earlier learning and teaching methodologies described as complicated, rather than complex. Echoes of earlier play-oriented teaching approaches can be discerned in contemporary lessons that are intended to be child-centred, experiential and guided through discovery. Qualities of emergence such as 'open-ended' rules that encourage creative and unpredictable responses to problems (Griffin & Butler, 2005) and an approach that recognizes and supports the cyclical nature of learning are highlighted, as are notions of the value of group participation and sharing, and adaptation to new experiences using previously learned skills. Physical skills are deconstructed into their constituent movement principles noted above and into actions that can be learned and applied to a variety of situations (Griffin & Butler, 2005; Stanley, 1977). Competition and winning are downplayed, and participation and progressive skill development using small-group modified games and activities are highlighted (Bean, 1985; Docherty, 1980).

An example of complexity-oriented physical education in this era is illustrated by the introduction of 'movement education' from Britain into North America in the 1960s and 1970s. Movement education is a highly analytical approach whereby physical educators are encouraged to incorporate into gymnastics, dance and games the physical principles of body awareness, space awareness, relationships and effort (including time, weight, space and flow) (Hill, 1979; Morison, 1969; Staniford, 1978; Stanley, 1977), as well as "the fundamental laws of motion and the biomechanical principles associated with their application" (Staniford, 1978, p. 387).

Group work is an essential aspect of this approach and student creativity is encouraged as students incorporate their growing awareness of movement principles into all of their physical education activities. Recursive learning as part of the student's developmental process is recognized as an essential aspect of learning. Movement education, with its reliance on many of the qualities associated with complex learning, may be directly linked to the constructivist approach of Teaching Games for Understanding found in contemporary elementary- and secondary-level physical education textbooks: "...the questions and complexities are legion and the solutions decidedly unsatisfactory" (Issitt, 2004, p. 685).

John Issitt (2004) has observed that textbooks

> present both the discipline's internal workings and its sense of self-identity as a coherent domain of study. They therefore function to create, trace and maintain the boundaries of a discipline by inclusion or exclusion of subjects and by expressing the disciplinary discourse that lays claim to a particular terrain of ideas.
>
> (p. 688)

Is there a future for physical education textbooks? Today, textbooks for physical educators are much less likely to display the evident dichotomies of the past. Where once behaviourist learning theorists moved to incorporate the most current knowledge about child and adolescent development, motor learning and skill acquisition, and the scientific basis of exercise into textbooks, they are now just as likely to also include research on intersecting issues of race, class, gender, sexuality, media and technology, once the exclusive territory of more 'politicized' learning theorists. And where constructivists advocate learning that is predicated on problem-solving through group interaction and conscious connections with previous experiences, they are also as eager to incorporate skill development built on progressive drills as they are to engage each student in small-group games highlighting a specific tactical problem to be solved (Griffin & Butler, 2005).

Even a quick glance through the Table of Contents and the Preface of many contemporary physical education textbooks illustrates the numerous ways in which many of the elements of complicated and complex learning theories have been enfolded together into 'hybrid' expressions of learning theory in physical education. Griffin and Butler (2005) argue in *Teaching Games for Understanding: Theory, Research and Practice* that "...instructional strategies should be based on learning theory because without a clear understanding of how students and teachers learn, one cannot expect to achieve clear learning outcomes [Kirk & MacPhail, 2002; Rink, 2001]" (Griffin & Butler, 2005, p. 10). They advocate building theoretical frameworks on information processing theory from cognitive psychology and incorporating research from sport pedagogy and motor learning. Further, they explore, with other contributing authors, the possibilities inherent in integrating a tactical games approach with other models of games instruction and with philosophical notions of enjoyment, thereby incorporating into TGfU additional elements of complicated and complex learning theories.

Peter Hastie, in his recent textbook, *Teaching for Lifetime Physical Activity through Quality High School Physical Education* (2003), goes further in his recommendations for the future. He states that it is necessary to "Start from Scratch—to completely reconceptualise the way in which physical education is delivered to students" (p. 5). If this is the case, then physical education textbooks in hardcover, paperback or virtual form should continue to serve physical educators for another 100 years to come.

Notes

1 William Henry, Duke of Gloucester, 1781 (Bartlett, 1980, p. 387).
2 Although 'textbook' has not yet been defined in this chapter, it is important to note that the subject area of this chapter is about physical education, and not health. Physical education is commonly taught in a gymnasium or other venue designated for activity, and focuses on the development of the student's physical abilities and knowledge through participation in various games, sports and pastimes. Health education is commonly taught in a classroom, with or without textbooks, and is concerned with teaching students how to make good decisions about their own healthy lifestyles.
3 The exception to this may occur if a student is medically exempt or, for some other reason, unable to participate in regular activity classes and is assigned alternative work.
4 Light (2008) contends that behaviourism grew out of Descartes's notion of the separation of mind and body. Early textbooks provide evidence that, as with other pioneer educators, physical educators struggling to establish their profession in the latter part of the nineteenth century were strongly influenced by this perspective as well.
5 Many female educators worried that unrestrained competition would lead young women to develop unattractive masculine qualities such as aggression and dominance. Interestingly, female sexuality was not called into question. As Ann Hall (2002) notes, "Any discussion about the sexuality of female athletes presumed heterosexuality. No one

suggested that masculine athleticism in women was indicative of homosexual love. ... The criticism of 'mannish women athletes' was not that they might be lesbians, but that they might be men" (p. 92).

6 ALT-PE or Academic Learning Time-Physical Education grew out of research into achievement in elementary mathematics and reading, where ALT was defined as "the amount of time a student spends engaged in a relevant learning task with a high success rate" (Marliave, 1976 in Metzler, 1982).

References

Apple, M.W. (1989). *Teachers & texts: A political economy of class and gender relations in education*. London, UK: Routledge.

Bartlett, J. (1980). William Henry, Duke of Gloucester. *Familiar quotations*. Boston, MA: Little, Brown and Company.

Bean, D. (1985). Movement education: Potential and reality. *Cahper Journal, 51*(5), 20–24.

Brandreth, W.G. (1931). *The Canadian book of games*. Toronto, ON: The Ryerson Press.

Cassidy, R., & Kozman, H.C. (1943). *Physical fitness for girls*. New York: A.S.

Davis, B., & Sumara, D. (2005). Complexity science and educational action research: Toward a pragmatics of transformation. *Educational Action Research, 13*(3), 453–464.

Davis, B., Sumara, D., & Luce-Kapler, R. (2000). *Engaging minds: Changing teaching in complex times*. New York: Routledge.

Dewey, J. (1899). *School and society*. Chicago, IL: University of Chicago Press.

Dewey, J. (1908). *The child and the curriculum*. Chicago, IL: University of Chicago Press.

Dewey, J. (1916). *Democracy and education*. Boston, MA: Houghton Mifflin.

Docherty, D. (1980). Effective development of games skills for elementary school children. *Cahper Journal, 46*(6), 30–36.

Griffin, L.L., & Butler, J.I. (Eds.). (2005). *Teaching games for understanding: Theory, research and practice*. Champaign, IL: Human Kinetics.

Hall, M.A. (2002). *The girl and the game*. Peterborough, ON: Broadview Press.

Hamilton, D. (1990). What is a textbook? *Paradigm, Journal of the Textbook Colloquium, 3*, no page numbers.

Hastie, P. (2003). *Teaching for lifetime physical activity through quality high school physical education*. San Francisco, CA: Benjamin Cummings.

Hill, L.E. (Ed.). (1903). *Athletics and out-door sports for women*. New York: Macmillan.

Hill, R. (1979). Movement education: What's in a name? *Cahper Journal, 46*(1), 18–24.

Hoskin, K. (1990). The textbook: Further moves toward a definition. *Paradigm, Journal of the Textbook Colloquium, 3*, no page numbers.

Houghton, E.B. (1891). *Physical culture: First book of exercises in drill, calisthenics, and gymnastics*. Toronto, ON: Warwick and Sons.

Issitt, J. (2004). Reflections on the study of textbooks. *History of Education, 33*(6), 683–696.

Kidd, B. (1996). *The struggle for Canadian sport*. Toronto, ON: University of Toronto Press.

Kinchloe, J.L. (2005). *Critical constructivism primer*. New York: Peter Lang.

Kirk, D., & MacDonald, D. (1998). Situated learning in physical education. *Journal of Teaching in Physical Education, 17*, 376–378.

Kirk, D., & MacPhail, A. (2002). Teaching games for understanding and situated learning: Rethinking the Bunker and Thorpe model. *Journal of Teaching in Physical Education, 21*, 177–192.

Lave, J., & Wenger, E. (1991). *Situated learning: Legitimate peripheral participation*. New York: Cambridge University Press.

Lenskyj, H. (1986). *Out of bounds*. Toronto, ON: The Women's Press.

Light, R. (2008). Complex learning theory – its epistemology and its assumptions about learning: Implications for physical education. *Journal of Teaching in Physical Education, 27*, 21–37.

Marliave, R. (1976). Observable classroom variables. *Technical Report 1–2, Beginning Teacher Evaluation Study*. San Francisco, CA: Far West Laboratory for Educational Research and Development.

Metzler, M.W. (1982). Adapting the academic learning time instructional model to physical education teaching. *Journal of Teaching in Physical Education, 1*(2), 44–55.

Michael, I. (1990). Aspects of textbook research. *Paradigm, Journal of the Textbook Colloquium, 2*, no page numbers.

Mitchell, E.D., & Mason, B.S. (1934). *The theory of play*. New York: A.S. Barnes.

Morison, R. (1969). *A movement approach to educational gymnastics*. London, UK: J. M. Dent and Sons.

Morrow, D., & Wamsley, K.B. (2005). *Sport in Canada. A history*. New York: Oxford University Press.

Mosston, M. (1966). Teaching physical education. Columbus, OH: A Charles E. Merrill.

Murray, N. (1981). Movement education: A factual statement. *Cahper Journal, 48*(2), 15–17.

Nichols, J. (2005). The philosophical underpinnings of school textbook research. *Paradigm, Journal of the Textbook Colloquium, 3*(1), 24–35.

Nixon, E.W., & Cozens, F.W. (1935). *An introduction to physical education*. Philadelphia, PA: W.B. Saunders.

Posse, N. (1890). *The Swedish system of educational gymnastics*. Boston, MA: Lee and Shepard.

Rink, J. (2001). Investigating the assumptions of pedagogy. *Journal of Teaching in Physical Education, 20*, 112–128.

Rosenberg, C.E. (1995). "Presidential address": Catechisms of health: The body in the Prebellum classroom. *Bulletin of the History of Medicine, 69*(2), 175–197.

Rovegno, I. (1998). The development of in-service teachers' knowledge of a constructivist approach to physical education: Teaching beyond activities. *Research Quarterly for Exercise and Sport, 69*, 147–162.

Schmidt, F.A., & Miles, E.H. (1901). *The training of the body for games, athletics, gymnastics, and other forms of exercise and for health, growth, and development*. London, UK: Swan Sonnenschein and Co.

Siedentop, D. (1983). *Developing teaching skills in physical education*. Palo Alto, CA: Mayfield.

Singleton, E. (2010). More than "just a game": History, pedagogy and games in physical education. *Physical and Health Education Journal, 76*(2), 22–27.

Staniford, D.J. (1978). Personalized physical education: A child centred movement approach to learning. *Cahper Journal, 44*(6), 3–5; 40–41.

Stanley, S. (1977). *Physical education: A movement orientation*. Toronto, ON: McGraw-Hill Ryerson.

Sumption, D. (1927). *Fundamental Danish gymnastics for women*. New York: A. S. Barnes.

Tinning, R. (1991). Teacher education pedagogy: Dominant discourses and the process of problem setting. *Journal of Teaching in Physical Education, 11*(1), 1–20.

9 Enabling constraints

Co-creating situated learning in Inventing Games

Joy Butler and Claire Robson

In this chapter, we explore the potential of encouraging students to invent their own games as a context for learning. This approach presents an alternative to the conventional approach where the teacher selects games and encourages active participation. By encouraging students to invent games, teachers can provide opportunities for students to understand how the nature of games and ethical game play emerge from the constraints imposed by each game form. We will first outline the concepts of Inventing Games and situated ethics. We then define the concept of enabling constraints and explore its potential in Teaching Games for Understanding (TGfU) in general and, more specifically, as teachers and students use them to co-create the rules and structures of Invented Games. We draw upon data from a research project conducted in the fall of 2007, which explored Inventing Games as a medium for learning about ethical behaviour.

Since we will be using the words 'sport' and 'games' quite frequently in the chapter, we will say at the outset that we are using the word 'games' to describe organized, physically active, rule-governed forms of play that have a specific purpose. When such games become highly institutionalized, in order to have histories, and governing bodies, they can be described as sports (Siedentop, 2008). It is important to note that sports and games exist on a continuum and have no clear conceptual boundary, and that sports are also games. In educational settings, teachers draw upon both sport and games as they design their curricula.

Inventing Games

Almond (1983), one of the originators of TGfU, published the first article on 'Games Making' (coined in this chapter as Inventing Games) in 1983, pointing to the fact that students felt a sense of ownership of, and involvement in, their learning as they got the chance to teach others, including their teachers. Learners' ability to make their own decisions is central to TGfU philosophy and pedagogy. Rather than executing skills 'correctly', learners are encouraged to make choices that may vary from moment to moment and situation to situation. Almond found that as students worked to create their own games, they began to understand the purpose and value of rules in shaping the nature of the game. In addition, as they explained their game to others and worked to invent them, they learned how to cooperate and communicate more effectively (Castle, 1990).

Inventing Games can be set up as a unit of TGfU in which learners create their own games based on the four games categories as they make up their own game rules that work as both prescriptive and proscriptive constraints on how game play emerges. In this way, game invention mirrors, in an accelerated fashion, the evolution of established games or sports. After playing their games, learners discuss ways in which the constraints they have negotiated (descriptive, prescriptive and proscriptive) might be developed or modified in order to make playing more inclusive and enjoyable (more enabling) for all participants (Almond, 1986a; Rovegno & Bandhauer,1994). The games evolve as learners explore them through play, and through group and self-reflection. For the researcher, this provides an interesting opportunity to investigate the processes of game invention, the social and ethical dimensions of game invention and their educational potential.

Situated ethics

Rather than springing directly from judgment and reason, the decisions we make about how to behave are usually the result of coping with what confronts us in the immediacy of the present moment, and are thus contextual (Varela, 1999). Ethical positions are thus a "commonsensical emergence of an appropriate stance from the entire history of the agent's life" (Varela, 1999, p. 11). Put another way, when we are faced with a moral choice, we operate from positions that have emerged from all of our previous choices and that are highly dependent upon our context, including the physical contexts we inhabit. In the same way that games afford varied responses from players in terms of strategies and tactics, they can also afford ethical situations and decisions such as whether or not to commit a deliberate foul in order to win. The Inventing Games process emphasizes moral or ethical decision-making in the physical context.

Moral positions are constructed over time as we act and react to our situations and these positions often become so entrenched that we are barely conscious of them. Varela (1999) suggests (and we agree) that even habitual or culturally-sedimented positions can be disrupted in moments of breakdown or aporia—those moments in which we become impossibly conflicted, confused or on the horns of dilemma. Though such moments may be challenging and difficult, they are also "the source of the autonomous and creative side of living cognition" (Varela, 1999, p. 11). When our habitual moral constructs are challenged as we find ourselves in these 'stuck spots', we are forced to pay conscious attention to our immediate situations. Since these moments of aporia are inevitable as groups strive for consensus, the researchers hoped to observe and analyse what happens as students encountered conflict and tried to regulate each others' behaviour, make good rules and reach compromise and consensus.

Enabling constraints

Before proceeding, it is important to introduce and clarify the concept of enabling constraints. Constraints that offer the system new possibilities for action are said to be *enabling*, in that they challenge the system to make creative adaptations. Far from being restrictive (as their name might initially suggest), such constraints are rather a precondition for learning, in that they disturb (or perturb) the status quo and invite the system to adapt, while preventing it from spiralling into chaos. For example, children playing an informal game with a soccer ball will self-organize to establish conditions for play, usually by determining that the ball must be moved only with the foot, and forbidding rugby-type tackling.

Such constraints can either be prescriptive or proscriptive. Prescriptive constraints or rules determine what *must* be done. For instance, you must stop play when the official blows the whistle, use a club to move the ball in golf and limit your actions to dribbling, passing and shooting with the ball in basketball. Proscriptive constraints determine what *must not* be done. For instance, in most games you cannot deliberately kick another player, golfers cannot move the ball by hand in order to improve their lie and cricketers may not use their lower legs to protect the wicket. There needs to be a balance of each type of constraint for the system to support an effective playing environment. Insufficient proscriptions lead to anarchy and chaos, yet too many will create stifling order or rigidity, thus rendering the game 'no fun'. As Shogan (2011, p. 6) suggests, "Although prohibiting some actions, proscriptive constraints make other actions possible."

Regulations of game play often use *descriptive constraints*. These are a type of enabling constraint that ordain such matters as ball size, playing areas and goal dimension. These also make up the rules and structure of a game. Like prescriptive and proscriptive constraints, descriptive constraints both restrict and enable particular patterns of play. In basketball, for example, a high goal offers a greater likelihood of success to taller players. A large hockey/ soccer field privileges players with good cardiovascular endurance. To a large extent, descriptive constraints are what teachers (and, by extension, students in an Inventing Games situation) manipulate to modify the challenge of the games experience in order to render it appropriate to the age, experience and ability of players.

When learners move from what they know into what they do not yet know, there is always risk and loss, as learners give up 'lovely knowledge' in favour of more 'difficult' understandings (Pitt & Britzman, 2003). Learning always happens on the edge, and no more so than when students are encouraged to play. As teachers consider the design of learning activities in the light of this delicate balance between creativity and control, they seek to offer learners the ideal opportunity to take a risk, solve problems, exceed present accomplishments and ignore prior limits, as intelligence and attention are focused and intensified (De Castell, 2011). In an educational setting that frames both the class and the individual learner as dynamic learning systems, enabling constraints offer a productive balance between freedom and structure, chaos and coherence.

Enabling constraints in games play

All games have evolved through the development of constraints that define their intentions. Most of these constraints were created along with the games themselves as they evolved during spontaneous play in social contexts. For example, though the origins of baseball are hotly debated, it has been suggested that it developed from various bat and ball games played in England in the seventeenth and eighteenth centuries, finding some coherence there in the mid-eighteenth century, at which time a version was brought to America by early settlers (Block, 2005). However, it was not until the nineteenth century that baseball settled into its current structure, and, even then, its rules continued to evolve (for instance, the counting of foul balls as strikes in the early twentieth century). Most of our traditional games were originally self-organized in this way, as constraints were invented and reinvented over a long period of adaptation and evolution. Though these descriptive constraints were not created by committees or organizations, they became codified as interested agents[1] sought consistency and predictability in game structures. Juarrero (1999) argues that, as individuals and communities evolve in this way, they generate second-order constraints—choices that become habitual for the system and thus operate top-down, rather than bottom-up, to influence behaviours. In the realm of game evolution, these second-order constraints can be framed as the rules and regulations of games. In this way, games mirror the complex evolution of societies, cities and human beings.

The primary purpose, intention or rule of a game can be said to serve as an overarching prescriptive constraint. In most competitive games, one must score more highly than one's opponent in order to win; in some, such as golf, a lower score is required for success. This intention to win in the prescribed way is what makes the game a game, rather than an activity (such as batting practice) or disorganized play (such as tossing a ball around). Each game is also uniquely defined by descriptive constraints that offer different equipment, playing areas, scoring, rules and regulations. The intention to win within the constraints offered generates a variety of strategies, concepts and tactical opportunities. In baseball, for instance, "players need to place the ball away from fielders in order to run the bases and score more runs than their opponents" (Butler, 1997, p. 44). Given the intention of the game, it would not usually make sense for a batter to deliberately hit the ball towards a fielder. However, it might be done inadvertently or even deliberately in some situations, for instance, if the fielder was considered to be a weak link and there were no better options. If this started to occur more frequently and interfered with game flow, the league might need to consider penalizing the practice by adding a proscriptive rule.

As we have suggested, game structures have usually been generated informally and refined by the needs and input of communities of interested agents. Since people usually play games in order to have fun and to compete against others, it is hardly surprising that players adapt rules and regulations as they go along, to ensure that the game is fair, enjoyable and (usually) safe. As players operate within the same constraints (a 'level playing field'), games that survive and endure often flow smoothly and generate excitement. Rules are changed in the interests of safety and sustainability—for instance, the removal of the 'sticks' rule in field hockey.

Enabling constraints in TGfU

Teaching Games for Understanding is a constructivist approach to sport or games education that was developed by Thorpe, Bunker, and Almond (1986). The TGfU

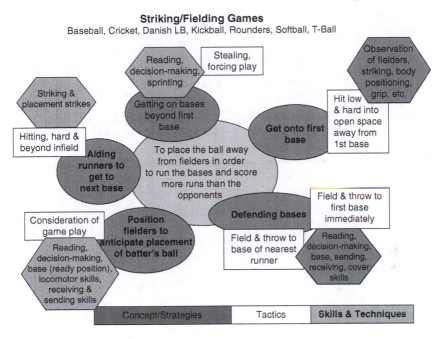

Figure 9.1 Striking fielding games.

classification system was developed by Thorpe, Bunker, and Almond (Almond, 1986b) building on the work of Margaret Ellis (1983, 1986), in order that games might be organized by intent or primary rule into four categories: target games, striking games, net/wall games and invasion games. For example, baseball falls into the classification of striking/fielding games, all of which are defined by the same intention: to place the ball away from fielders in order to score more runs than opponents[2] (strategic intent). Figure 9.1 shows the subcomponents of concepts, strategies and tactical actions generated in the striking/fielding classification. The combination of prescribed and proscribed rules give each category in the TGfU classification the same basic structure (primary rule) and provide insight into how each game is shaped by its constraints. So, for example, by limiting the actions in net games to one side of the net or the other, the concept of a rally becomes unique to that category of games. Not allowing the ball to touch the floor (a proscription used in volleyball) or attempting to reduce the time the ball is on the floor (as with other net games) produces a set of problems to which actions such as the spike, set, serve and drive serve as solutions.

When primary intentions are classified in this way, educational advantages for both teachers and learners result. As teachers design curricula, they can maximize their effectiveness by working within classification systems, rather than concentrating on the minutiae of specific games. As they move away from a seasonal curriculum dedicated to traditional sports (such as rugby, soccer, baseball, basketball) and into a TGfU curriculum organized around common tactical themes, teachers are able to focus more consciously on tactical play, game concepts, decision-making and movement competencies that will support play in the variety of games within each classification (Butler & McCahan, 2005). As teachers focus on aspects of game play such as sending and receiving, stealing bases, throwing to the base nearest the runner or defending bases, they are teaching more deeply and more systematically for understanding. As students work within a unit that identifies these competencies, concepts and tactics across a range of sports, they have the capacity to learn (by doing and with the help of an attentive teacher) to transfer them from one game within the category to others. They achieve conceptual understanding, rather than becoming adept at a series of unrelated movement patterns or techniques.

Manipulation and invention of enabling constraints in TGfU

Thus far, we have considered the role of constraints in games that have evolved over time and through the combined efforts of interested parties. It is also possible for educators to manipulate enabling constraints as they seek certain intentions or outcomes for students.

In TGfU, teachers can alter existing constraints in order to focus student attention on the movements, tactics and concepts demanded within different game classifications. In 'modified' representations of traditional games, the number of players (descriptive constraints) might be reduced to encourage passing and focus attention on off-the-ball play, tactics and strategy. Modifications to existing games include such alterations to rules and regulations as lengthening and narrowing the tennis court. In this way, particular game problems can be emphasized and students are encouraged to blend reading the situation with tactical decision-making to effect a movement outcome that successfully solves the problem. Games can also be modified to promote their accessibility to students at different levels of development (including students who are differently able) by changing equipment. Staying with the net game example, paddle bats might be used so that less skilled or less able students encounter success, or students might practise by throwing (rather than striking) balls of differing weights and sizes. All these are examples of descriptive constraints.

Research goals

We turn our attention to a research project that investigated these ideas in an applied setting of Inventing Games. We will argue that, as we consider learning through the lens of complex dynamic systems operating within enabling constraints, such outcomes may be better served and more easily observed.

In this research project, our goals were not fixed, but rather emergent and revisited in a recursive cycle. For the purposes of this chapter, however, we concentrate upon two areas of our preliminary findings. The first is the 'appropriateness' of the evolution of the games invented. Here, we wondered if learners would be successful in Inventing Games that were suited to their developmental needs, in terms of fairness, flow and fun. For this reason, we have compared two games—one created by experienced players and one by less experienced players—in order to determine whether their invented games serve their different developmental needs. We studied the invented games as they evolved in accordance with the enabling constraints set by their game classification and the rules and regulations designed by their players.

The second area of focus is the potential of Inventing Games and enabling constraints to enable learning in a specific area, which we are calling *situated ethics* or *democracy in action*. Though physical educators have assumed that such activities as playing in teams, winning, losing and striving for excellence help students develop ethical consciousness and awareness, there has been little research to substantiate these assumptions, and little conscious curriculum planning for such learning outcomes. As observed, the teacher in our project was experimenting with manipulating enabling constraints to focus student attention upon social and ethical situations. Bourdieu (1984) has emphasized the social dimensions of games and sport, indicating that our judgments and values are often embodied and prereflexive; thus Inventing Games offers learners a way to examine these judgments and values as they negotiate and strive to reach consensus about game structures.

Situated ethics in Inventing Games pilot project

Butler (2007) focused on two groups (each comprised of three boys and three girls) as they engaged in sixth-grade physical education classes in Vancouver, British Columbia. The rest of the students in the class participated in the activities, but were not studied. Their regular teacher taught the class an Inventing Games unit in the category of invasion games. At the beginning of the unit, the teacher organized the members of the class into groups, two of which were researched. One was a group of more experienced players (involved in playing games during extra-curricular activity) and one was a group of less experienced players (game playing limited to physical education classes).

Each group was invited to create a game, using Invasion Game structures, and then to discuss the following questions: Does your game flow? Is it structured? Is it safe for everyone? Is it fair for everyone? Is everyone involved? Is it fun? As they considered these questions, the students were invited to consider possible changes in the constraints that made up their game structures in order to produce a better game (in the senses defined above). They were asked to negotiate consensus around their decisions, and to make sure that this consensus was representative of the entire group. Their process in doing so was videorecorded three times: as their student groups decided on the structure of their games and revised them; during game play; and as they observed other games being presented. The researchers sat with each of the groups as they reviewed videorecordings of themselves playing their games and as they observed the other group playing theirs. The students were videorecorded as they responded to questions posed by the researchers on their decision-making processes and games learning.

Preliminary findings

Players developed their own rules in order to design their games. In the analysis below, these have been divided into prescriptive and proscriptive constraints in order to show whether or not learners were successful at using them to construct a creative balance between the two. We have focused on three other areas in our findings: game evolution, decision-making and moments of aporia leading to teachable moments in the area of situated ethics.

The more experienced group

Game evolution

The more experienced players reverted to traditional forms of dodge ball in the early stages of their process, perhaps reflecting their greater interest in and respect for traditional forms of sport, or the fact that, as more highly-skilled students, they anticipated success. The purpose of the game that they eventually settled upon—a combination of dodge ball and capture the flag—was to score goals by throwing a ball into a soccer-type net. Table 9.1 lists the enabling constraints used by the more experienced group in the design of their game.

The game was an ideal match for the more sophisticated skills and abilities of these more experienced players. It put them in situations where they had to make rapid decisions, pass on the move, maintain and use peripheral awareness and move into space. Since the play environment was quite open, movement sequences were mainly continuous. The game was challenging in that there was a great deal of interaction and contact between opponents (such as dodging and tagging). Some sophistication in game tactics and strategies (such as offensive and defensive positions) became apparent. The more experienced players worked primarily as individuals in order to score goals. Though the group lacked team cohesion, they compensated for this by designing a game that lent itself to individual play.

Table 9.1 The enabling constraints developed by the more experienced players

Prescriptive constraints	Proscriptive constraints
• Points were scored by throwing one of 18 balls into a soccer net • A maximum of two steps could be taken when holding the ball • Teams were organized by gender • When tagged by an opponent, players had to go to 'jail' • Team-mates could free opponents by touching them	• Players were not allowed within the goalie's semi-circle • No body checking was allowed

Decision-making

Within the game itself, decisions during play had to be made and implemented quickly, as did the performance of skills and manoeuvres. Since defenders were allowed to interfere with opponents in the act of throwing, pressure was placed on the shooters. The use of no less than 18 balls further complicated the game. Quick decision-making was imperative.

As far as decision-making about game design, the more experienced players, particularly the boys, were so eager to engage in active game play that they preferred to keep discussion to a minimum, with interesting consequences. They were less able to share ideas and work cooperatively. Rules were changed as the game proceeded, often with a minimum of discussion. A rift between the girls and boys emerged as the boys were less disposed than the girls to discuss or process game invention. Some of the boys dropped out of the first conversation after about ten minutes, and the girls became frustrated with them. Eventually, the girls and boys worked independently of each other to create two games with a view to combining them later. The experience of game play seemed to get the boys re-engaged in the process and the game was eventually played—girls against boys.

Aporia

During the debriefing after the unit had ended, the teacher observed that the members of the experienced group appeared to be locked in conflict, as its members engaged in loud and angry debate. As she approached, she heard an exchange of hostile accusations and asked what was going on:

TEACHER Q: There seems to be some disagreement amongst you as far as the presentation goes. What's the problem?

A. BOY 1: The game stank. I hated it.

A. GIRL 1: It was great. It (inaudible, several people speaking at once)

A. BOY 1: No one listened to me from week one!

A. GIRL 2: You just sulked just cuz we didn't take your idea one time. You had … plenty of times to make other suggestions. But you didn't. If you don't join in, then you have to suck it up! You have to do what everyone else decided.

A. GIRL 1: You just sulked cuz you didn't get your way like you usually do. This game rocked!

(Butler, Hopper, & Robson, 2012)

The less experienced group

Game evolution

The game invented by the less experienced players afforded comfort and security to its players. The environment was partly open and partly closed, allowing for a slower pace, though the game was in constant motion. Interactions with opponents

Table 9.2 The enabling constraints developed by the less experienced players

Prescriptive constraints	Proscriptive constraints
• Points were scored by knocking down one or more of eight pins on opponents' back line • Floor hockey sticks were used to move the ball • There was no limit (time or steps) on moving while carrying the ball or on passing	• Players could not cross the half-way line

were minimal and rarely physical. Skill actions such as shooting were discrete since defenders could not interfere with the shot, and passes could only be intercepted. Table 9.2 lists the enabling constraints used by the less experienced group in the design of their game.

Decision-making

These constraints left ample time for players in the less experienced group for decision-making and skill execution during game play. They only used one ball, thus reducing the game's complexity, and they built in the capacity to spend time in secret huddles before play in order to discuss strategies. Defenders were only allowed to the halfway line, allowing offensive players to aim and shoot at targets without distraction, an activity that they took turns to execute.

As they processed their game invention, the less experienced group appointed a leader, shared ideas cooperatively and listened to each other without too much interrupting. They made decisions by voting, and invented a unique method of casting votes that afforded anonymity to players, and a concomitant reduction of conflict or coercion about how people voted. When they played, they offered encouraging comments upon each other's play and invited each other to participate more fully. No apparent distinctions were drawn between girls and boys. They spent more time than the experienced group deciding on their game and adapted rules as they went along by reaching clear consensus. As we speculate about the observed differences in process between the two groups, we wonder if the less experienced players had less ego investment in being perceived as 'good' games players. Experienced players might be expected to be more familiar with a games culture in which the coach directs the action, and less used to making their own decisions, rendering the IG process disconcerting. For the inexperienced players, there was no reputation to give up and they could respond with reason and logic! What a novelty.

Aporia

As they encountered situations that demanded change, the less experienced players developed constraints that allowed them to work through aporia constructively.

They looked for clear consensus, invited input from all players, and focused on the greater good as they concentrated on what was best for the game.

Q: So what were you discussing right now? Is this when you were deciding who the referee was?
A: Yeah. Yep.
Q: And you were deciding to be fair. Is this how you make most of your decisions?
A: Yeah. We asked for opinions and the best for the game.
Q: The best for the game? That how you make your decisions?
A: Yeah.
Q: And what if somebody doesn't agree?
A: Then we … it changes. If there's only one person that doesn't agree then … and we have to have a reason why she doesn't agree. And we keep on going.
Q: So one person doesn't like it.
A: And if they have a good reason, we'll change it. But if it's not that good, we won't change it.
Q: OK. But what if three people don't like something?
A: We'll change it. It has to be three.
Q. It has to be half?
A: Yes.
Q. OK. So if it's 50% of people don't agree, then you'll change that?
A: Yeah. It's happened before.

Conclusion

The students in the research project were highly successful in their manipulation of enabling constraints. If their class teacher had spent time trying to create two games that would both challenge and engage his two groups of differently abled students, s/he would have been hard put to come up with better alternatives. Their games were engaging, fun and fair, and offered opportunities to develop transferrable skills and strategies. We are encouraged to believe that when students invent game structures by manipulating constraints, they can create games that offer just the right balance between challenge and comfort. In this way, they place themselves on the productive intersection of chaos and order—that place where learning can occur. As they experiment with different ways of negotiating, discussing and eventually making decisions, learners gain a more conscious and embodied understanding of how rules contribute to fun experiences and make them accessible to all.

The less experienced group developed some impressive democratic structures as they listened to each other, made suggestions, voted on decisions and refined their game structures. As part of this process, they were able to experience ethical dilemmas first-hand as they struggled to achieve balance between the needs of the individual and the greater good of the group, process and outcome, challenge and safety. The more experienced group encountered considerable conflict. Rather than regarding this as problematic, we believe that it opened up highly-charged issues that have tended to lie hidden in the physical education curriculum. These include the influence of professional sport on skilled students, which leads to an undue emphasis on outcome and a consequent reluctance to engage in creative play for its own sake. We suspect that the gender division that occurred in the more experienced group is related to this, and we look forward to exploring these issues in our future research.

Just as students are often challenged by the more open learning environment offered by Inventing Games, so the teacher is challenged to teach differently. As students disagree and argue, the teacher's role may not be to provide quick solutions, but rather to intensify and prolong debate. The focus shifts from individual learning to group learning, from outcome to process, from physical to holistic, and from an ontology rooted in disciplinary mastery to a more ecological and emergent learning-focused ontology.

The role of the teacher is key to the success of this approach. As the class discussed the importance of rules in the debrief, for instance, the following exchange occurred:

T: How many groups who have started their game have rules? (*Hands go up.*) Okay. Somebody tell me what a *rule* is. Because everybody says, 'yeah we got those, we got those' but I wonder if you think that a rule is the same thing I do.
A: Well … a rule is something you can't do in the game.
T: Something you can't do?
S: Or can.
T: Or can do. Okay. And what's *the point* of having rules? Why would a game want to have rules? Terry?
S: To keep order and also to keep people from cheating.
T: That's a really good answer. To keep order to the game and maybe to keep them from cheating. Are people *cheating* if they break the rules? Is that kind of what you're saying?
S: Yeah.

As we analyse this conversation, we believe that the teacher missed an opportunity as he settles for an easy and obvious answer to his question. That this is the answer he expects and desires, the only answer permissible, is indicated by his initial question: "I wonder if you think that a rule is the same thing I do?" But this, of course, is not the only possible answer. Though the prevention of cheating is an important function of rules, it is far from being the only one, or even the most important one, and even if this were not the case, the notion of cheating requires unpicking. Why is it wrong to cheat? What is the line between savvy game play and dishonest game play? If the ball falls outside the line and the official doesn't see it and the player doesn't 'fess up', is *that* cheating? More importantly, how did the rules of this particular invented game prevent cheating? Were they doing an efficient job? What is the learning process for the students as they rotate their turn to be official of the game? Does their experience as referee enhance their understanding of the rules as players, allow them to be empathetic for the referee as they play? Or does it create a binary of seen–not seen and get away with it–not get away with it?

Teacher questions should serve to open, not close the debate of ideas, just as enabling constraints open a range of possible responses to a perturbation or intervention, rather than the execution of a skill performed exactly the 'right' way. In his examination of Ethical Know How, Varela (1999) compares the actions of the 'village honest man' (who obeys the rules without questioning them) with the truly virtuous actions that flow from an 'activated disposition'. It is this disposition that we seek to explore in our future research, as we also examine how teachers may activate it through openness to emergent learning.

Notes

1 Players, officials and spectators, and, as sports became more commercially oriented, promoters, vendors, sponsors and advertisers.
2 Though players also strike the ball in other games, it is the intention of the play, rather than the method, that is key. For instance, although players strike the ball in soccer, the intention, as for other territorial games, is to protect one's own territory and invade the territory of the opponent in order to score goals.

References

Almond, L. (1983). Games making. *Bulletin of Physical Education*, 19, 1.

Almond, L. (1986a). Games making. In R. Thorpe, D. Bunker & L. Almond (Eds.), *Rethinking games education* (pp. 67–70). Northamptonshire, UK: Woolnough Bookbinding.

Almond, L. (1986b). Reflecting on themes: A games classification. In R. Thorpe, D. Bunker, & L. Almond (Eds.), *Rethinking games education* (pp. 71–72). Northamptonshire, UK: Woolnough Bookbinding.

Block, D. (2005). *Baseball before we knew it: A search for the roots of the game*. Lincoln: University of Nebraska Press.

Bourdieu, P. (1984). *Distinction: A social critique of the judgment of taste*. Translated by Richard Nice. Cambridge: Harvard University Press.

Butler, J. (1997). How would Socrates teach games? Constructivist approach to teaching games. *Journal of Physical Education, Recreation and Dance*, 68(9), 42–47.

Butler, J. (2007). Using decision-making to improve the learning, understanding and playing of games. Humanities and Social Sciences Research Council Funding Grant.

Butler, J., Hopper, T., & Robson, C. (2012). *Back in the curriculum race: (Re)inventing teaching and learning through physical education*. Paper presented at the 2012 American Education Research Association Conference, Vancouver, Canada.

Butler, J., & McCahan, B. (2005). Teaching games for understanding as a curriculum model. In L. Griffin & J. Butler (Eds.), *Teaching games for understanding: Theory, research and practice* (pp. 33–54). Champaign, IL: Human Kinetics.

Castle, K. (1990). Children's invented games. *Childhood Education*, 67(2), 82–85.

de Castell, S. (2011). Ludic epistemology: What game-based learning can teach. *Journal of the Canadian Association for Curriculum Studies*, 8(2), 19–27.

Ellis, M. (1983). *Similarities and differences in games: A system for classification*. Paper presented at the AIESEP Congress, Rome, Italy.

Ellis, M. (1986). Modification of games. In R. Thorpe, D. Bunker, & L. Almond, (Eds.), *Rethinking games education* (pp. 75–78). Northamptonshire, UK: Woolnough Bookbinding.

Juarrero, A. (1999). *Dynamics in action: Intentional behavior as a complex system*. Cambridge, MA: MIT Press.

Pitt, A., & Britzman, D. (2003). Speculations on qualities of difficult knowledge in teaching and learning: An experiment in psychoanalytical research. *Qualitative Studies in Education*, 16(6), 755–776.

Rovegno, L., & Bandhauer, D. (1994). Child designed games: experienced teachers' concerns. *The Journal of Physical Education, Recreation and Dance*, 65(6), 60–64.

Shogan, D. (2011). *The making of high-performance athletes: Discipline, diversity and ethics*. Toronto, University of Toronto Press.

Siedentop, D. (2008). *Introduction to physical education, fitness and sport*. Dubuque, IA: McGraw-Hill.

Thorpe, R., Bunker, D., & Almond, L. (1986). *Rethinking games education*. Northamptonshire, UK: Woolnough Bookbinding.

Varela, F.J. (1999). *Ethical know-how: Action, wisdom and cognition*. Stanford, CA: Stanford University Press.

10 Effective learning design for the individual

A nonlinear pedagogical approach in physical education

Jia-Yi Chow, Ian Renshaw, Chris Button,
Keith Davids and Clara Tan Wee Keat

Skill acquisition is a complex process that is dependent on numerous factors such as the presentation of instructions, provision of feedback and the organization of practice schedules (Magill, 2011). Effective learning design is, therefore, critical to the retention and transfer and extent of learning. Undoubtedly, the learning design adopted in physical education should be underpinned by a clear theoretical model reflecting the advancements in motor learning research so that the learning activities are delivered in a sound and functional approach (Davids, Button, & Bennett, 2008).

One of the major challenges that physical educators face is how to structure learning processes for classes of 30–40 students to meet the needs of individuals who do not learn the same way, nor find the same movement solutions in the same learning context (Chow, Davids, Hristovski, Araújo, & Passos, 2011). A functional approach should be a focus on planning and structuring effective learning at the level of the individual. For example, individual differences in growth, development and maturation in children clearly impact on how we should design appropriate individualized learning activities that can account for such individual variations (Thelen & Smith, 1994). A focus on the individual suggests that, from a skill acquisition and motivational perspective, bottom-up and student-centred approaches rather than top-down, teacher-centred approaches should be the cornerstone of effective learning designs in physical education (Chow *et al.*, 2011; Davids *et al.*, 2008).

Goal-directed movements that a learner exhibits emerge as a consequence of the interaction among key constraints in the learning context. Specifically, constraints have been defined as boundaries or features which shape the emergence of behaviour by a learner seeking a stable state of organization (Newell, 1986). As espoused by a constraints-led approach (see Renshaw, Davids, Chow, & Hammond, 2010), the dynamic interaction among key constraints such as the performer, task and environment leads to the emergence of specific movement behaviours (Davids *et al.*, 2008). For example, the Western grip, in which tennis players place their hand on the top of the racquet handle during performance of the forehand drive (performer constraint), emerged as a functional coordination solution in players performing on the hard, sun-baked courts of California (environmental constraint). This grip allowed the players to get over the high-bouncing ball and to drive it deeply into an opponent's court (task constraint). Conversely, a player learning to drive on the generally damper, slower courts of the eastern states of America tended to use the Eastern forehand grip, in which the hand was placed on the bottom of the handle, allowing them to get under the low-bouncing ball to lift it over the net (Brown, 2004).

In many situations the emergence of movement behaviours tends to be specific to an individual since the various constraints interact in different ways for different individuals. The dynamic interactions present in learning situations also signify that we should not expect learning processes to take a linear progression. For example, for a child trying to learn how to ride a bike and having little success, a parent may add safety wheels, thus allowing the child to practise riding the bike. The child can then develop leg strength and form a sense of how to balance on the bike, learning that the bike needs to attain a basic minimum speed in order to maintain stability. As leg strength develops, along with confidence in maintaining balance and functional speed from trial and adaptation, the safety wheels can be removed, with the cycling skill emerging as a nonlinear transition in behaviour.

A pedagogical approach based on the tenets of complexity and a dynamical systems perspective is well-suited to provide the theoretical foundations to structure learning designs for the individual learner conceived as a nonlinear complex system (Chow *et al.*, 2007). In the following sections of this chapter, we will explain in detail how learning can be classified as a nonlinear process and will also explain the key features of a nonlinear pedagogy (Davids, Araújo, Hristovski, Passos, & Chow, 2012). Further discussion will also be undertaken to explain how learning can be designed based on theoretical insights from nonlinear dynamics and how these ideas might generate principles to support effective pedagogical practices for physical education in schools.

The case for learning as a nonlinear process

The key differences between nonlinear and linear systems are described in Table 10.1 and adapted from Chow *et al.* (2011). The main features of the learner as a

Table 10.1 Key differences between linear and nonlinear systems as descriptors of human learning (adapted from Chow *et al.*, 2011)

Nonlinear	Linear
• Non-proportional change in response to inputs in the learning environment	• Proportional change in response to inputs from the learning environment
• Multi-stability (single cause may have multiple behavioural effects)	• Mono-stable (only one behaviour outcome is expected)
• Parametric control—factors external to individual alter behaviour	• Centralized control—factors within the individual alter behaviour
• Functional role of variability in behaviour	• Variability in behaviour is viewed as undesirable

nonlinear dynamical system have been elucidated in past research (Chow *et al.*, 2011; Davids, Chow, & Shuttleworth, 2005) and have implications for teaching and learning games skills that differ from those inferred from a perspective of the learner as a linear system. The assumptions of linear learning have been drawn from the experimental psychology legacy of motor learning where the unit of analysis was the group, with the increases and decreases due to individual differences in performance 'flattened out', resulting in a performance curve that looked relatively linear. The characteristics of linear systems, when modelled in the human learner, neglect essential components that are present during skill acquisition for individuals within a group.

A major feature of nonlinear systems identified in Table 10.1 is that changes to the inputs into the system may produce a non-proportional response to the inputs. If the learner behaves in the manner of a nonlinear system, then the inputs that we provide in the learning context (e.g., spatial constraints or verbal feedback) *may lead* to non-proportional and unexpected changes in performance in response to these inputs. This expectation contrasts with the perspective of the learner as a linear system in which it is assumed that any change in practice task constraints leads to a proportional, additive change in performance (Chow *et al.*, 2011). The level of change resulting from exposure to a key specific constraint such as a new training method, higher-quality practice partners or a minor rule change is sometimes difficult to predict and will be determined by the intrinsic dynamics (current predispositions) of the individual (Renshaw, Davids, Phillips, & Kerherve, 2012). Essentially, everyday real-time events set the scene for the next stage and the real-time causal force behind change (Smith & Thelen, 2003, p. 347), resulting in the smallest movement triggering small or vast changes in the world we make and remake together (Kauffmann, 1995, p. 243). As a result, there is considerable indeterminacy by which athletes achieve similar performance outcome levels. As self-organizing systems they remain poised on the edge of stability and instability, ready to produce creative movement solutions to performance challenges when exposed to a significant constraining influence (Kauffmann, 1995; Phillips, Davids, Renshaw, & Portus, 2010a).

A second key difference is that nonlinear systems are *multi-stable* (one constraint in nonlinear systems may result in multiple behavioural effects) while linear systems are mono-stable (a single constraint will result in a single behavioural effect). In addition, the same learner can utilize different movement solutions (multi-stable) to achieve the same performance outcome brought about by manipulation of constraints for nonlinear systems (Chow *et al.*, 2011). For example, when a boxer is positioned at a certain distance from a punching bag, his or her position at that distance affords or allows several variations on a punching action (i.e., there are multiple stable preferred patterns of behaviours afforded to the boxer) (see Hristovski, Davids, & Araújo, 2006).

Parametric control suggests that, by manipulating certain parameters, physical educators can guide learners to explore various functional organizational states within the learning context. For example, the manipulation of instructions or the change in equipment enables learners to display new or different movement behaviours in learning situations. A badminton coach, focused on working on overhead clear and drop shot, can manipulate the playing area by keeping the length of the regulation playing area, but narrowing the width of the playing area to accentuate the long and short play afforded to players in a 1v1 badminton game. Such task manipulation is an example of parametric control (i.e., manipulating a practice task constraint or modification by exaggeration) having an influential role in skill acquisition.

Last but not least, variability or noise is not always detrimental to performance and can play a crucial role in learning a new skill (Chow *et al.*, 2011). For example, in multi-stable nonlinear systems, *noise can play a functional role* by increasing the likelihood of a system transition between multiple states. Specifically, the inclusion of variability can encourage the learner to explore multiple solution possibilities for a task goal (Chow *et al.*, 2011). For instance, it is through executing a skill in different ways (e.g., kicking a ball with different parts of the foot) that a learner can refine and acquire new movements (e.g., kicking for height, distance or spin) which could be more effective. Variability in practice, therefore, encourages the learner to explore and, perhaps, find a movement solution that meets the needs of his/her own performer constraints, as well as the specific objective of the task.

The preceding discussion on features of nonlinear systems and the associated examples on its relevance to human movement behaviour provide suggestions that the learners behave like nonlinear systems. While performance and learning are different processes, the basis of a human movement system functioning like a nonlinear system would suggest that, in terms of learning, specific pedagogical strategies to accommodate features of nonlinear behaviour are needed to enhance learning of movement skills. Undoubtedly, acquisition of movement coordination is not typically a linear process. Instead, depending on the strength of cooperative and competitive mechanisms, it may involve nonlinear and abrupt transitions, progressions and regressions (see Chow *et al.*, 2007; Kelso, 2003; Newell, Liu, & Mayer-Kress, 2001).

From a nonlinear dynamics perspective, motor learning or the acquisition of coordination is viewed as a process of searching for stable movement patterns, into which a system can settle during a task or activity (Button, Chow, & Rein, 2008). Although learning is usually defined as a relatively permanent change in behaviour (Magill, 2011), from a coordination dynamics perspective, learning is seen as the process of change when a learner moves from one stable preferred movement pattern to another (Beek & van Santvoord, 1992; Mitra, Amazeen, & Turvey, 1998; Zanone & Kelso, 1992). For example, Chow, Davids, Button, and Rein (2008) observed how learners 'transit' from one preferred kicking pattern to a new kicking pattern in a soccer kicking task during four weeks of intervention where the participants were required to kick a ball over a height barrier and have the ball land accurately as well as comfortably at a live receiver's feet in the absence of any specific technical instructions on the kicking action. The period of transition was evidenced by increased kicking variability for the more successful participants. During learning, the inherent repertoire of movement behaviours of the learner acquired previously through practice or experience is modified so that it can meet the needs of a new movement task. Therefore, the acquisition of a new movement skill should not be seen as just attaining the new movement pattern. The acquisition of a new movement pattern for a learner would have implications on altering the whole control system of the learner, such that other movement behaviours and learning will be impacted. Even small, seemingly minor, rule changes can have a major impact on the coordination of highly-skilled athletes. A good example of this was the difficulty that the US basketball team had in scoring three pointers during the Beijing Olympics in 2008. The three-point line was 6.25 m from the basket in comparison to 7.24 m in the NBA league in America. Although it might be expected that supremely talented athletes should be able to adapt to an apparently minor rule change, against Angola, the US team scored 5 from 21 shots from the three-point range, and 3 from 24 against China.[1]

Recognizing that learners behave like a nonlinear system makes it important to consider pedagogical approaches that leverage on these features of nonlinearity to structure learning designs that may better meet the needs of our learners in physical education. Below, we discuss aspects of nonlinear pedagogy that could underpin effective pedagogical strategies in teaching movement skills.

What are the principles of a nonlinear pedagogy?

Nonlinear pedagogy provides practitioners with key principles to employ in teaching situations, such as how to assess performance, how to structure practices and how best to deliver instructions and provide feedback. Recent work in nonlinear pedagogy has demonstrated that the theoretical principles underlying nonlinear pedagogy can be adopted to address the key question, "How should we design conditions for learning in physical education?" (Chow et al., 2009). This involves considerations not only for *what* activities are designed, but also *how* they are taught in a physical education setting.

From a nonlinear pedagogical perspective, the learner, learning environment and teacher form a complex system. The interaction between system components and the constraints of each specific performance situation provide the platform for functional movement behaviours to emerge, and no single component (e.g., the teacher) is seen as the over-riding factor in prescribing how movements should be performed. Consequently, a nonlinear pedagogist has no one common optimal movement pattern in mind towards which each individual learner should aspire during practice (Chow et al., 2007). Instead, the practitioner's role is to create a challenging, yet supportive, learning environment in which individually appropriate movement solutions are encouraged and subsequently stabilized. This approach essentially supports the manipulation of performer–environment interactions, through identifying and altering relevant task, environmental and performer constraints (e.g., the earlier discussion on accentuating the long and short play by changing the dimensions of the badminton playing area is one example of how a coach could change the task constraints) (Newell, 1986).

Nonlinear pedagogy differs in many ways to the more typical and traditional methods that are regularly seen in teaching and coaching of movement skills

(Chow *et al.*, 2006). The hallmarks of the traditional approach include an over-focus on reproduction of a putative optimal movement pattern to which all learners should aspire, the use of too many verbal instructions and corrective feedback, the use of repetitive skill drills in which learners are required to repeat movement skills rather than solve movement problems, and the decomposition of tasks which could perturb the acquisition of information–movement couplings in children (Davids *et al.*, in press; Renshaw, Davids, & Savelsbergh, 2010). In terms of skill development, the role of the teacher has too often been associated with presenting tasks that employ practice drills to perfect performance in relation to an idealized motor pattern, evaluating technique, giving instruction and feedback and carefully managing the learner's practice environment. For example, Curtner-Smith, Todorovich, and McCaughtry (2001) confirmed in their research that physical education teachers spend up to 78% of their interactions with students engaging in such teaching strategies. Ironically, such strategies may limit the amount of time that learners are engaged in meaningful physical practice where the skills can be transferable to real game contexts. For example, recent evidence suggests that children in physical education classes on average spend only 25% of the time actually engaged in physical activity (Tinning, 2006). Tinning identified research on teaching effectiveness across a number of countries (i.e., France, Canada, Australia, New Zealand and the USA) to examine Academic Learning Time in Physical Education (ALT-PE), which revealed that, on average, children spend 28% of their time "waiting for something to happen" (Tinning, 2006, p. 235) (e.g., standing in a line waiting for a turn), 20% of their time involved in managerial tasks such as being organized for practice or being moved from one place to another, and 20% of their time receiving information from the teacher about how to perform a skill better or how to play the next game. Interestingly, Tinning (2006) noted that most of the interactions teachers have with children is to provide 'corrective feedback', presumably with the aim of helping them achieve the perfect reproduction of a skill, or to 'nag' them into organizational or managerial tasks like getting equipment out or getting into groups. Sadly then, over 80% of total interactions are focused on what the children are doing incorrectly, often while attempting to perform activities that are beyond their current ability level (Tinning, 2006). This has important implications for enhancing intrinsic motivation, as discussed later in the chapter.

From a nonlinear pedagogical perspective, progression from the blocked repetition of simple, isolated movement patterns to more complex practice activities is typical of traditional approaches in physical education and assumes proportional changes as practice advances. In fact, it is somewhat ineffective and erroneous in its basic assumption. Constraints upon action exist on short (i.e., within a practice session, e.g., goal orientations), intermediate (i.e., over months of practice, e.g., growth spurts) and long time scales (i.e., years of practice, e.g., attunement to key affordances through education of attention), and consequently both motor learning as well as motor development processes are typically punctuated by nonlinear 'jumps' of varying magnitudes to more mature motor patterns (Newell *et al.*, 2001), reflecting the nonlinear features of non-proportionality and multi-stability.

Nonlinear pedagogy highlights the importance of designing practice tasks and modified games that provide a viable platform for adaptive movement patterns to be acquired during learning. Thus, instead of designing static practice drills with specific teaching cues for repeated practice so that students can replicate the movement skills as presented by the physical educator, the role of the physical educator is to create a supportive learning environment in which each student's movement solutions are encouraged and subsequently stabilized; this can be achieved by careful manipulation of task constraints. For example, raising the height of the badminton net will force the learners to execute overhead clears rather than smashes without providing explicit instructions to do so. Similarly, using larger and softer balls will encourage learners to throw and catch with both hands (if chest pass is to be encouraged in basketball as an example).

A nonlinear pedagogical approach to practice also suggests the need for learners to interact with a variety of individuals of different body-scaled dimensions and action capabilities so that they can develop perceptual awareness of informational constraints on movement. Experience gained in dynamic and continuous interactions with other individuals can help develop awareness of opportunities to act (e.g., probabilities, options and movement directions) which can provide better multi-sensory information for learners. Changes in body dimensions and physical abilities inherently affect the nature of inter-individual relationships between groups of learners (Ulrich, Thelen, & Niles, 1990). By faithfully representing performance environments during practice (and thus providing practice specificity), learners can engage in exploratory behaviour and become attuned to key perceptual information sources (e.g., their position on the playing area or the relative position of team-mates or opponents) available in specific performance environments (Beek, Jacobs, Daffertshofer, & Huys, 2003).

Challenges in adopting a nonlinear pedagogical approach in physical education

In this section we consider some of the key issues and challenges that practitioners face when designing learning based on nonlinear learning principles applied to physical education in schools. As highlighted earlier, according to nonlinear pedagogy, physical educators also need to design tasks to meet the individual's needs and differences; the planning and structuring of effective learning designs should be undertaken at the level of the individual. As various constraints interact in different ways for different individuals, and different learners may progress at different rates, it is imperative for physical education teachers to be ready to adjust the complexity of tasks by manipulating appropriate task constraints to challenge learners to achieve success. For example, changing the rules to decrease difficulty levels or, from a nonlinear perspective, task simplification (see Renshaw *et al.*, 2010; Tan, Chow, & Davids, 2011) would allow students to achieve success and potentially acquire a better fit between their own intrinsic dynamics and the dynamics of the task. In tennis, shortening racket handles, increasing racket head area and using larger projectiles would certainly fall into the category of task simplification and act to enhance the self-efficacy of beginner tennis players (Pellett & Lox, 1998). However, within a physical education context, structuring learning design for the individual is likely to raise several concerns, not the least of which is the practicability of designing learning for up to 30–40 individuals that may form a standard physical education class. Within the limited scope of this chapter, we provide some ideas related to the organization of practices and delivery of instructions. A suggestion for the organization of practices may be for the physical education teacher to consider having multiple pairs or groups of students with similar needs and abilities (see Renshaw *et al.*, 2010). In this way, the physical education teacher can carefully and appropriately manipulate task constraints to continually challenge the different pairs/groups of students with similar 'abilities'/ characteristics to overcome specific movement challenges in modified games. Alternately, game rules can be modified for individuals' needs for informal back-yard games (see Renshaw, Oldham, & Bawden, in press). Based on students' learning and performance during the lesson, students may be regrouped (or regroup themselves) accordingly whenever necessary. Another suggestion is for physical educators to design tasks where students within a pair/group can have different goals with different degrees of success, as previously mentioned in this chapter. Hopper (2011) also highlighted that it may even be better if game constraints can be adapted by a simple modification by adaptation condition whereby the "game is modified to increase the challenge to the player who was successful on the previous game encounter" (p. 6). Such a condition allows the challenge of diversity in a class setting to become an asset as students learn to adapt to the variability from playing opponents of different abilities but with a more equitable chance of success (see Richardson, Sheehy, & Hopper, Chapter 14 in this book). In addition, providing opportunities for learners to access an array of relevant equipment that they could use in a modified game setting adds to their sense of ownership and autonomy in game play, leading to a potential for greater success.

A closely linked concern is the delivery of instructions for a physical education class with multiple pairs/groups with different design tasks. While teachers may be able to move from pair to pair or group to group to present the different tasks, teachers may also consider 'delivery' of instruction through task cards. For example, physical education teachers can devise and prepare task cards for practices or small-sided games that include practice/game conditions, goals, tactical target/purpose and organization.

From an ecological perspective, a key challenge for practitioners is the need to create learning tasks that are representative of the task constraints of the performance environment (Davids *et al.*, 2012; Pinder, Davids, Renshaw, & Araújo, 2011). Practice task constraints and games should mimic the actual performance environment adequately so that students can learn to adjust to the dynamic environmental demands and be able to make appropriate and quick selective decisions as they adapt to the evolving environment. For example, passing and receiving should be practised in the context of a sub-component of an actual game. Small-sided and conditioned games that incorporate most aspects of the actual rules of the game with smaller numbers of players will be representative of the actual perceptual–action dynamics present in the full game. It is a struggle for physical educators to design representative learning contexts in sport and physical activity within the resourcing and diversity of students within a typical physical education class. Too often this has led to an oversimplification of the learning process, with a focus on skill or rather, technique learning in easy to control environments, with repetition of the desired motor pattern.

Though repetition of skill to enable the action to become automatic is a common sense notion in skill acquisition, how the skill is practised is critical to lead to its eventual use in a game. This idea was exemplified with reference to performance in cricket by Pinder, Renshaw, and Davids (2009), who showed that batting against a ball projection machine is not representative of batting against a bowler in a performance environment. They reported clearly distinct emergent movement patterns under the two conditions, predicated on the capacity of participants to use information from the bowler's actions. Against the ball projection machine, participants could only use ball flight information. These findings imply that the tendency to design simplistic and highly-controlled practice drills in physical education may not provide a requisite level of representative design to enhance learning.

Finally, we suggest that a key challenge for physical education teachers is the need to create variability in practice rather than the traditional focus on repetition of practice. Students should be engaged in learning design where teachers create conditions for variability in practices that allow students to find functional relationships between their actions and the performance environment. This approach allows students to learn how to dynamically adapt their movement patterns to achieve their performance goals rather than attempting to reproduce a prescribed movement solution presented by the teacher. When designing tasks, physical educators can manipulate task constraints (such as relevant instructions) to guide students in their search for a solution(s) to overcome specific movement challenges in modified games. For example, asking students to focus on the movement outcome (rather than a prescriptive movement form) allows less conscious control of movement. In executing a badminton serve, the student could focus on the flight trajectory (inverted U) rather than how the arms and body should move. Such movement–outcome-based instructions allow an external focus of attention (see Peh, Chow, & Davids, 2011), encouraging the student to explore and acquire individualized movement patterns that leverage on the intrinsic movement dynamics of the student.

Clearly, the principles underlying nonlinear pedagogy are applicable to physical education and the challenge is for practitioners to explore how features of nonlinear pedagogy can be presented to allow students to learn new movement skills in an ecologically valid context. The highlighted practices emphasize an individualized learning approach that is student-centred and which connects well with the insights provided from a nonlinear pedagogical approach. Nevertheless, more empirical work in physical education settings is required to confirm the perceived benefits of nonlinear pedagogy, even though aspects of nonlinear learning are evident in many motor learning investigations (see Chow *et al.*, 2011). Still, it is heartening to know that various researchers are currently working on exciting and meaningful investigations. Below we suggest that one area ripe for further exploration in physical education is the potential impact of nonlinear pedagogy on motivating students to learn in a physical education setting.

Creating intrinsically motivating physical education via nonlinear pedagogy

One area that, over time, has received plenty of attention in education is the importance of creating motivating learning environments. Unfortunately, as highlighted in our earlier discussion of the work of Tinning (2006), the typical way physical education seems to be operating may not be best placed to fulfil the motivational needs of students to engage in games.

Drawing on Deci and Ryan (2000), self-determination theory, a well-recognized theory on motivation, implies a key requirement for a curriculum that aims to educate children through the medium of physical activity and sport is to ensure that chosen activities and pedagogical approaches underpin learners' attempts to always act to satisfy the basic psychological needs of autonomy, competence and relatedness. These needs can only be met if lessons are perceived as being interesting and important to the students (Deci & Ryan, 2000). However, as one of the author's trainee physical education students put it, the typical games lesson focused on a direct instructional approach consisting of "50 minutes of pain, for 10 minutes of game!" As such, the ability of the direct instructional model that seems to dominate physical education lessons (Metzler, 2005), in terms of its ability to meet the self-determination needs of children, is questionable. Typically, lessons taught with a focus on direct instruction:

- fail to provide opportunities to undertake autonomous behaviours;
- do not facilitate perceptions of competence due to a focus on attaining the perfect *adult* technique (impossible for many children) via inappropriate drills (where perception is separated from action, resulting in the development of non-functional movement patterns or inappropriate decision-making) (Renshaw *et al.*, 2010) and the accompanying emphasis on corrective feedback (seen as criticism by many children);
- can also result in a less functional level of relatedness between teacher and student, as the majority of teacher-led verbal interactions are about what the student didn't do (correcting) (see previously and Tinning, 2006), rather than on what she/he did well (reinforcing perceptions of competence).

The implication for teachers is that it is not only important *what* activities or sports are chosen to be taught, but it also matters *how* it is taught. Consequently, while choosing to focus on rugby union in a New Zealand school may initially create high levels of intrinsic motivation due to the high cultural significance of rugby to most New Zealanders, the way in which the skills of the game are taught will moderate the emotions and motives expressed, as well as the movement skills that emerge as a result of the teaching intervention. As such, teaching methods should facilitate opportunities to pursue autonomy, competence and relatedness which will result in intrinsic, motivated behaviours such as effort, persistence and problem-solving with respect to goal tasks. Some pedagogues have attempted to address these issues, developing new, more holistic approaches to games teaching. For example, Bunker and Thorpe indicated that they developed the Teaching Games for Understanding (TGfU) approach in an attempt to make games lessons more 'exciting' and to allow children to 'learn and enjoy themselves' (Thorpe, 2005). The constraints-led approach is an approach that implicitly meets the requirements for addressing the self-determination needs of children in that it is a learner-centred approach that has, as its central focus, the emergence of skills through self-organization. This approach acknowledges that there are many individually specific solutions to meet game problems and promotes the use of representative learning design through task simplification (meaning that tasks are provided that enable success for all students). Adopting task simplification in team games lessons means that small groups of children are required to work together to solve game-related problems, while the use of 'time-outs' to allow the teacher to ask focused questions to develop awareness promotes a climate of relatedness where teacher and student work together to facilitate learning.

In summary, by adopting the principles of nonlinear pedagogy, teachers of physical education can design learning environments that provide opportunities to achieve and enhance individual perceptions of competence, enhance related-ness and facilitate autonomous supportive behaviours. This approach facilitates the development of intrinsic motivation for all pupils, not just the talented few in each class. To exemplify, we will consider the pedagogical approach of playing small-sided games with associated questioning that underpins both nonlinear pedagogy and TGfU approaches. In terms of developing competence, creating small-sided practice games increases goal proximity to the 'real game' and has the advantage of maintaining important informational aspects of game play and associated perception action links. Additionally, games that involve small numbers of players offer more opportunities for achievement by virtue of greater inclusion; it is easier to be involved as the number of performers decreases. In relation to enhancing percep-tions of autonomy, adapted games, as opposed to repetition of skills, requires more decisions to be made by the learner. These decisions can be seen as self-endorsing acts and are, therefore, autonomy supportive. Finally, the greater proximity to other players and the degree of interaction demanded by small games will encou-rage greater interpersonal exchange which, in turn, should lead to greater feelings of relatedness. Questioning is a powerful teaching tool and can act to increase feelings of competence through the enhancement of task-related knowledge and by reinforcing the notion that important information resides within the performer. This, in turn, reflects on self-esteem, confidence and efficacy. Additionally, ques-tions devoted to the development of individual action and planning may be seen as autonomy supportive. The reader is directed towards Renshaw *et al.* (in press) for more examples of how teachers could take ideas from sports coaching to integrate the ideas and concepts of nonlinear pedagogy and self-determination theory into their learning design.

Conclusion

In conclusion, adopting a nonlinear pedagogical approach in physical education to enhance learning design for our children may create a more functional and supportive learning, as well as an intrinsically motivating, environment. Individual students can learn to adjust to the dynamic environmental demands more successfully and are able to make appropriate and quick, selective decisions as they adapt to their evolving environment, as well as enhance individual perceptions of competence, relatedness and autonomy. The approach is likely to facilitate the development of movement behaviours, games skills and intrinsic motivation for all students in the physical education context.

Note

1 http://www.examiner.com/golden-state-warriors-in-san-francisco/nba-players-on-team-usa-are-at-disadvantage-olympics-when-it-comes-to-international-3-point-line.

References

Beek, P.J., Jacobs, D.M., Daffertshofer, A., & Huys, R. (2003). Expert performance in sport: Views from joint perspectives of ecological psychology and dynamical systems theory. In J.P.L. Starkes & K.P.A. Ericsson (Eds.), *Expert performance in sport: Advances in research on sport expertise* (pp. 321–344). Champaign, IL: Human Kinetics.

Beek, P.J., & van Santvoord, A.A.M. (1992). Learning the cascade juggle: A dynamical systems analysis. *Journal of Motor Behavior, 24*(1), 85–94.

Brown, J. (2004). *Tennis: Steps to success*. Champaign, IL: Human Kinetics.

Button, C., Chow, J.Y., & Rein, R. (2008). Exploring the perceptual-motor workspace: New approaches to skill acquisition and training. In Y. Hong & R. Bartlett (Eds.), *Handbook of biomechanics and human movement science* (pp. 538–553). London: Routledge.

Chow, J.Y., Davids, K., Button, C., & Rein, R. (2008). Dynamics of movement patterning in learning a discrete multi-articular action. *Motor Control, 12*, 219–240.

Chow, J.Y., Davids, K., Button, C., Rein, R., Hristovski, R., & Koh, M. (2009). Dynamics of multi-articular coordination in neurobiological systems. *Nonlinear Dynamics, Psychology and Life Sciences, 13*(1), 27–52.

Chow, J.Y., Davids, K., Button, C., Shuttleworth, R., Renshaw, I., & Araúo, D. (2006). Nonlinear pedagogy: A constraints-led framework to understanding emergence of game play and skills. *Nonlinear Dynamics, Psychology, and Life Sciences, 10*(1), 71–103.

Chow, J.Y., Davids, K., Hristovski, R., Araújo, D., & Passos, P. (2011). Nonlinear pedagogy: Learning design for self-organizing neurobiological systems. *New Ideas in Psychology, 29*, 189–200.

Chow, J.Y., Davids, K., Shuttleworth, R., Button, C., Renshaw, I., & Araújo, D. (2007). From processes to principles: A constraints-led approach to teaching games for understanding (TGfU). *Review of Educational Research, 77*(3), 251–278.

Curtner-Smith, M.D., Todorovich, J.R., & McCaughtry, N.A. (2001). Urban teachers' use of productive and reproductive teaching styles within the confines of the national curriculum for physical education. *European Physical Education Review, 7*, 177–190.

Davids, K., Araújo, D., Hristovski, R., Passos, P., & Chow, J.Y. (2012). Ecological dynamics and motor learning design in sport. In A.M. Williams & N. Hodges (Eds.), *Skill acquisition in sport: Research, theory & practice* (2nd ed., pp. 112–130). London: Routledge.

Davids, K., Button, C., & Bennett, S. (2008). *Dynamics of skill acquisition: A constraints-led approach*. Champaign, IL: Human Kinetics.

Davids, K., Chow, J.Y., & Shuttleworth, R. (2005). A constraints-based framework for nonlinear pedagogy in physical education. *Journal of Physical Education New Zealand*, 38, 17–29.

Deci, E.L., & Ryan, R.M. (2000). The "what" and "why" of goal pursuits: Human needs and the self-determination of behavior. *Psychological Inquiry*, 11(4), 227–268.

Hopper, T. (2011). Game-as-teacher: Modification by adaptation in learning through game-play. *Asia-Pacific Journal of Health, Sport and Physical Education*, 2(2), 3–21.

Hristovski, R., Davids, K., & Araújo, D. (2006). Affordance-controlled bifurcations of action patterns in martial arts. *Nonlinear Dynamics, Psychology & the Life Sciences*, 10, 409–444.

Kauffmann, S.A. (1995). *At home in the universe: The search for laws of self-organization and complexity*. Oxford: Oxford University Press.

Kelso, J.A.S. (2003). Cognitive coordination dynamics. In W. Tschacher & J.P. Dauwalder (Eds.), *The dynamical systems approach to cognition* (pp. 45–67). River Edge, NJ: World Scientific.

Magill, R.A. (2011). *Motor learning: Concepts and applications* (9th ed.). New York: McGraw-Hill.

Metzler, M. (2005). *Instructional models for physical education* (2nd ed.). Scotsdale: Holcomb Hathaway.

Mitra, S., Amazeen, P.G., & Turvey, M.T. (1998). Intermediate motor learning as decreasing active (dynamical) degrees of freedom. *Human Movement Science*, 17, 17–65.

Newell, K.M. (1986). Constraints on the development of coordination. In M.G. Wade & H.T.A. Whiting (Eds.), *Motor development in children: Aspects of coordination and control* (pp. 341–360). Dordrecht, Netherlands: Martinus Nijhoff.

Newell, K.M., Liu, Y.T., & Mayer-Kress, G. (2001). Time scales in motor learning and development. *Psychological Review*, 108(1), 57–82.

Peh, S.Y.C., Chow, J.Y., & Davids, K. (2011). Focus of attention as an instructional constraint on movement behavior. *Journal of Science and Medicine in Sport*, 14, 70–78.

Pellett, T.L., & Lox, C.L. (1998). Tennis racket head-size comparisons and their effect on beginning college players' achievement and self-efficacy. *Journal of Teaching in Physical Education*, 17, 453–467.

Phillips, E., Davids, K., Renshaw, I., & Portus, M. (2010a). Expert performance in sport and the dynamics of talent development. *Sports Medicine*, 40(3), 1–13.

Phillips, E., Davids, K., Renshaw, I., & Portus, M. (2010b). The development of fast bowling experts in Australian Cricket. *Talent Development and Excellence*, 2(2), 137–148.

Pinder, R.A., Davids, K., Renshaw, I., & Araújo, D. (2011). Representative learning design and functionality of research and practice in sport. *Journal of Sport & Exercise Psychology*, 33, 146–155.

Pinder, R., Renshaw, I., & Davids, K. (2009). Information-movement coupling in developing cricketers under changing ecological practice constraints. *Human Movement Science*, 28(4), 468–479.

Renshaw, I., Davids, K., Chow, J.Y., & Hammond, J. (2010). A constraints-led perspective to understanding skill acquisition and game play: A basis for integration of motor learning theory and physical education praxis? *P.E. & Sport Pedagogy*, 15(2), 117–131.

Renshaw, I., Davids, K., Phillips, E., & Kerherve, H. (2012). Developing talent in athletes as complex neurobiological systems. In J. Baker, S., Cobley, & J. Schorer (Eds.), *Talent identification and development in sport: International perspectives* (pp. 64–80). New York: Routledge.

Renshaw, I., Davids, K., & Savelsbergh, G.J.P. (2010). *Motor learning in practice: A constraints-led approach.* London: Routledge.

Renshaw, I., Oldham, A., & Bawden, M. (2012). Nonlinear pedagogy underpins intrinsic motivation in sports coaching. *The Open Sports Sciences Journal,* 5, 88–99.

Richardson, K., Sheehy, D., & Hopper, T. (2012). Modification by adaptation: Proposing another pedagogical principle for TGfU. In A. Ovens, T. Hopper, & J. Butler (Eds.), *Complexity in physical education: Reframing curriculum pedagogy and research* (pp. 181–193). London: Routledge.

Smith, L.B., & Thelen, E. (2003). Development as a dynamic system. *Trends in Cognitive Sciences,* 7(8), 343–348.

Tan, C.W.K., Chow, J.Y., & Davids, K. (2011). "How does TGfU work?": Examining the relationship between learning design in TGfU and a nonlinear pedagogy. *Physical Education and Sport Pedagogy,* 1–18. DOI:10.1080/17408989.2011.582486.

Thelen, E., & Smith, L.B. (1994). *A dynamic systems approach to the development of cognition and action.* Cambridge, MA: The MIT Press.

Thorpe, R. (2005). Rod Thorpe on teaching games for understanding. In L. Kidman (Ed.), *Athlete-centred coaching: Developing inspired and inspiring people* (pp. 229–243). Christchurch: Innovative Print Communication Ltd.

Tinning, R. (2006). Thinking about good teaching in physical education. In R. Tinning, L. McCuaig, & L. Hunter (Eds.), *Teaching health and physical education in Australian schools* (pp. 232–242). Frenchs Forest: Pearson Education Australia.

Ulrich, B., Thelen, E., & Niles, D. (1990). Perceptual determinants of action: Stair climbing choices of infants and toddlers. In J. Clark & J. Humphrey (Eds.), *Advances in motor research,* Vol. 3 (pp. 1–15). New York: AMS Press.

Zanone, P.G., & Kelso, J.A.S. (1992). Evolution of behavioral attractors with learning: Nonequilibrium phase transitions. *Journal of Experimental Psychology: Human Perception and Performance,* 18, 403–421.

11 A nonlinear pedagogy for sports teams as social neurobiological systems

How teams can harness self-organization tendencies

Chris Button, Jia-Yi Chow, Bruno Travassos, Luís Vilar, Ricardo Duarte, Pedro Passos, Duarte Araújo and Keith Davids

Many team sports implicitly share similarities in the collective movements of players during the ebb and flow of offensive and defensive phases of play (Dutt Mazumder, Button, Robins, & Bartlett, 2011). At elite levels, team sports demonstrate a high level of movement organization and coordination within and between players. As an example, one might think of the way in which players from top football clubs such as Barcelona and Manchester United (the 2011 European Football Champions' League finalists) move and support team-mates, as well as fluidly co-adapt to actions of opponents. Whilst movements of novice players or early learners are less obviously structured, it is useful to know how these behavioural patterns are governed by the collective actions of the social and physical environment.

Some common principles of collective behaviour have already been identified in the organization of different social neurobiological systems[1] in nature such as swarming insects, flocking birds, schools of fish and herds of animals (Sumpter, 2006). Whilst humans have greater capacity to act autonomously than many other living organisms, it is likely that common, functional principles may partially explain collective behaviours in team sports because they represent dynamical systems. In this chapter we explain why team games adhere to the principles of dynamical systems and also what practical value this complexity perspective can offer physical educators. Although specific task constraints (i.e., rules, equipment, numbers of opponents) of different sports shape the evolution of behaviours that players manifest (for example, rule-based restrictions to certain parts of the playing area, as in netball, or strong adherence to specific playing positions or formations, as in American football), our discussion of teams as social neurobiological systems will be exemplified with reference to the collective organization of players in association football and futsal. We conclude by considering how physical educators can best influence skill acquisition of teams using the theoretical principles of nonlinear pedagogy (see also Chow *et al.*, Chapter 10).

Principles of collective organization amongst social neurobiological systems

Collective behaviour of social neurobiological systems is ubiquitous in nature. For example, whilst animals are individual, autonomous agents, evolutionary pressures and learned experience have revealed that behaving as groups can often be a more successful strategy than behaving as individuals acting independently. A crucial point is that collective behaviour amongst groups of individuals is the result of self-organization. In self-organizing systems, it is well-established that organization emerges[2] from the interactions of the mass of individuals rather than from one or a few agents (Kauffman, 1993); but how is this possible? Amongst others, Sumpter (2006) has argued that simple principles underpin the apparently complex arrangements of different animal groupings during common behaviours such as nesting, hunting, predator avoidance and courtship. It has been known for some time now that mathematical models of such rich, asymptotic behaviour can be formulated on the basis of relatively few, ordinary differential equations (Nicolis & Prigogine, 1977). For example, Couzin, Krause, James, Ruxton, and Franks (2002) modelled the dynamics of schooling fish and showed that three simple rules could explain the emerging pattern formation: (i) move away from nearby neighbours; (ii) adopt the same direction as those that are close by; and (iii) match velocity of nearby agents to avoid becoming isolated.

Interestingly such organizational principles have been also identified amongst groups of humans. Helbing, Farkas, and Vicsek (2000) showed how human evacuation behaviour in buildings can be predicted and strongly influenced by relatively simple factors like corridor width and exit size. More specifically in team sports, such as rugby union, it has been revealed that the interpersonal distances between agents within an attacker subunit are context dependent; the range of interpersonal distances between attackers increase after the subunit passes the first defensive line (Passos *et al.*, 2011). This means that, once attackers break through the first line of defence to penetrate the opponents' territory, they take advantage of the space behind the defence to spread the areas that the defenders have to guard to prevent a score. Within critical regions of a game, typically characterized by low values of interpersonal distances between players, actions do not result from preplanned rules but rather emerge from continuous player interactions as a game evolves, resulting in fast-paced exchanges that cannot be predetermined. Such findings are initial indications that groups of individuals acting according to simple principles can organize themselves into complex and extremely effective pattern configurations, without the need for a central controlling agent.

Self-organizing systems have the *capacity to output more than the sum of their parts*. Due to positive feedback loops, a critical mass of individual agents acting with a common purpose can accomplish functional behaviours that would be beyond individuals (such as building a nest or a large building) (Beekman, Sumpter, & Ratnieks, 2001). Such systems are also *sensitive to the initial conditions* under which they are formed. For example, large numbers of humans now interact through social communication networks such as Facebook and Twitter. It is doubtful whether such powerful networking systems would have propagated under the social constraints 20 years earlier, when e-mailing and phone-texting communication modes were in their infancy.

In attempting to understand collective behaviours in different social systems, it is important to acknowledge that an individual human's behaviour may not always conform to simple rules and that spontaneous patterns of behaviour can emerge and destabilize quickly. Perhaps more so than any other living organism, humans possess many individual differences in terms of their capacity to: act in certain ways; detect relevant informational cues; plan ahead and strategize; and lead rather than be led to a goal/solution.

In sports there are many influential individuals (e.g., coaches, captains, play-makers) who have the skill, knowledge and motivation to strongly influence performance outcome. This important distinction leads us to the classification of different kinds of agents amongst groups of individuals—namely, informed leaders vs. naïve followers (Merrifield, Myerscough, & Weber, 2006). Informed leaders possess prior knowledge of the final desired goal of the collective group and help coerce and guide their more naïve counterparts to achieve this outcome. For example, a spontaneous round of applause amongst an audience may be initiated by a few individuals but is swiftly picked up and synchronized by the larger group. Passos, Araújo, and Davids (2012) discuss the implications of self-organization processes for leadership in sport. They note that preconceived tactical formations can constrain the organization of players somewhat during games. Hence we do not suggest that all patterns of players spontaneously emerge; instead, the pattern-forming dynamics of groups of players can be strongly influenced (e.g., by tactical instructions) under certain conditions. It is likely also that informed leaders are most sensitive and react swiftly to response thresholds; in other words, they collectively change their behaviour in response to a stimulus reaching some critical value. In summary, whilst humans possess many differences to other organisms (most notably, the obvious capacity to behave autonomously), they also have the tendency to exhibit collective organization when they form groups. The extent to which they do so within structured team sports is the question we consider next.

Modelling team sports games as dynamical systems

Team sports can be conceived of as dynamical systems as they share common characteristics. There are numerous component parts (i.e., players) constituting degrees of freedom which are loosely coupled via energy (e.g., sound, light, gravity) flowing through the system. Whilst a game's outcome can be heavily influenced by a preconceived plan of a coach or a practiced set-play, the complex, dynamic movement behaviour of athletes is an emergent phenomenon. The organization of such a system is emergent, yet it is attracted towards stable, recurring states that are dependent on other players and the game situation. Recurring patterns of behaviour (e.g., expansion and contraction towards and away from a target invasion area) have been observed at multiple levels of analysis such as at the level of the team, sub-groups and amongst individual players (i.e., Bourbousson, Seve, & McGarry, 2010; Frencken, Lemmink, Delleman, & Visscher, 2011).

Performance analysts can provide fascinating insights into how team players interact and respond to sudden attacks (perturbations) and reorganize themselves to stop such instabilities (Dutt Mazumder et al., 2011). Increasing attention is being directed towards the study of team games as dynamical systems realized through the formulization of synergetic and nonlinear equations to model the dynamics of human movement (Davids, Glazier, Araújo, & Bartlett, 2003). In the past few years, team sports such as association football (Gréhaigne, Bouthier, & David, 1997), futsal (Travassos, Araújo, Vilar, & McGarry, 2011), basketball (Bourbousson et al., 2010) and rugby union (Passos et al., 2009) have received this kind of analysis. For example, Gréhaigne et al. (1997) employed video analysis of elite (i.e., international level) player positions in order to identify whether general principles of play were met and whether these were observed in the antecedents to goals. Based on the simple parameters of player position, direction and speed of movement, 'sectors of play' for each player were determined. It was noted that, in general play, the behaviour of players in possession of the ball was to respect the principle of passing into open sectors of their team-mates' space (out of 110 sequences of play, 102 adhered to this state). In other words, the ball was typically passed into free sectors where a team-mate can control the ball and did not cross 'interceptable' sectors en route. On the few occasions where this constant state was not met, either possession was lost or goal-scoring chances resulted from the loss of system stability (often resulting from defender mistakes).

In relation to small-sided games in soccer, Frencken et al. (2011) have shown that the dynamics of the centroid position of each team are strongly related. The centroid is calculated from the average position of all of the outfield players on the pitch at any one time. Interestingly, in the build-up to goals, specific character-istics of the forward–backward motion of the centroid positions were apparent (Frencken et al., 2011). Whilst systems-based modelling seems an intuitively pro-mising approach in football, surprisingly few studies have sought to extend it and identify coordination variables at lower skill levels. However, Gréhaigne, Caty, and Godbout (2010) recently performed an observational performance analysis amongst young (11–18 years old), less-skilled football players. Eight prototypic offensive configurations of players were found in 4 vs. 4 small-sided games. In terms of the configuration of players, the effective play-space (EP-S) was defined as the polygonal area that one obtains by drawing a line that links all involved players located at the periphery of the play at a given instant. The eight common configurations largely depended upon where, on the pitch, ball possession was lost/attained. Perhaps, unsurprisingly, the stability of games contested by less-skilled players fluctuates within shorter timescales as a consequence of more mistakes being made and higher frequencies of possession turnover. Nevertheless, some regular patterns of behaviour, such as ball-focused swarming of players, are common observations under certain playing conditions (Button, Chow, Dutt Mazumder, & Vilar, 2011). The examination of small-sided games (such as futsal) seems to represent a promising approach with which to test these ideas through research.

Interpersonal coordination tendencies under performance constraints in futsal

> I played futsal growing up in Baurd. In futsal you need to think quick and play quick so it's easier for you when you move to normal football. (Pélé, Brazilian footballer)

A complex systems approach to collective behaviours in team sports provides an understanding of interpersonal coordination by examining the information that guides player interactions during performance. For example, although game strategies defined by teachers or coaches may constrain performance, players' goal-directed behaviours emerge as they interact with key features of the performance environment (Davids, Kingsbury, Bennett, & Handford, 2001). Opportunities for players to act (or affordances) are revealed by these interactions (Araújo, Davids, & Hristovski, 2006). Since futsal is played on a small pitch (42 × 25 m), the average player density across the playing area is generally high and, therefore, time and space are crucial factors. Here, affordances are defined as a relationship between players' capabilities and the physical conditions of the performance environment to achieve a certain goal. Affordances also exist at the collective level. For example, when a futsal player in possession of the ball becomes isolated, with no passing options, opposing players need to recognize that brief opportunity to increase defensive pressure on the ball carrier and force a turn-over in possession during that brief time window. Hence, performance is grounded on the players' ability to identify and actualize opportunities to act collectively as well as for themselves based on interpersonal spatial–temporal relations (Araújo *et al.*, 2006; Richardson, Marsh, & Baron, 2007). So what may be the key constraints of the performance environment that influence these interpersonal coordination tendencies in team sports like futsal?

Location of the goal as a constraint on interpersonal coordination

In futsal, the aim of each attacker is to achieve his/her interactions with an immediate marking defender in the most beneficial way for the team (Vilar, Araújo, Davids, & Travassos, 2012). The attacker may act in order to destabilize coordination with his/her opponent or he/she may 'fix' (capture the attention of) an immediate defender in a stable dyad so that other dyads may attain looser coordination (allowing other attackers to exploit the attacking potential in other 1v1 sub-systems without a covering defender) (Vilar, Araújo, Davids, & Button, 2012). Either way, the goal of an attacker is to lead the system organization to less stable regions of behaviour. Conversely, each defender seeks to counteract the movements of immediate attackers to maintain system stability (to prevent the attacker from gaining a positional advantage that allows him/her to threaten the goal) (Davids, Araújo, & Shuttleworth, 2005; McGarry, Anderson, Wallace, Hughes, & Franks, 2002; Vilar *et al.*, 2012). Simultaneously, defenders can coordinate to re-stabilize other dyads broken by an attacker's movements by switching positions with each other.

In order to understand how players use information from the locations of the opponents and the goal to maintain or disrupt stability in attacker–defender dyadic systems, Vilar, Davids, Araújo, and Travassos (2012) examined the distances and angles between the four outfield attackers and their nearest defenders involved in futsal matches. Interpersonal coordination tendencies were accessed through relative phase between players. This variable considers attacker and defender displacements as two (informational) coupled oscillators (repetitive variations between different states) that capture the players' coordination states. The relative phase dynamics refer to common patterns of relative phase in sport which include in-phase patterns (0° and multiples of 360°) in which both players in a dyad moved closer/further from the same place at the same time, and anti-phase patterns (180° and multiples of 360°) in which both players in a dyad moved in opposite directions at the same time (Palut & Zanone, 2005).

Figure 11.1 demonstrates how a dyadic system's stability in one exemplar trial was continuously forged and broken until the attacker scored a goal. The players' distances to the goal showed that the defender always tried to remain closer

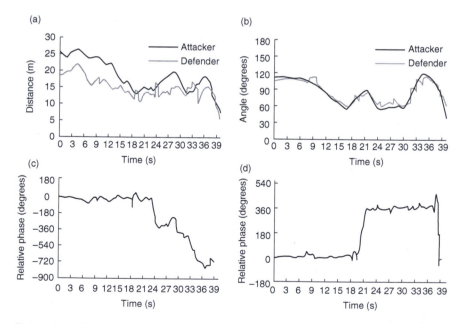

Figure 11.1 Goal location as a constraint on coordination processes in dyadic systems presented in decomposed format: Left column: distances of each player to the centre of the goal; right column: angles of each player to the centre of the goal; upper row: exemplar data from attacker 5 and nearest defender; bottom row: dynamics of the relative phase of the exemplar data from attacker 5 and nearest defender (adapted from Vilar *et al.*, 2012).

to the goal than the attacker (Figure 11.1a). Simultaneously, the two players' angles to the goal were similar throughout the sequence, suggesting that the defender tried to remain between the attacker and the centre of the goal (Figure 11.1b). Relative phase analysis suggested that, while the attacker was in possession of the ball and the defender was between the goal and the attacker, stability between the players was maintained (Figures 11.1c and d). The defender's efforts to maintain the stability of this dyadic system were often insufficient and critical fluctuations (or instability) precipitated more than one system phase transition. As the sequence of play evolved towards its end (24–36 s), the distance of both the attacker and the defender to the goal decreased until they reached similar values, and the angular differences of both players relative to the goal increased, suggesting that a misalignment of the defender's positioning between the attacker and the centre of the goal may have precipitated a successful shot on goal (36–39 s). A common characteristic of such sequences taken from competitive games is that, only when there is a change in dyadic system coordination near the goal and the defenders do not have the collective ability to re-establish dyadic system stability, are goal opportunities presented. This research explains how players in futsal regulate their performance by using spatial-temporal information about their relative positioning to the nearest opponent and the goal (Vilar et al., 2012).

Ball dynamics as a constraint on interpersonal coordination

Emergent patterns of coordination in futsal result from cooperation and competition among players to achieve favourable spatial-temporal conditions during performance (McGarry et al., 2002). Whilst attackers try to disrupt the defensive structure by exploring different spatial-temporal relations, defenders try to couple their displacements to protect the goal (Travassos et al., 2011). Based on this synergistic relationship, the analysis of intra-team (across players of the same team) and inter-team (between players of the opponent team) couplings between dyads is considered the basis for understanding team game dynamics (McGarry et al., 2002).

Following this logic, Travassos and colleagues (2011) studied the reciprocal relation between the ball and players by considering their lateral and longitudinal movement trajectories in a futsal game. Results showed that defenders demonstrated the strongest stability in relation to the ball (27% at −30° relative phase), whereas attackers revealed high variability in their mode of coordination with the ball (14% at −30° relative phase) (Figures 11.2a. and b). In Figure 11.2a, stability in the defenders' ball relations between 0 s to 15 s and 30 s to 70 s can be observed. A decrease in stability of relations was observed in Figure 11.2b in which relative phase presents few moments of stability with different types of relations (0 s to 10 s in-phase and 40 s to 47 s anti-phase), although, with weaker stability levels, similar relations were also observed for the relations between defenders (20% in-phase) and defender–attacker relations (12% in-phase). The relations between attackers of the same team revealed the lowest stable relations with no preferable mode of

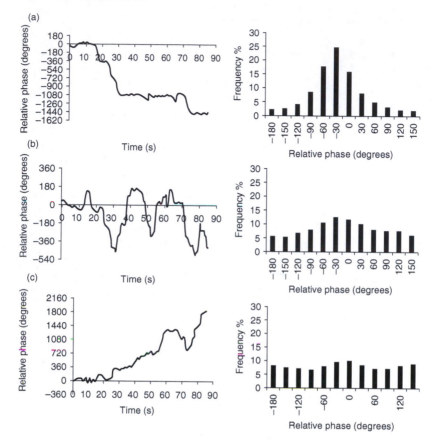

Figure 11.2 Ball dynamics as a constraint on coordination of: (a) defenders and ball; (b) attackers and ball; (c) attackers–attackers. Left column: dynamics of the relative phase of an exemplar trial; right column: frequency histograms of relative phase (adapted from Travassos *et al.*, 2011).

coordination (Figure 11.2c). In Figure 11.2c it is possible to observe a continuous variation in relative phase, without stable relations.

These findings revealed that relations between futsal players and the ball typically revealed high levels of stability. Therefore, ball dynamics can be assumed as a key constraint on players' performances, especially for defenders. These results suggest that, in order to protect the goal area, the positioning of defenders should be coupled with their team-mates and attackers, and more predominantly with the movement of the ball. The differences between the coordination dynamics of defenders and attackers may be interpreted as additional evidence for different team objectives (intentionality). Whilst defenders need to couple their behaviour with the ball dynamics to consistently protect the goal, attackers need to promote variability in their spatial-temporal couplings to promote instability in defensive structure and score a goal. For example, they can make runs into spaces around the goal to open up areas for other attackers to exploit.

Harnessing inherent self-organization processes in football practice

> My position is this: street soccer is the most natural educational system that can be found. (Rinus Michels, Dutch national player and team coach, credited with the invention of the "Total Football" playing strategy, 2002, p. 175)

How can knowledge of the self-organizing properties of sports teams help practitioners to enhance skill acquisition in physical education? In this section we reflect on the information discussed in this chapter and offer some practical ideas for implementation, particularly amongst early and young learners. Emerging research is starting to identify the critical variables that influence the organizational properties of sports teams (Frencken *et al.*, 2011; Travassos *et al.*, 2011; Vilar *et al.*, 2012). Furthermore, it seems that important interpersonal variables, such as the defender–attacker alignment, may be symbolic of the simple principles that govern agent movements in team games as social collectives. Whilst practitioners may not be able to measure such variables with the same level of sensitivity/accuracy as researchers, they can certainly use such knowledge to inform their practice design.

Combining the concepts of self-organization (for emergent behaviour) and teaching (based on developing certain behaviours through instruction) may appear at first glance to be an uncomfortable partnership. Indeed, it is quite possible that, by providing too much instruction and repetitive practice of certain team formations, teachers may, in fact, circumvent the inherent self-organizing tendencies that exist in social collectives. For example, a teacher could design a football practice activity in which small groups of players are restricted to certain areas of the pitch in order to develop a rudimentary team shape or formation. However, whilst possibly effective in the short term, such a heavily-constrained task modification may be somewhat artificial (and possibly frustrating for players) in attempting to promote awareness of space in relation to other players and the ball dynamics. Furthermore, the activity of restricting players to areas of the field does little to promote their independent-thinking and problem-solving. In our view, self-regulated, spontaneous learning *coupled* with modified practice games can be developed to allow learners sufficient freedom to organize themselves and still provide sufficient guidance to develop from restrictive (anarchical) to more open-ended (elaborate) styles of play (see Table 11.1). Note how in the examples below the dyad is set-up to encourage attacking players to explore and exploit the use of space, with changes in shape of playing area and use of extra players. Defenders are then encouraged to counter this exploitation to regain stability. Also note how constraints associated with environment and rules are altered to challenge players' skill selection and execution.

Unstructured practice environments and spontaneous learning: the case of street football

There is some indicative evidence in the literature on the emergence of expertise in players who have received little systematic and structured coaching during their development (Araújo *et al.*, 2010; Phillips, Davids, Renshaw, & Portus, 2010). For

Table 11.1 Exemplar teaching concepts and activities to help learners in team games to harness existing self-organizing tendencies

Teaching concept	Activity	Rationale
Developing or defending shooting opportunities	1. Set up small player dyads (i.e., 1v1, 3v3) in different sizes/shapes of playing area relative to the goal. 2. Assign the players into pairs—the player in possession of the ball must carry the ball to a target zone; the defending player tries to jockey them (without tackling) away from the target.	Develop awareness of interpersonal distance, ball dynamics and location of goal. Encourage attacking players to explore, maintain and break the stability of symmetry relationships.
Creating time and space for team-mates	1. Manipulate size of playing area. 2. Set up simple rotations of player position (e.g., circle, triangle) to draw defending players away from the ball-carrier.	Change the spatio-temporal demands upon players. Draw defenders away from target zones and create space to attack.
Increasing effective play space area	1. Change playing surfaces (i.e., start on grass or sand then transition to a wood floor or concrete). 2. Impose a rule that players can't dribble with the ball; they must control and pass.	Alter the frictional characteristics of ball and playing surface to perturb the swarm's stability. Adapt simple rules of swarm agents thereby inducing alternative behaviours.
Defending as a team	1. Four attackers play against three defenders. The defenders must try to prevent attackers from passing to each other through a marked target zone. 2. Set up 5 × 2 m 'goals' in one half of a pitch. Four defenders attempt to stop the attacking team (6) passing through the goals and scoring points.	Awareness of passing affordances and location of goal. Defending multiple target zones, cooperating together to nullify attacks.

example, Salmela and Moraes (2004) identified that many talented Brazilian football players aged 16–17 years tend to have received little, if any, structured coaching in programmes, in contrast to a multitude of unstructured football experiences played on the streets. In a series of interviews with elite players and coaches, Fonseca and Garganta (2008) provided qualitative data on the general perception that unstructured football played on the streets had a crucial role in learning game skills for these elite players. The pleasure and the passion that a child gains from playing football and the possibilities for free exploration, creativity and goal achievement under unpredictably variable performance conditions were considered essential for developing football expertise by these expert coaches and players (see Araújo *et al.*, 2010 for other illustrative examples of street football). We should acknowledge that, whilst the self-organizing tendencies of teams can be promoted through street football, this environment may also foster undesirable technical/tactical and even negative social/affective outcomes for less able players in the complete absence of any formal coaching or adult supervision. Rather than simply replacing the teacher or coach, we suggest that the introduction of 'street play' can be blended with structured practice activities to optimise learning, as is being recommended in blending teaching approaches such as sport education and Teaching Games for Understanding (Alexander & Penney, 2005).

The findings of Araújo and colleagues (2010) suggest that characteristics of learning environments like 'street football' and 'backyard games' (Phillips *et al.*, 2010) can constitute powerful tools for practitioners to enhance the acquisition of skill and learning in team games. Their data suggest that key characteristics of learning design in team games should include: (i) not relying on formalized games and training drills all the time; (ii) designing activities for fun and enjoyment; (iii) creating learning environments that encourage search, discovery and exploration in movements; (iv) enhancing adaptive behaviours by creating opportunities for learners to satisfy different constraints (playing in different weather conditions, against children from different age groups, gender, number of players, etc.); (v) varying equipment and facilities for practice, varying surfaces and textures, footwear, ball types; (vi) not conceptualizing an idealized target movement pattern as *the* way to perform a skill; (vii) making sure that skill practice encompasses 'repetition without repetition'; and (viii) ensuring that practice tasks are always dynamic and never static or decomposed (such as in traditional practice drills). These key features will ensure that learning design is able to harness inherent self-organizing tendencies in team game training programmes, capturing skill performance during continuous spatio-temporal interactions of learners.

Changes in within- and between-team coordination patterns during learning

Another interesting manifestation of self-organizing processes in team sports occurs when a group of players participate together in small-sided games (SSGs). Different types of play can be observed from groups of players of distinct skill levels (Mombaerts, 1999) and when different SSG formats are used in practice (Folgado, 2010). In a recent study, Folgado (2010) investigated changes in inter-team coordination (identifying variations in the distances between geometrical centres of competing teams) and intra-team coordination (establishing a length by width ratio within each team) from U9 to U13 age groups, in 3v3 and 4v4 formats of small-sided games. Variations in the length by width ratio can explain how team players coordinate their movements on the field of play when creating or restricting space (in width and length). Data revealed that team game players increased the distance between the geometrical centres and their synchrony with length and width expansion/contraction movements as a function of age. These findings indicated that, with increasing age and physical capacity, grouping of players transited from a prototypical cloud shape around the ball to a more distributed positioning around the playing space. This more advanced collective behaviour induced an increase in the effective play-space explored by each team (i.e., the surface area covered by each team). Moreover, Folgado's (2010) findings also suggested that older players tended to increase their ability to coordinate the expansion and contraction of collective movement patterns over the length and width of the playing area, in a synchronized manner. In contrast, younger players typically showed a preference to explore the length of the playing area and focused on a direct path to the goal, to the detriment of the breadth. The extent to which variables such as age, playing experience or physical fitness are driving these changes should be explored in future research.

Learning team games through a constraints-led approach: a nonlinear pedagogy

An important question concerns the pedagogical implications of these previous findings (i.e., Folgado, 2010). The players' expertise in football is considered to evolve from the prototypical game level illustrated in the left panel of Figure 11.3 (anarchical game) to the more elaborated level shown in the right panel. The 'anarchical game level' represents the initial phases of learning in team games. Learners typically display a low capacity to play collectively due to their continuous spatial concentration around the ball (e.g., the ball-focused cloud or swarm) and their difficulties in controlling the ball when performing basic skills such as passing. At this level, the game is often characterized by a single player (the 'dribbler') rushing individual plays until ball possession is lost. These plays are more commonly observed at the periphery of the effective play-space because learners typically are not capable of exploiting space in critical areas of play in a more direct approach to goal. At this stage there are numerous involuntary exchanges in ball possession between competing teams. The main performance aspects for physical educators to focus on at this level are: (i) ball control under basic temporal and spatial constraints, (ii) rational structuring of space, in which team members are encouraged to expand and contract the effective play-space, and (iii) exploiting depth in direct play to approach the field where learners are constrained to play depth passes to team-mates positioned ahead of the ball in the field.

In contrast to the 'anarchical' stage of play, the 'direct playing game' appears when learners are able to occupy more longitudinal space. Learners are often positioned ahead of the ball and ball displacement trajectories frequently occur from back to front in the team structure (see middle panel of Figure 11.3). There are not many alternatives to the direct play approach that results in numerous losses in ball possession. The relevant aspects of play to focus on at this stage are: (i) to create opposition to an opponent dribbling a ball by adopting a defensive positioning between the ball and the goal axis, as well as to stop the progression of the ball dribbler in the field, (ii) to provide support for the ball carrier by moving into space and creating opportunities for passing the ball, ensuring the continuity of ball possession progression up the field which the

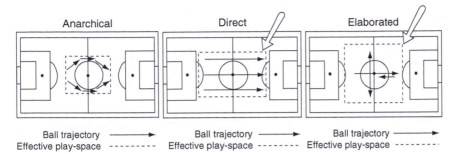

Figure 11.3 The evolution of game level according to players' expertise: from the 'anarchical game' (left panel), to a 'direct playing game' (middle panel) and to a more 'elaborated game' (right panel). Game levels can be characterized in practical terms according to two collective performance indicators: predominant ball trajectory and effective play-space (adapted from Mombaerts, 1999).

defending team is seeking to prevent, (iii) to develop the use of width on field by constraining learners to continuously play in wing channels on the field during practice and (iv) to maintain ball possession in small groups of players, constraining learners to continually move into space and create new passing opportunities.

Finally, the 'elaborated game' is characterized by an increase in the width of the effective play-space that appears when support for an attacking player with the ball is frequently created and used by learners. Ball displacement trajectories tend to increase in the width dimension of the field during this stage of learning (see right panel of Figure 11.3). The main performance features to focus on at this game level are: (i) defensive support in which defending players need to position themselves to support the nearest defender to a ball dribbler and to maintain the cohesiveness of a defensive formation, (ii) defensive support to build up a collective spatial concentration in critical performance areas between the goal being defended and the ball axis and (iii) the creation and use of space by continuously moving the ball around the playing area and using changes of direction and surprising moves to destabilize the opposition team.

To summarize, an important strategy to promote skill acquisition and learning in team games is the use of small-sided and modified games (e.g., Fenoglio, 2003; Mitchell, 1996). This type of practice task constraint promotes a more frequent functional involvement of players in the game due to the high density of players and number of actions performed in a smaller area of play compared with full-sided games (Capranica, Tessitore, Guidetti, & Figura, 2001). Going back to the examples listed in Table 11.1, physical educators need to identify and adjust key task constraints of small-sided games in order to promote the acquisition of specific game skills or tactical behaviours (e.g., limiting the number of touches to improve passing game and support movements). In so doing, physical educators have a valuable, but challenging, role to play in learning to step back, yet facilitate, self-organizing behaviour.

Notes

1 We occasionally use the term 'social neurobiological system' when referring to groups of humans as a broad classification to signify that collective organizational principles have been identified in many groups of living organisms including other animals and insects. We acknowledge that humans are somewhat unique amongst social neurobiological agents in their developed capacity to strategize, plan, improvise and act autonomously.

2 It is important to note that self-organizing behaviour (e.g., flocking in birds) does not result purely by chance; instead, key control parameters drive the whole system towards more stable solutions (or attractor states).

References

Alexander, K., & Penney, D. (2005). Teaching under the influence: Feeding games for understanding into the sport education development-refinement cycle. *Physical Education and Sport Pedagogy*, *10*(3), 287–301.

Araújo, D., Davids, K., & Hristovski, R. (2006). The ecological dynamics of decision making in sport. *Psychology of Sport and Exercise*, *7*, 653–676.

Araújo, D., Fonseca, C., Davids, K., Garganta, J., Volossovitch, A., Brandão, R. et al. (2010). The role of ecological constraints on expertise development. *Talent Development and Excellence*, *2*, 165–179.

Beekman, M., Sumpter, D.J.T., & Ratnieks, F.L.W. (2001). Phase transition between disordered and ordered foraging in Pharaoh's ants. *Proceedings of the National Academy of Sciences*, *98*(17), 9703–9706.

Bourbousson, J., Seve, C., & McGarry, T. (2010). Space-time coordination dynamics in basketball: Part 1. intra- and inter-couplings among player dyads. *Journal of Sports Sciences*, *28*(3), 339–347.

Button, C., Chow, J.-Y., Dutt Mazumder, A., & Vilar, L. (2011). *Exploring the swarming effect in children's football*. Paper presented at the World Congress of Science and Football, Nagoya, Japan, 26–30 May.

Capranica, L., Tessitore, A., Guidetti, L., & Figura, F. (2001). Heart rate and match analysis in pre-pubescent soccer players. *Journal of Sports Sciences*, *19*(6), 379–384.

Couzin, I.D., Krause, J., James, R., Ruxton, G.D., & Franks, N.R. (2002). Collective memory and spatial sorting in animal groups. *Journal of Theoretical Biology*, *218*(1), 1–11.

Davids, K., Araújo, D., & Shuttleworth, R. (2005). Applications of dynamical systems theory to football. In T. Reilly J. Cabri, & D. Araújo (Eds.), *Science and Football V* (pp. 547–560). London: Routledge.

Davids, K., Glazier, P., Araújo, D., & Bartlett, R.M. (2003). Movement systems as dynamical systems: The role of functional variability and its implications for sports medicine. *Sports Medicine*, *33*, 245–260.

Davids, K., Kingsbury, D., Bennett, S., & Handford, C. (2001). Information-movement coupling: Implications for the organization of research and practice during acquisition of self-paced extrinsic timing skills. *Journal of Sports Sciences*, *19*(2), 117–127.

Dutt Mazumder, A., Button, C., Robins, A., & Bartlett, R. (2011). Neural network modelling and dynamical system theory: Are they relevant to study the governing dynamics of association football players? *Sports Medicine*, *41*(12), 1–15.

Fenoglio, R. (2003). The Manchester United 4 V 4 pilot scheme for under 9's: Part II – the analysis. *Insight: The Football Association Coaches Association Magazine*, *6*(4), 21–24.

Folgado, H. (2010). *Towards an understanding of youth football teams' tactical performance by analysis of collective positional variables during small-sided games.* Unpublished masters thesis, UTAD, Vila Real, Portugal.

Fonseca, H., & Garganta, J. (2008). *Futebol de rua, um beco com saída. Jogo espontâneo e prática deliberada* [Football on the street, an alley with escape. Spontaneous game and deliberate practice]. Lisboa: Visão e Contextos.

Frencken, W., Lemmink, K., Delleman, N., & Visscher, C. (2011). Oscillations of centroid position and surface area of soccer teams in small-sided games. *European Journal of Sport Science, 11*(4), 215–223.

Gréhaigne, J.F., Bouthier, D., & David, B. (1997). Dynamic-system analysis of opponent relationships in collective actions in soccer. *Journal of Sports Sciences, 15,* 137–149.

Gréhaigne, J.F., Caty, D., & Godbout, P. (2010). Modelling ball circulation in invasion team sports: A way to promote learning games through understanding. *Physical Education & Sport Pedagogy, 15*(3), 257–270.

Helbing, D., Farkas, I., & Vicsek, T. (2000). Simulating dynamical features of escape panic. *Nature, 407*(6803), 487–490.

Kauffman, S.A. (1993). *The origins of order: Self-organization and selection in evolution.* New York: Oxford University Press.

McGarry, T., Anderson, D., Wallace, S., Hughes, M., & Franks, I. (2002). Sport competition as a dynamical self-organizing system. *Journal of Sports Sciences, 20,* 771–781.

Merrifield, A., Myerscough, M.R., & Weber, N. (2006). Statistical tests for analysing directed movement of self-organizing animal groups. *Mathematical Biosciences, 203*(1), 64–78.

Michels, R. (2002). *Teambuilding: The road to success.* Spring City, PA: Reedswain.

Mitchell, S. (1996). Improving invasion game performance. *Journal of Physical Education Recreation and Dance, 67*(2), 30–34.

Mombaerts, E. (1999). *Pédagogie du football: Apprendre à jouer ensemble par la pratique du jeu* [Pedagogy of football: Learning to play through game practice]. Paris: Vigot.

Nicolis, G., & Prigogine, I. (1977). *Self-organization in non-equilibrium systems.* New York: Wiley.

Palut, Y., & Zanone, P.G. (2005). A dynamical analysis of tennis: Concepts and data. *Journal of Sports Sciences, 23*(10), 1021–1032.

Passos, P., Araújo, D., & Davids, K. (2012). Self-organization processes in team sports: Implications for leadership. *Sports Medicine, 42,* In press.

Passos, P., Araújo, D., Davids, K., Gouveia, L., Serpa, S., & Milho, J. (2009). Interpersonal pattern dynamics and adaptive behavior in multiagent neurobiological systems: Conceptual model and data. *Journal of Motor Behavior, 41*(5), 445–459.

Passos, P., Milho, J., Fonseca, S., Borges, J., Araújo, D., & Davids, K. (2011). Interpersonal distance regulates functional grouping tendencies of agents in team sports. *Journal of Motor Behavior, 43*(2), 155–163.

Phillips, E., Davids, K., Renshaw, I., & Portus, M. (2010). Developmental trajectories of fast bowling experts in Australian cricket. *Talent Development and Excellence, 2,* 137–148.

Richardson, M., Marsh, K., & Baron, R. (2007). Judging and actualizing intrapersonal and interpersonal affordances. *Journal of Experimental Psychology: Human Perception and Performance, 33*(4), 845–859.

Salmela, J.H., & Moraes, L.C. (2004). Coaching, families and learning in Brazilian youth football players. *Insight: The FA Coaches Association Journal, 2,* 36–37.

Sumpter, D.J.T. (2006). The principles of collective animal behaviour. *Philosophical Transactions of the Royal Society B, 361,* 5–22.

Travassos, B., Araújo, D., Vilar, L., & McGarry, T. (2011). Interpersonal coordination and ball dynamics in futsal (indoor football). *Human Movement Science, 30*, 1245–1259.

Vilar, L., Araújo, D., Davids, K., & Button, C. (2012). The role of ecological dynamics in analysing performance in team sports. *Sports Medicine, 42*(1), 1–10.

Vilar, L., Araújo, D., Davids, K., & Travassos, B. (2012). Constraints on competitive performance of attacker–defender dyads in team sports. *Journal of Sports Sciences, 30*(5), 1–11.

12 Emergence in school-integrated teacher education for elementary physical education teachers

Mapping a complex learning system

Tim Hopper

when we started to go into
little PE classes
all the time
a light was going on in my head
oh yeah …
we are supposed to be doing this …
oh yeah …
this is what we learned.
actually seeing it
an environment that was safe
I wasn't the centre
of the teaching show
was a safe place to start
having the things
that would prove me
to be a good teacher
(Hopper & Sanford, 2008, p. 38)

The opening extract on the school-integrated teacher education (SITE) experience focuses on how student engagement in a school context created the conditions for learning how to teach. In this chapter this experience will be interpreted with a complexity lens, considering how learning can be considered as an emergent process (Osberg & Biesta, 2008). As described by Hopper (2010), SITE courses allow students "through continued participation in a school culture" to "gradually take responsibility for teaching episodes within a lesson" as they "continually reflect on shared experiences from a school context through systematic observation, active participation and joint reflection on practice" (p. 12). The SITE course creates the conditions for learning to be framed as an emergent interplay of what the person brings to the situation as they engage in the challenges of the tasks and the outcomes of these interactions.

Mason (2008) frames complexity theory as creating a dynamic system whereby diverse elements, interacting in a particular environment, show emergent "properties and behaviours, which are not necessarily contained in the essence of the constituent elements or able to be predicted from a knowledge of initial conditions" (p. 35).

In essence, in a complex system the whole is greater than the sum of the parts; the *interactions* and products of the interconnecting parts enables a person's learning, as adapting and re/forming skills and knowledge, to emerge in a way that is unique to the system. The aim of this paper is to try to capture the benefit of these interactions through a process of mapping complexity features onto the SITE course.

To understand a complex learning system I draw on Mennin's (2010) definition of the terms 'agent' and 'attractor' (commonly used in physics to describe patterning behaviours of particles) to metaphorically explain the patterning behaviour of human activity. An agent is something that takes part in an interaction of a system and is itself subsequently changed—for example, a person, a team, a nerve cell or a student. Individual agents interact at the local level; they do not know the system as a whole nor does a central agent have responsibility for overall control of the system. The term 'attractor' is used to describe the "pattern or activity in time in a region of space that 'appears' to draw the energy of a system to it" (p. 838). It is the attractor that brings agents together to form a complex system. It is the premise of this paper that the school experiences in the SITE course creates the attractor that draws together the energy of the students as agents to form a complex learning system.

Conditions necessary for complex emergence

This section will briefly outline the key features of a complex system that were established in the course. Referencing multiple sources on complex learning systems (Davis & Simmt, 2003; Davis & Sumara, 2006; Davis, Sumara, & Luce-Kapler, 2008; Johnson, 2001; Morrison, 2008; Osberg & Biesta, 2008), the following features of a complex system have been woven into the SITE courses.

1. *Enabling constraints—opening possibilities by limiting choices*
    As noted by Davids, Button, and Bennett (2008), a key condition for a complex system to form is the idea of enabling constraints. This condition means that constraints placed on agents of a system are opening them to possibilities by limiting choices. This idea plays out in the SITE courses by creating complete/incomplete assignments, setting tasks integrated with experiences in the school and working within the course rules of engagement.
2. *Feedback loops—positive and negative*
    A complex learning system is modulated by a variety of feedback loops that amplify (positive) or dampen (negative) the actions of a system. Such "a 'feedback loop' is a continuous and recursive process that takes part of a system's output and feeds it back as input" (Davis *et al.*, 2008, p. 204). In a physical education lesson this is done through encouraging exploration, demonstrations to focus attention on key ideas or through reminders in regards to safety and appropriate behaviour. In the SITE course the forum, blog, video-clips and peers' and instructor's feedback offered these continuous feedback loops.
3. *Creating memories—remembering and forgetting (collective memory)*
    A complex system that learns must have the ability to select memories and preserve memories. A system cannot remember everything but it must have

the ability to recall. So a complex system must have the ability to embody its own history. In essence, the MOODLE platform, especially the blog and video journal, offer these memory spaces.

4. *The simultaneity of diversity and redundancy among agents of a system*
For a complex system to adapt it must contain enough internal diversity in the agents of the system to allow it to respond innovatively to novel circumstances. The intelligence of a complex system can therefore be seen as related to the diversity of the system. For the complex system to form there must be enough internal redundancy (that is, duplication and excesses between agents of the system) so that they can connect and compensate for each other. As Davis and Simmt (2003) note, this "sameness ... is essential in triggering a transition from a collection of me's to a collective of us" (p. 150). The forum and blogs allowed diversity to be valued as well as commonalities to be realized.

5. *Recursive elaboration—iterative processes and nested systems*
Learning systems unfold recursively by constantly invoking and elaborating established associations in a cyclical, dynamic process. At the individual level, an iterative process, rather than linear process, is always present as "one's history both enables (and constrains) one's perceptions of new experiences" (Davis *et al.*, 2008, p. 201). The same is the case for social groups of humans where, as suggested by social constructionist theories, "the knowledge needed to deal with a new topic is usually present in the classroom collective" (p. 201).

6. *Enabling decentralized control through neighbourly interactions*
As Johnson (2001) speculates, there is a tendency that observers of groups suspect the existence of a coordinating agent. Such a perception may be rooted in cultural habits of interpreting phenomena in cause–effect rather than complex emergent terms. In nature, birds, insects and animals operate in complex and intelligent ways without an organizing agent. The same has been interpreted for human "intelligent behaviour, especially with regard to social and cultural collectives" (Davis & Simmt, 2003, p. 152). Agents in a complex system must also be able to affect another's activities. This means that structures need to be in place to allow ideas to come across one another as agents share insights. Course structures were set up to trigger interpretations between agents that trigger still further interpretations so that, as Davis *et al.* (2008) describe, "the center [is] not the teacher, a student, or an object, but an emerging possibility" (p. 200).

School-integrated teacher education (SITE) as an attractor for situated learning

The purpose of SITE courses is to prepare generalist students to teach physical education in elementary schools. As we, and others, have noted (Brouwer & Korthagen, 2005; Darling-Hammond, 2006; Hopper & Sanford, 2004, 2008), the integrative approach to teaching course content in schools offers powerful transformative experiences for students to learn how to teach (Hopper, Brown, & Rhodes, 2005). This is especially the case when courses maintain a tight coherence and integration with coursework and school-based field experiences, effectively linking theory and practice. For example, as one student in an earlier study on the SITE course commented:

> My many positive experiences have turned my attitude of, "I don't like physical education, don't want to teach physical education and I would like to work in a school with a physical education specialist" to "I love physical education, I can't wait to teach physical education, and it would be fun to be a physical education specialist".
>
> (Hopper & Sanford, 2005, p. 7)

The SITE PE courses are part of the last three years of a four-year bachelor of education degree in which students take a practicum each year and take courses in an array of subject areas plus courses in other areas such as psychology, special education and administration. Figure 12.1 captures the critical elements of the elementary course content which focused on (1) understanding child development, (2) the teaching process and (3) physical education curriculum areas linked to the provincial guidelines (BC IRP) and planning (Allison & Barrett, 2000; Gallahue, 1996; Rink, 1998; Wall & Murray, 1994). This content is progressively developed in relation to critical experiences in the school when observing, working with and teaching children.

For a complex system to form it needs an attractor for the agents but also the agents need to come together by obeying simple rules that enable their system to

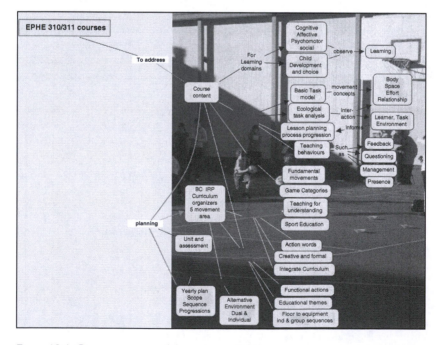

Figure 12.1 Course concepts of the content of the course.

generate from the bottom-up (Davids *et al.*, 2008). A set of simple rules allows the system to form in relation to the agents' interactions with the environment and with the attractor that gives coherence to their interactions (Holland, 1998; Johnson, 2001). It is my opinion that too many students in university courses tend to work to get the highest mark for the least effort, work as individuals and are somewhat reluctant to work in groups for a shared mark. To shift from this focus on competition for marks and individual learning, I have adopted a contract grading process in my courses. As shown in Figure 12.2, in SITE courses activities are framed around three indigenous teaching and learning principles for class engagement (Williams, 2008). To encourage students' collective identity, shared learning and co-operation, the rules of engagement in the course were given as: (1) put the learning of their peers before their own learning; (2) create work that will benefit seven generations to come; and (3) find their own passion in physical education and use it to energize the community.

The learning activities in the course initiated by the instructor were: (1) teaching practical experiences focused on fundamental movement skills for games, dance and gymnastics; (2) using the basic task model to develop task progressions (Rink, 1993; Wall & Murray, 1990) with a focus on how constraints shape the learning process (Davids *et al.*, 2008); and (3) planning focused on cognitive, affective, psychomotor and social learning in lessons, units and yearly plans.

The teaching episodes modelled the same practices and tasks that were then used by the instructor when teaching in the school with the children. The lessons were video-recorded by students, with commentary, then compressed by the instructor and uploaded on the learning management system MOODLE (Moodle, 2010). All reflections (written, visual and audio) by students were submitted and shared with their peers on the interactive features of the MOODLE. Finally, the contract grading process led to a mastery approach to assignments where students were expected to submit all work at a B+ level or higher, a grade recognized as an acceptable mark

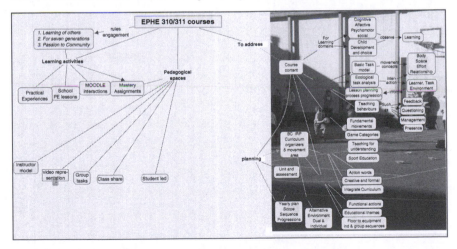

Figure 12.2 Learning activities and pedagogical spaces.

(defined in the university calendar as "good work, high knowledge level and good application of information").

These learning activities then interacted with the pedagogical spaces for student engagement. These were set up with: (1) students leading some activities such as forum discussions; (2) group tasks including peer teaching and teaching in the school; (3) video creation task to review course material; and (4) the instructor modelling developmental physical education drawing on movement education (Carline, 2011), Teaching Games for Understanding (Thorpe & Bunker, 1989) and sport education (Siedentop, Hastie, & Van der Mars, 2004).

The common goal of becoming a generalist teacher formed the basic attractor for all the students, especially as the SITE course was the only course in the elementary programme that worked with children in a school. The physical education environment allowed 30 children and 30 adult students to simultaneously share the same space. It created a more authentic experience for students as they observed and worked with children. For the students, the anticipation of going to the school created purpose to the learning that enabled the students to imagine themselves teaching physical education, since they knew that they would soon be given the opportunity. This 'attractor' formed the core for a complex learning system to unfold.

SITE and conditions for complexity

The two SITE PE courses are spread over two terms with 36 contact hours from 24 classes each term. Six classes each term are integrated in the school. The courses have been developed to create the conditions for emergence and a collective awareness between students. Data reported here are from my reflections (memory and written notes) and insights from students in the most recent iteration of the SITE courses.

Enabling constraints and forming a new system for different pedagogical encounters

The evaluation system in SITE courses places constraints on students with the agents (students) of a system (course) being open to possibilities by having their choices limited. Initially, when I taught SITE courses in 1999 to 2003, I focused on graded assignments and mid-term/end-of-term exams. However, I consistently felt that this system simply afforded student compliance that was not compatible with what I saw as good professional learning. Most students focused on learning content only for the exam rather than for application, and students would always tell me that they learned so much more in the course than was assessed by the examinations. The revised assignments were designed to connect the learning experiences with the pedagogical spaces (Figure 12.3), shifting the assessment process from assessment-of-learning to more assessment-for-learning (criteria-based) and assessment-as-learning (self-reflection) (Earl, 2003). Students *observed* children in lessons taught by their instructor and wrote an analysis of the child's development levels drawing on the informed literature. The weekly student-led class *forums* focused on course readings. The students' *blogs* were weekly notes

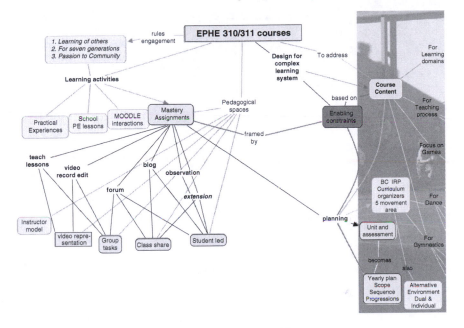

Figure 12.3 Learning activities and assignments as enabling constraints.

entered by each student but shared with their peers. Students were encouraged to copy from each other as long as they acknowledged their peer. In groups of three, students created a *video journal* of the first month of the course and then, in the same group, they prepared, taught to their *peers* and then taught in the *school* a games lesson designed for the developmental level of the students they had previously observed. In the second term students did more *peer/school teaching* and developed *unit overviews* and a *year plan*. If the mandatory assignments were done to a professional level, the student got a B+ grade. All assignments had detailed criteria (assessment-for-learning) with examples available of previous assignments done by students. To obtain an 'A' range grade students were expected to complete a proposal template for an *extension* assignment. As shown in Figure 12.3, these enabling constraints channelled much of students' learning and, through the interactive nature of the insights produced, they caused the collective potential of the learning system to expand exponentially as the students shared and encouraged each other's learning about teaching physical education.

Feedback loops: positive and negative

The assignments shown in Figure 12.4 allowed ongoing feedback loops through the course via MOODLE. This shifted the learning process from a typical, hierarchical teacher-to-student manner to a recursive exploration for students, then selection and sharing process with peers and instructor. In addition, the basic task model used by the instructor in practical activities modelled a feedback process of the teacher

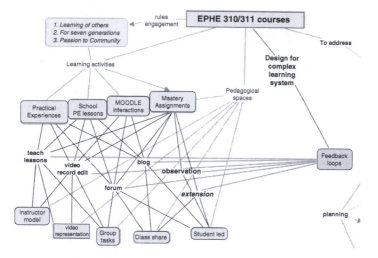

Figure 12.4 Assignments as feedback loops on the learning process.

responding to students' actions to tasks, feeding back ideas to the group based on individual actions of group members. This basic task approach focused on refinements, simplifications and extensions to application tasks, enabling continuous constraint-led feedback loops within the lesson. In this process the teacher encourages the students to experiment, drawing on each others' responses to tasks as they consider what moves, where it moves, how it moves and in relation to what. As the students select the movement action, they then refine the movement further as the teacher extends the elements of the activity. This process can be repeated as needed, developing movement actions that are applied to games, dance and gymnastics. As noted in Hopper (2010), experiencing this process as learners at the university, then seeing this modelled with children in the school, enabled the students to adopt a more responsive approach with their peers as they practised for teaching the children in the local school. Feedback from their instructor, peers and then teachers in the school allowed the complex learning system of the class to increasingly become aware of, and able to use, these approaches. Two students noted the following about task progressions and the teaching process:

> Through working with my peers in learning new skills, activities and task progression, I became enthusiastic about my learning even though I am not in any way athletic or skilful at physical education. This completely surprised me and showed me just how effective it is ... creating spaces in which students are able to explore their abilities and are challenged appropriately for their skill level.
>
> (Laura blog summary)

> It is amazing what a good task progression can do in terms of organizing yourself, making an effective lesson and creating a dynamic learning environment.
>
> (Bry blog summary)

Creating memories: remembering and forgetting (collective memory)

For a system to learn and to maintain its viability, it must have a means to remember (Davis *et al.*, 2008). Regarding selection, a living and learning system must be able to forget/discard as well as to remember/collect. Keeping track of every interpretive possibility is just as debilitating as keeping track of none. As shown in Figure 12.5, the MOODLE system allowed the collective consciousness of the group to form—selecting from and orienting towards the interpretive possibilities they encountered in the practical experiences, school lessons and the readings. These memories were created by:

1. Threaded discussion forums in groups of ten with each student leading a discussion based on course readings. The final ideas were summarized on a cross-group Wiki.
2. Personal blogs co-constructed using their own notes and peers' blog entries.
3. Shared directories created by the instructor containing:

   a. digital video from all classes
   b. video journals created by groups of students
   c. audio-reflections (podcasts) on field experiences
   d. video-tutorials on available software and access to open source software.

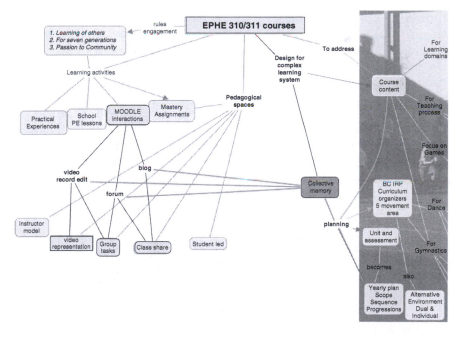

Figure 12.5 Collective memory: the ability to recall and forget.

Students demonstrated ongoing engagements with MOODLE with interactions ranging from 550 to 1,660 hits during one term. Typically students request that the MOODLE stay up for two years after the course so that they have access to it in the final year of their programme. Many also commented that they could not believe that they now felt confident about teaching physical education. Representative responses are listed below:

> I never expected to get as much hands-on teaching and experience learning about the course material—and learning about the cognitive and affective aspects of the physical education environment. I have learned so much, and it seems awfully difficult to try and say it all in words.
>
> (Ally blog)

> I had to miss Monday's class and I must say, as I watched the videos from class, I was really sorry that I had to miss it. This is a big realisation for me as I have never been sad about missing a physical education class before. This really tells me how much I am enjoying this class and that my feelings towards physical education classes have probably gone from a 4 to a 10.
>
> (Laura blog)

What was noteworthy for me as the instructor was the quality of the work submitted by students within the B+ contract grade. For example, for the observation assignment students received clear submission guidelines and exemplars papers from previous years. This resulted in all of the observation papers being completed with a high degree of professionalism, correctly referenced and incorporating appropriate quotes from the informed literature and clear examples linked to the literature. In addition, several students took risks with their forms of representation, utilizing new technologies and integrating images, videos and even music into their analysis.

Recursive elaboration: iterative processes and nested systems

As shown in Figure 12.6, the recursive elaboration was most evident in the SITE course with students planning lessons, practising them at the university with their peers, and then teaching the same lessons to a class of children in the school. In a school lesson plans inevitably had to be adapted to the children and context, sometimes changing radically from the lesson modelled at the university. The university students grasped this need for adaption, conceptualizing planning as a process of planning the teacher to teach so that the teacher could respond to the children's actions in the lesson. As Bry commented, "the lesson plan is planning the teacher—it isn't something to be followed to the 'T'." As Laura noted, "To promote learning for all students, the physical education teacher needs to plan lessons that can be adapted for students of all abilities."

Students learned to adapt their lessons, drawing on a recursive elaboration to their understanding of teaching as they self-organized around the lesson content

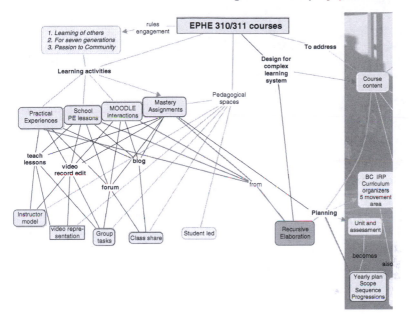

Figure 12.6 Recursive elaboration throughout the course.

and the responses of the children, coming to see learning as a bottom-up process. Teaching physical education then became less linear and more iterative. Students learned to draw on the repertoire of possibilities in the class, and began applying movement concepts to discern the relative effectiveness of these possibilities. Ultimately they learned to set tasks for children and then to respond as the movement qualities of the children emerged. As Emily wrote on the blog about her own learning when asked to coach a peer

> we played games that involved a coach. It was interesting to hear feedback and to give feedback. I felt that I learned a lot more being able to watch other people and then apply things that I had seen other people do.

After students taught in the school they also realized that learning happens because you allow children to shape the conditions for learning. For example, Courtney commented after her school teaching experience

> The students demonstrated that they understood the game as they were able to articulate how to modify the game to make it easier or harder for the runner or tagger.

The simultaneity of diversity and redundancy among agents of a system

Redundancy between agents, that is, the common abilities and understandings, allow effective interaction and the ability to compensate for another agent in the

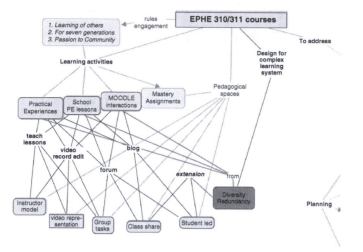

Figure 12.7 Diversity to inform learning and redundancy to connect agents.

system. As highlighted in Figure 12.7, the common readings and shared experiences in the course both in practical lessons and observations of the lessons being taught in the school, allowed a language of learning to develop in the class. This language was subsequently shared on course blog, forum and video journal. These common experiences allowed a core understanding to develop for the students that reassured them and gave them a way of sharing insights as they worked in groups to create a video, then plan and teach lessons in the school. This shared learning was promoted from the rules of engagement in the course that played out through all the shared activities. As Bry reflected:

> Dr. H. told us on the first day of class, "Focus on the learning of your peers." At first, I was kind of confused by this ... learning, I thought, was something of a personal activity. But through peer assessment and teaching, I came to recognize just how important it is to focus on the learning of your peers—a huge part of personal growth comes from working with others and doing what you can to support their learning.

The diversity amongst the students enabled generative abilities as students' integrated their prior knowledge and understanding into course planning. At times this diversity caused issues with students disagreeing about what they should teach and repeating lessons that they had deemed successful in other roles as coaches or summer camp leaders. Sometimes these ideas worked well, but often they did not transfer. However, the collective wisdom of the group, referencing the readings and course instructor's feedback, combined with the authentic experiences in the school, led to coherence and a sense of confidence in what and how to teach physical education. Often students totally revised their lesson after teaching their peers, and every group voiced appreciation for the opportunity to try out an idea, adapt it and re-plan for the school experience.

Most notably, the extension assignment allowed the diversity in the student population to be an asset in the class as new content emerged from students' passions. As an example, here is a typical list of extension assignments from one class:

- content overviews with assessment strategies on student passions such as health and fitness, soccer and multiple forms of dance;
- teaching behaviour analysis from systematic data on teaching experiences with peers and in schools;
- video journals on course experiences.

The breadth of these assignments was huge. Occasionally edits were required to pass, but the majority of assignments were of a high-quality and easily met the 'A' range standard. Even when assignments were passed, several students indicated they intended to edit them based on my feedback before uploading them to their certification ePortfolios. As one student commented after receiving feedback on her extension assignment: "Thank you for your feedback on my teaching behaviour analysis assignment … I will resubmit an updated version to be used as an example for future classes."

The learning extended beyond the confines of the course curriculum with the *extension* assignment process enabling a very different instructor–student relationship. No longer was I the judge of their work, trying to find fault to justify a mark to an 'objective' external measure, forcing me to compare one student to another. I offered encouraging feedback and suggestions for improvement; I became a facilitator who shared readings with students based on their interests. I often sent out praise to students for their work and helped them share it with the rest of the class. I felt genuinely enriched by the students' insights and was excited by the ideas that they had infused into the course.

Networking systems: neighbour interactions enabling decentralized control

As noted in the previous section, the interactive nature of the course, with practical experiences in class and group work in schools, created the potential for decentralized control. For example, working in groups of three, the students conducted peer teaching sessions in preparation for teaching a class of children in the school. This created a comingling of the students' ongoing histories with the emergent activity of teaching children in the school. A structural coupling of learning how to teach formed as the students related their observations of children being taught and the expectation of being responsible, albeit as part of a group, for teaching a class of children. Learning to teach, then, developed as a complex networking of experiences, prior history and the anticipated role of being a teacher. Figure 12.8 shows how the student-led components gave each student the role of

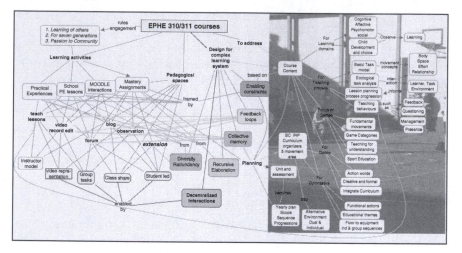

Figure 12.8 Decentralized control and neighbourly interactions.

being a hub for their group members by mediating the reading materials. A typical exchange on the forum is shown below.

> Great comments Rachel! I really like your comment that, "Even if planning can seem very time-consuming, it makes teaching more time-effective and valuable." I think that we are all guilty of sometimes trying to find the easy way out of things but, as teachers, we cannot do this since we are responsible for the learning of others.

The class sharing process flourished when students were not competing for marks. Group tasks became engaging as students regularly took risks and tried new ideas such as in the video-journals where they integrated movie trailers, played with slow-motion replay, introduced commentary on events along with transitions and music— all for the same mark. Working as a group, networking on MOODLE and developing more control of the teaching role resulted in students: (1) encouraging each other to try out new ideas, (2) continuously connecting back to course material, and (3) sharing the joy of teaching a physical education lesson through the blog. The list of comments from students on the blog captures this uniting energy.

- "Our experience at Haro[1] School teaching was awesome!!"
- "I think our group did really well. We worked hard on revising our lesson plans and trying to work well as a team ... I had a lot of fun and can't wait to teach some more."
- "Peer teaching this week has been great! It's been awesome to watch everyone assume the role of teachers ... I really see my peers in a new light now."
- "On Monday, we were at Haro to teach our lessons. Holy camoles! That was exciting! It was great to get feedback from Emma. I learned that I was doing things I wasn't even consciously thinking about."

Initially when I taught the SITE courses I would teach five lessons and oversee the students' experiences in the class. They would get opportunities to work with small groups under my direction. I came to realize that many students were ready to take on classes of children. I set them the task of teaching a games lesson in the first term and then a series of four creative dance lessons in Term Two (Hopper & Sanford, 2010). With the ongoing support of the teachers in the school, accommodating their curriculum to the students and then mentoring them during the lessons on class management, the students all surpassed themselves, as was evident in their personal reflections such as "I never knew I could have so much fun teaching a lesson", "Who would have thought I could teach physical education, and enjoy it to boot?"

Sarah summarized how the creative dance concert really created the sense of a physical community. As she said, "I really enjoyed watching all the grades' creative dances. The children, parents and teachers were engaged throughout the whole concert. It was really rewarding when many of the Grade 5 students thanked us and gave us a huge hug at the end of the performance. This was an awesome experience for me that I will remember forever."

As shown in Figure 12.8, the interactions, mapped in relation to a complex system, show how the school and the university combined around a mutual commitment to child learning. The neighbourly interactions between students and instructor, between students and teachers and between students and children created networking systems that became decentralized from the university instructor. These systems are now enmeshed within the university course and an annual expectation within the local school community.

Conclusion and future directions

As noted by Morrison (2008), "Complexity theory is alluring; once we are aware of it we see it happening everywhere" (p. 32). Indeed, I may be accused of being allured by complexity theory, however, I have found mapping the features of complexity thinking within my courses to be very rewarding in reconfiguring the pedagogical system of my university instruction. Increasingly my course design is less based on traditional and linear assumptions about learning that perennially seem to create theory and practice gaps. No longer do I feel compelled to offer an expert-to-novice dialogue with the students. The opportunities in the course allow many to achieve lessons I could not have imagined. Complexity theory challenges "conventional epistemology, cognition, simple and reductive certainties, linear causality", suggesting that learning is an emergent process. It advocates "holism, autonomy and creativity" calling "constantly to create new knowledge; it forces creativity, rather than recycling the old and familiar; it is a theory of perpetual novelty, disequilibrium" and creativeness (p. 33). Complexity thinking may offer a way of building a conceptual frame for a more-than-human understanding of learning, educating a new generation of teachers who draw collectively from a context of teaching and learning as they integrate established knowledge into their situated knowing.

Exploring the learning processes in a SITE course presents the opportunity to investigate how to create the conditions for complex emergence. The indigenous teaching and learning principles offered the engagement rules that have refocused the reason for doing work as not just for grades, but for a collective wisdom. Complexity thinking as demonstrated in the SITE course encourages us to frame teaching as creating the conditions for learning as an occasion where the unexpected comes together (Davis, 2004; Hopper & Sanford, 2010). The SITE course offers critical insights on teaching practice. As Jane noted after her first creative dance lesson, "We had made a lesson plan to use for today, yet I don't know if I even used it. I did all the moves we were planning on doing, however, kind of just experimented (saw what the kids needed at the time) and went with it. This worked fabulously." Such insights, centred on child learning, not self-as-teacher, allow the *unanticipated* to be embraced by students as they learn to see emergent moments as critical to enabling engaged learners.

Note

1 School name changed for confidentiality.

References

Allison, P.C., & Barrett, K.R. (2000). *Constructing children's physical education experiences: Understanding the content for teaching.* Boston, MA: Allyn and Bacon.

Brouwer, N., & Korthagen, F. (2005). Can Teacher Education Make a Difference? *American Educational Research Journal, 42*(1), 153.

Carline, S. (2011). *Lesson plans for creative dance: Connecting with literature, arts and music.* Champaign, IL: Human Kinetics.

Darling-Hammond, L. (2006). Constructing 21st-century teacher education. *Journal of Teacher Education, 57*(3), 300–314.

Davids, K., Button, C., & Bennett, S. (2008). *Dynamics of skill acquisition: A constraints led approach.* Windsor, ON: Human Kinetics.

Davis, B. (2004). *Inventions of teaching: A genealogy.* London: Lawrence Erlbaum Associates.

Davis, B., & Simmt, E. (2003). Understanding learning systems: Mathematics education and complexity science. *Journal for Research in Mathematics Education, 34*(2), 137–167.

Davis, B., & Sumara, D. (2006). *Complexity and education: Inquiries into learning, teaching and research.* London: Lawrence Erlbaum Associates.

Davis, B., Sumara, D., & Luce-Kapler, R. (2008). *Engaging minds: Changing teaching in a complex world.* New York: Routledge.

Earl, L. (2003). *Assessment as learning.* Newbury Park, CA: Corwin Press.

Gallahue, D.L. (1996). *Developmental physical education for today's children* (3rd ed.). Madison, WI: Brown and Benchmark.

Holland, J. (1998). *Emergence: From chaos to order.* Reading, MA: Helix Books Addison-Wesley.

Hopper, T. (2010). Complexity thinking and creative dance: Creating conditions for emergent learning in teacher education. *PHEnex, 2*(1), 1–20.

Hopper, T., Brown, S., & Rhodes, R. (2005). Augmenting the aptitude of learning how to teach physical education: Situated learning and an application of the theory of planned behaviour. *Physical and Health Education Journal, 71*(3), 44.

Hopper, T., & Sanford, K. (2004). Representing multiple perspectives of self-as-teacher: Integrated teacher education course and self-study. *Teacher Education Quarterly, 31*(2), 57–74.

Hopper, T., & Sanford, K. (2005). *'Teacherly conversations' within school integrated teacher education courses: Creating intersecting communities of practice for transformative education* (p. 14). Montreal: American Education Research Association (AERA).

Hopper, T., & Sanford, K. (2008). Using poetic representation to support the development of teachers' knowledge. *Studying Teacher Education, 4*(1), 29–45.

Hopper, T., & Sanford, K. (2010). Occasioning moments in game-as-teacher: Complexity thinking applied to TGfU and Videogaming. In J. Butler & L. Griffin (Eds.), *More teaching games for understanding: Moving globally* (pp. 121–138). Windsor: Human Kinetics.

Johnson, S. (2001). *Emergence: The connected lives of ants, brains, cities, and software.* New York: Scribner.

Mason, M. (2008). What is complexity theory and what are its implications for educational change? *Educational Philosophy and Theory, 40*(1), 35–49.

Mennin, S. (2010). Complexity and health professions education: A basic glossary. *Journal of Evaluation in Clinical Practice, 16*(4), 838–840, doi: 10.1111/j.1365–2753.2010.01503.x

Moodle. (2010). *Moodle: Philosophy.* Retrieved May 15, 2010, from http://docs.moodle.org/en/Philosophy.

Morrison, K. (2008). Educational philosophy and the challenge of complexity theory. *Educational Philosophy and Theory, 40*(1), 19–34.

Osberg, D., & Biesta, G. (2008). The emergent curriculum: Navigating a complex course between unguided learning and planned enculturation. *Journal of Curriculum Studies, 40*(3), 313–328.

Rink, J. (1993). *Teaching physical education for learning* (2nd ed.). St. Louis, MO: Times Mirror/Mosby College Publishing.

Rink, J. (1998). *Teaching physical education for learning* (3rd ed.). St. Louis, MO: McGraw-Hill.

Siedentop, D., Hastie, P. A., & Van der Mars, H. (2004). *Complete guide to sport education.* Champaign, IL: Human Kinetics.

Thorpe, R., & Bunker, D. (1989). A changing focus in games teaching. In L. Almond (Ed.), *The place of physical education in schools* (pp. 42–71). London: Kogan/Page.

Wall, J., & Murray, N. (1990). *Children and movement.* Dubuque, IA: Wm. C. Brow Publishers.

Wall, J., & Murray, N. (1994). *Children and movement.* Dubuque, IA: Wm. C. Brown Publishers.

Williams, L. (2008, September 5). *Storysticks: Learning and teaching in an indigenous world.* [University course].

13 The complex thinking paradigm in physical education teacher education

Perspectives on the 'reflective practitioner' concept in France

Nathalie Wallian and Ching-Wei Chang

The world one faces nowadays has become, at times, very complex, unpredictable and difficult to understand. Even in such diverse predicaments as a nuclear power plant meltdown, an airplane crash or a major earthquake, the main goal is to find appropriate solutions when faced with a situation that is complex in nature, unique by its context and time-constrained (Atlan, 1979; Foucault, 1966; Olssen, 2008). The human way of interpreting the world is nowadays in need of change because globalized events are no longer compatible with a closed autopoïetic (i.e., self-creating) system conception (Le Moigne, 1984, 1995, 2004; Morin, 1973, 1990, 2004). The dialogue between the subject and complex events is vital and drives the need for new heuristics for decision-making (Bourdieu, 1980).

Post-modern societies shape citizens to be active interpreters of a changing world and no longer individuals able to apply pre-determined procedures or hyper-specialized competencies. New models that allow creativity and divergence reshape the professional's posture and background to enable a reflective practitioner to emerge, capable of acting competently in response to situated practical problems. As a result, in French educational sciences, a phenomenological approach to the interpretation of action (Gadamer, 1960) and the corresponding constructivist approaches (Cobb, 1994; Fosnot, 1996; Glasersfeld, 1995) to understand learning redefine the teacher's role as a 'reflective practitioner' (Schön, 1983) able to link the complex setting to intended actions by an interpretative posture. Especially in the area of physical education and sport pedagogy, the target in France is to shape an educational practice that lets this reflective practitioner solve practical problems encountered during sport practices and/or physical education lessons through a complex decision-making process. This new emerging model of 'capability' (Sen, 2003) claims that the agent responsible for reflection in/on action and finally for providing autonomous and adaptable professionals rests with the teacher education institution.

This chapter's aim is to link the paradigm of complexity thinking with physical education teacher education perspectives as provided in France. We will first outline seven properties that contribute to the complexity of the physical education lesson setting, then explore teaching/learning as a complex system. Finally, we expand the paradigm in the contemporary physical education teacher training and educational research field.

Thinking about education as a complex process

It is increasingly the contemporary mode of thinking to conceive of the teaching/ learning process as a system that is both determined and determining; the processes involved are both socially constructed and inscribed within historical processes (Vygotsky, 1962) and produced and determined by individual/collective constructions and actors that co-determine the relationships about the knowledge-to-be-taught. This dialectic implicates the intricacy of the teaching and of the learning as being co-influenced and co-constructed within, and by, classroom interactions (Fleener, 2005; Lani-Bayle, 2008). The consequence for research is that one has to consider simultaneously the teaching process in terms of its impacts on learning and the learning as a major factor for planning and/or regulating the teaching process, instead of as a knowledge transmission process. In the following section we discuss the evolution of constructivist epistemologies and consider how these provide the properties that characterize complex educational settings.

Complex thinking and constructivist epistemologies in Europe during the twentieth century

Constructivism evolved in the early part of the twentieth century in response to the perceived limitations of behaviourist and cognitivist approaches to learning. The Swiss approach to constructivist theory defines knowing as a process instead of a result and proposes the notion of circular causality, where the relationships between the subject and objects co-determine the elaboration of the interpreted and embodied world. Knowing is based on former experiences and serves as a basis for shaping future experiences: 'The act of knowing does not start from some inner knowledge contained by the individual, nor is it contained as some essential poverty of an external object, but rather by the relational manner in which the individual and object interact; it is by simultaneously orienting towards the two poles of this interaction that the world is organized in the act of organizing oneself' (Piaget, 1937). So the subject does not 'know things' but 'knows the act by which he/ she enters into interaction with things' (Marquardt, 1999). In the Russian approach, Vygotsky gave a social and historical colouration of this constructivist approach (Clot, 1999). The social environment consists of co-acting with peers inside a community of practice while the individual historicity inscribes the learning trajectory into continuity and rupture. In his translated book *Thinking and Language*, Vygotsky (1962) outlined the role language played and the action for/during learning.

Based on modelling the dynamics of system theory (Foerster, 1973; Geert, 1994, 1998; Poincaré, 1892), Maturana and Varela (1987) considered that cognition is the ability provided by a living organism of adapting in an ever-evolving environment. An autonomous living system is capable of self-creation (autopoïesis) and is therefore able to develop strategies for problem-solving. Through a complex environment one can exhibit coherent behaviour: the parts co-ordinate in the relationships between the organic components and the constraints/opportunities offered by the environment. The self-organization for problem-solving will be later replaced by a more efficient solution of varying dynamic stability. Links form the structure of a new developmental state of order in the mind through a process called *scalloping* that alternates the building up and the collapsing of complex performance. Morin and Le Moigne (1999, 2007) focused their work on constructivist epistemology based on complex thinking and emerging from the critical rationality and the teleologic assumption that action sciences are generated as a new emerging field characterized by pluri-disciplinary approaches (Abdelmalek, 2010; Alhadeff-Jones, 2010; Pena Vega & Proutheau, 2011). In developmental psychology, Thelen (1992) formulated, in congruence with Varela, Thompson, and Rosch (1991), the 'embodiment hypothesis' whereby complex systems are composed of very many individual elements embedded within.

These groundings help reconsidering the classroom setting as a system where the learning appears to be the expression of an adaptation process. During learning the student reaches a state of disequilibrium (dissonance or obstacle) where old patterns have broken down and re-constructed in a more coherent-for-the-situation pattern. Complexity thinking is linked with the constructivist approach to learning in the sense that the conception of transformation processes is similar and the dialectic dynamic of interactions is the basis for studying the dynamics of the teaching/learning system in a situated classroom setting (Terhart, 2003). Based on this, it is now possible to consider some of the properties that characterize the complexity of educational settings.

Seven properties of the classroom setting

The process of studying educational processes needs to take into account the following properties that characterize the complexity of the classroom setting. First, the didactic setting (Brousseau, 1998) provides *multi-determined facts:* many variables interact within the teaching/learning system and it is impossible to isolate them from an authentic ecology of class activity. So, the causal attribution of facts becomes quite impossible because the standardization and the stabilization of variables are hazardous. At the very core is the question, "does the teacher fully contribute to the students' success?" This becomes irrelevant because many variables interfere with the process of learning. This supposes at a time: (1) to cross the scientific points of view and the subjects' (teacher/learners/observers) points of view, (2) to define available indicators of change and/or of learning, (3) to multiply observations in a long-term perspective and (4) to cross by triangulation the sources of data collection. Even if the researcher tries to control the educational variables, the rigorous methodology cannot control all of the events that could happen in the classroom setting. Thus the researcher will have to expect the unexpected and rely on the relevant facts (i.e., critical events).

Second, the didactic setting is *highly situated* (Brown, Collins, & Duguid, 1989; Clancey, 1997; Fosnot, 1996; Hutchins, 1995; Suchman, 1987), especially in physical education (Gal-Petitfaux & Durand, 2001; Gal-Petitfaux, Sève, Cizeron, & Adé, 2010; Kirk & Macdonald, 1998). This means that any event has to be interpreted in context and that this situation will denote the meaning of any participant activity. So, the difficulty for interpreting an action rests on the quality of the dialogue between teacher/learner activity and the learning. This process will be studied by inference in context. The quality of the analysis-in-situ of the learning activity taken as a process will determine the relevance of the allocated plausible meaning. The interaction between subject/setting is constantly evolving, forcing the interpreter to constantly reformulate the interpretations from time to time. A structural coupling of the action provided by an actor is included within a circular process that makes the setting the genesis and the issue of the learning. The subject interaction within context becomes the key point of the research interest so as to infer from the subject's single experience his/her meaning of interpretation and his action strategies. As a result, studying the teacher activity has to be completed by the same instructor provided to the students because, if not, the transfer from laboratory to classes bears no meaning because the teaching/learning system is highly-situated.

Third, the facts that occur in a didactic setting are essentially *unique and fleeting*. The impermanence of events in a classroom implies the impossibility for repeating or even replicating the facts that occur. So, if phenomena are not replicable, it becomes difficult to validate general laws and to generalize research products. The second consequence is that the researcher has to work on singularities and from authentic practices in order to model the collection of observations from qualitative as well as quantitative data (Denzin, 2009; Denzin & Lincoln, 2003). In an ecologically current class, the researcher will collect data that will help model regularities and exceptions and will process the data by inference in order to describe the observed facts; the heuristic descriptive process for understanding will overtake the project to generalize the tendencies.

Fourth, the classroom environment is inscribed within a very *normalizing institution*—the school. This normative institution has a wide impact on the way individuals behave and interpret the rules and the actions. The relationship between teacher and students is, in essence, asymmetrically organized into a hierarchy from the 'knower' to the 'learner'. When the student is implicated within a very constraining system, the teacher will also have to satisfy the expectations of the school. So these normalized relationships pre-determine events that will occur in classroom settings and, in return, are determined by this system. The process appears to be cyclical, determining as well as determined.

Fifth, *the dynamics* of exchange within a classroom are interactive and therefore constantly evolving. The subjects constantly co-determine and adjust to others in the process, redefining the relationship towards knowledge, others and oneself according to the issues of the exchanges (Bronckart, 1996). As a result, the process is fleeting so that any event may determine further interactions. This dynamic may, of course, generate learning, but it may also generate conflict, exclusion, opposing relationships and differentiation. This process may be continuous or not, discrete or not, linear or not.

Sixth, the classroom setting is inscribed within a *community of practices* (Lave & Wenger, 1991) comparable to an entity that can be identified because of 'boundary' objects. Because the class is a network, the boundary is very permeable and only serves to help identify the class of students as an entity. Exchanges among partners (peers, teacher/students) allow the sharing of practical knowledge and/or mutual experiences. This social dimension, highlighted by Vygotsky (1962), involves individuals among a peer community that appears fully characterized by an identity and a collective collusion that wears a strong identity constructed on shared experiences (i.e., tacit knowledge and habits, secrets, common history and stories).

Finally, the classroom setting is included within a longitudinal process that inscribes the learning within a duration of a before/after. Considering this *historical dimension*, (Cobb, 1994; Vygotsky, 1962) implicates the collection of a data to the present and it is significant for understanding the learning process from a dynamic, temporal point of view. So the continuity/rupture of events has a long-term inscription and impact, especially when regarding the educational phenomena. The question of the temporal scale of observation is very pertinent for research protocols.

Complex thinking and PETE paradigms

Three main models of Physical Education Teacher Education (PETE) can be described in connection with the complexity of PETE. These models are strongly linked with research designs in PETE and, depending on the model that is used, French research issues are contextualized by different research teams and located in different institutions. The first model is the 'companionage model' that postulates that professional learning is situated and decomposed into stages and initiation rituals. The second model of 'task scheduler' is based on planning so as to reduce uncertainty and to foresee events that may occur. The third model of 'reflective practitioner' supposes expanding a posture that focuses on the problem-solving encountered within professional activity.

The three models of PETE may be compatible and appear simultaneously or concurrently in the representations of teacher educators, as well as of novices. Sometimes, these models lead to misrepresentations or to obstacle-representations when students returning from practical teaching assume that academic courses are disconnected from professional preoccupations, and, therefore, not valuable or useful.

The 'companion', the 'task scheduler' and the 'reflective practitioner' in physical education

First, 'the companionage model of PETE' (Adell-Gombert, 2004) derives from the Middle Ages. The workers learned their jobs by the progressive induction to a strong corporation or guild. Simultaneously, the corporation was based on traditions transmitted by initiation rites and on the companionage process within a community of practice. Secrets and techniques were learnt by participating alongside experienced members of the corporation. The expert master showed a novice the steps for shaping the product, and, as time wore on, the novice themselves became a master. Under such tutelage, the novice is able to appropriate the practical knowledge of the master and replicates the required level of expertise. Research paradigms, influenced by this companionage model, are now actively debated in France and promote the masterization process of PETE. It is based on a specific set of social values and on the active socialisation of the novice in to the culture of the guild. The process of becoming a competent member of the corporation or guild is done by oral tradition, practice and comparison.

The second paradigm, of 'the task scheduler', postulates that the rationality of professional decision-making can be modelled as a form of artificial intelligence. Two models applied from sciences are used. The first model is from the field of thermodynamics and is based on the various observations of a closed, autonomous system (for example, a nuclear power plant, a swimming pool or the central-heating system in a house). Entry values (in-puts) and exit values (out-puts) characterize this functioning system (Shannon & Weaver, 1949; Wiener, 1948). The detection of error process identifies the differences between expected and effect data. It then regulates the process by feedbacks and error reduction. The second model comes from the theory of games (Von Neumann & Morgenstern, 1944) applied to war strategies and to natural or financial risk management strategies. The success of Napoleon's or of Von Clausewitz's thinking applied to enterprise management strategies postulates that human reasoning is hyper-rational and that action planning is effective. The decision-making process is included within an evidence-based approach where the projection of probable issues supposes the repertoire of all decisional algorithms in order to foresee events, to reduce uncertainty and to correct errors by comparison between expected and observed values.

According to this model, generic reasoning is defined under stabilized constraints and very little uncertainty is taken into account. The simulation of the scenario provides action programmes. The repetition of adaption in the case of critical events is valued. Critical events are taken as opportunities for achieving the pattern of decision-making. This model explains, for example, the strong persistence for finding and extracting the black boxes from crashed airplanes in order to avoid the repetition of these events and to serve as a basis for further pilot training. If the stimulation of standardized action programmes helps regulate the debriefing post decision-making process, then the problem is that sometimes professionals use, in complex situations, false reasoning to find right issues. For example, novice nuclear engineers, while correctly applying academic rules and reasoning in stimulation activities, would cause a nuclear incident. In reality, how would they transfer their knowledge to manage complex events (Pastré, 2002).

The 'reflective practitioner': the present PETE French paradigm

The third model of professional training, called 'the reflective practitioner', may be inspired by the Chinese war strategist Sunzi (544–496 BC) who recognized the relevance of taking into account the propensity of unanticipated events which also occur. In this way of thinking, the military official is never action-planning but tries to read and interpret the natural tendency of events; he studies the states of degradation, assesses the levels of danger or disorder, defines areas for decision-making and cross-checks the interpretation with peers. As a result, he does not reason with general laws but with the circumstances present in this current context. This reasoning is extracted from the practical situation and uses what ancient civilizations called 'ingenio' (creativity) along with practical intelligence developed through reflective practice when confronted with unchartered territory (Jullien, 1996).

The Canadian Donald Schön (1983, 1991) made a strong impact in France in terms of teacher education because he rehabilitated the idea of 'knowledge-in-action' extracted from experience and not from academia. This reflective practitioner paradigm, relayed by the prestigious CNAM (National Conservatory of Arts and Professions in France), involves professionals working in an authentic, complex setting, providing a detached posture (like the 'mirror' provided by Lacan), extracted by induction heuristic models. The case study becomes a way for initiating the reflection, for cross-checking points of view (i.e., novice, expert, teacher trainer, student, etc.) and for interpreting a co-constructed and negotiated reality. The key-point of the professional training is the definition of the problem-solving area (see the example of architecture expertise provided by Schön, 1983).

Exploring the complex teaching/learning system in educational research

The question that emerges from this discussion is how to characterize the complex teaching/learning system in a relevant manner. Several options are provided in the 'professional didactics' field as developed in the French-speaking educational research. Depending on the emphasis given to one of the aspects of the considered system, researchers may choose to focus on: (1) the activity of the teacher, (2) the impact in terms of student learning and development and/or (3) the effectiveness of taught knowledge in terms of development and modifications. In the 'cognitive-situated anthropology' approach (Durand, 2002; Gal-Petitfaux, 2011), the key assumption is to focus on effective teacher activity so as to describe and to model typical functioning repertoires of the practitioner. This very heuristic and sophisticated approach involves research methods based on systematic observations linked with interviews (Vermersch, 2000) and different video-based protocols (Theureau, 2006) allowing the practitioner to be reflexive. The French 'professional didactics' field (Amade-Escot, 2007; Brousseau, 1998; Sensevy, 2007) and the working psychology from Parisian CNAM (Clot, 1999; Lémonie, 2010; Pastré, 2002) postulate that the teacher's effectiveness has to be studied in an indirect, inductive way in order to consider the effective impacts on students confronted with the learning task. The gap between formal/taught/learned curricula has to be well-matched-up and reduced by appreciating that it is not sufficient to teach, but that students also have to learn. Therefore, it is necessary to study the teacher's decision-making strategies as a project of influence because such decision-making is oriented with regards to students' scheduled impacts. Therefore, these researchers focus on the professional activity within the single classroom context while solving practical problems, focusing on case studies and qualitative research designs.

Teachers' professional activity: a process of interpreting student activity

Merleau-Ponty (1960, p. 56) states that "language signifies when, instead of copying the thinking, it bears the meaning like the pencil for a drawing or like the foot prints reflect the movement and the body effort." The moving and embodied individual is open to meaningful interpretation through a 'semiosis process'. This process occurs not only according to the action content (i.e., observation of the produced gestures and techniques) but also according to its effects (i.e., intended/effective action strategies, reasoning and mental states) (Anscombe, 2000; Courtès, 2001; Ricoeur, 1989; Searle, 1983). From this perspective, motoric action is not only a succession of observable sequences of technical movements and gesture, it also has an intention-in-action that is inferred from the representational system in the situation that enables such movements to be meaningful (Iser, 1975; 1980). In addition, it is socially normalized and historically relevant (Sperber, 2011). When conceptualized in this way, a teacher's professional activity may be redefined as a situated project of influence on others (students) and on the world (school task systems and constraints). Consequently, it is the condition for evolving the professional identity of the teacher.

Interpreting the actions of the student teacher consists of inferring the relevance of their actions according to the individual's subjectivity and the situated context (Sperber, 2011; Sperber & Wilson, 1989). The difficulty for the teacher-practitioner and the researcher is to identify the events that are relevant for the student so that the decision-making and the intervention can be taken at the right time and ways. The question now is, "how is it possible to investigate the student-teacher activity so as to facilitate becoming an expert teacher?"

Complex thinking as a paradigm in PETE: perspectives

The complex thinking approach to PETE implies that novice teachers learn how to link relationships in the teaching/learning system. Based on the discussion so far, we suggest that five postulations are available for exploring the student activity by a semio-constructivist approach (see also Wallian & Chang, 2006). First, the opportunity to experience all aspects of the teaching role during professional practices must be provided. This means that not only the act of teaching be performed, but a certain posture of teacher reflection-on-action has to be developed by several means (i.e., portfolio, reflective written reports, prospective/critical professional writings, self-observation in video-recorded pertinent sequences, systematic observation tools and grids and crossed interpretations on class events among novices, experts and teacher trainers, etc.). Second, the student teacher needs to experience authentic problems that enable pedagogical knowledge and problem-solving to be mobilized. In such situations the student teacher is then encouraged to identify the problem to be solved in order to consider plausible ways of understanding the problem and possible ways of pro-ceeding as a solution. For example, when confronted with a student behaving in an unexpected way, the student teacher can analyse the behaviour from a psy-chological perspective as well as considering their movements from a physiological or biomechanical approach so as to get a multi-dimensional representation of the learner activity. Third, any professional knowledge is highly situated. No general rules or laws provide ready-made answers in each specific educational context. For example, it is questionable that a general rule exists that effectively guides the teacher on how to provide effective feedback that facilitates the student transfor-mation of activity in the very single task system and classroom setting. Fourth, the student teacher attributes a relevant-for-him/her value to facts. The difficulty is to cross the interpretations in order to enrich the frame of interpretation and the expectation horizons. Fifth, the interpretation varies according to the representa-tional system that has to be constructed/deconstructed at a higher level of complexity: so the resistance against change is very strong and the reshaping of representations supposes a true emotional and cognitive effort when confronted with the field of professional practices.

Crossed case studies as a repertoire for learning how to interpret the student activity

The case study of meaningful sequences from physical education practices can serve as a basis for helping the student teacher to construct the professional expertise and identity. There are meanwhile conditions for making this approach propitious. In these conditions, we propose the linking of the terms 'semiotics' and 'motricity' within the new term 'semiot®icity' that contracts the idea of mean-ingful motor activity of the individuals.

The 'semiot®ic approach to student learning' (Wallian in Rabatel, 2010) postu-lates that the motor production is a kind of writing (a 'text') when recorded, stabilized and situated; a semiotic study of the non-verbal and verbal language productions becomes possible under these conditions in terms of content/discourse analysis (Charaudeau & Maingueneau, 2002; Schiffrin, Tannen, & Hamilton, 2001). The opportunity to interpret actions in terms of pertinent-for-subject activity ensures the student teacher acts in the full teaching role and as a reflective practi-tioner within the teaching/learning system (Wallian, Poggi, & Chauvin-Vileno, 2012). Many possibilities are available for collecting information about the student teacher's action and reflection in/on action, such as systematic observations of professional practices, verbal data collection (i.e., expressing interviews, video-based tests, ante/post interviews) (Chi, Bassorck, Lewis, Reinmann, & Blaser, 1989), and professional written reports about practice (i.e., written preparation of lessons, field notes and written reports before/after action). This information collection would be cross-checked with systematic observations of the classroom events so as to give a multidimensional view of the processes involved; it would allow insights into some of the dissimulated or subjacent aspects of the school phenomena underlying the mutually-determined process of the teaching/learning. As a result, PETE could be based on the cross-checked interpretation of student case-study activity in simulated video-based contexts. The practical modalities would aim to link: (1) the observed facts, (2) the plausible interpretations and (3) the professional intervention in terms of decision-making. This modality for PETE has recently been introduced in France; the analysis of video-based sequences on situated student activities in school contexts has become a front-and-central examination for the national state enrolment of physical education teachers.

Conclusion: complex thinking and the challenges for PETE

Complexity thinking stems from the assumption that educational phenomena are inherently complex. It supposes progressing the positivist conception of PETE research in order to change the conception of knowledge via a constructivist approach. In an ever-evolving world, the challenge is to give student teachers the opportunity to think about, in, for and with their own professional practice and to expand a reflective posture on the events occurring in their classrooms in order to train them how to adapt. The challenge is to learn how to expand a reflective posture, to solve practical problems in multi-determined settings and to move from a teacher-centric approach to a student-centric approach. There are countless opportunities for understanding what makes sense for the student teacher and to understand how she/he reshapes the representational system during their professional lifespan. The main condition is to link inter-disciplinary studies in order to shape complex professional teachers in the same way that McMurtry (2011, p. 33) states for "complex learners".

The paradigm of complex thinking in physical education teacher education is nowadays reshaping French conceptions, practices and university curricula, while redefining the relationship of 'uncertainty' on educational events. It invites the conception of the teaching/learning system on reliance, contextualization and globalization without forgetting the singular, embodied, situated and dis(con)crete aspects of events. It re-envisages the teacher–subject reality construction as a key basis and a prior construction for studying the professional decision-making, not with reference to the expert teacher, but with regards to the constrained/contradictory activities produced by the student teacher at a moment of professional identity construction. Complex thinking in education follows the process from practical problem-solving gleamed from practice to a sort of reflection on/by action through a dialectic interpretative process between practice and theory. If many schools of philosophy of the mind have formalized this paradigm according to diverse research fields that span far back in history, the implications for sport pedagogy is open-ended because of the extreme diversity and heterogeneity of the classroom settings.

Acknowledgement

The authors warmly thank Alan Ovens for his very perceptive and relevant proofreading.

References

Abdelmalek, A. (2010). *Edgar Morin, sociologue de la complexité*. Paris: Apogée.

Adell-Gombert, N. (2004). Les sentiers de l'orient. Initiation chez les compagnons du tour de France. *Ethnologie Française, 3*, 34.

Alhadeff-Jones, M. (2010). The reduction of critique in education: Perspectives from Morin's paradigm of complexity. In D. Osberg & G. Biesta (Eds.), *Complexity theory and the politics of education* (pp. 25–38). Rotterdam: Sense Publishers.

Amade-Escot, C. (2007). *Le didactique*. Paris: Ed. EPS.

Anscombe, G.E.M. (2000). *Intention* (2nd ed.). Cambridge, MA: Harvard University Press.

Atlan, H. (1979). *Entre le cristal et la fumée*. Paris: Seuil.

Bertalanffy, L.von (1968). *General system theory: Foundations, development, applications*. New York: Braziller.

Bourdieu, P. (1980). *Le sens pratique*. Paris: Minuit.

Bronckart, J.P. (1996). *Activité langagière, textes et discours*. Genève: Delachaux et Niestlé.

Brousseau, G. (1998). *Théorie des situations didactiques*. Grenoble: La Dispute.

Brown, J.S., Collins, A., & Duguid, P. (1989). Situated cognition and the culture of learning. *Educational Researcher, 18*(1), 32–42.

Charaudeau, P., & Maingueneau, P. (2002). *Dictionnaire d'analyse du discours*. Paris: Seuil.

Chi, M.T.H., Bassrock, M., Lewis, M.W., Reimann, P., & Blaser, R. (1989). Self-explanations: How students study and use examples in learning to solve problems. *Cognitive Science, 13*, 145–182.

Clancey, W.J. (1997). *Situated cognition: On human knowledge and computer representations*. Cambridge: Cambridge University Press.

Clot, Y. (1999). *Avec Vygotski*. Paris: La Dispute.

Cobb, P. (1994). Constructivism in mathematics and science education. *Educational Researcher, 23*(7), 4.

Courtès, J. (2001). *La sémiotique, comprendre l'univers des signes, le langage*. Paris: PUF.

Denzin, N.K. (2009). *Qualitative inquiry under fire. Towards a new paradigm dialogue*. Walnut Creek, CA: Left Coast Press.

Denzin, N.K., & Lincoln, Y.S. (2003). *Collecting and interpreting qualitative materials*. London: Sage.

Durand, M. (2002). *L'enseignement en milieu scolaire*. Paris: PUF.

Fleener, M.J. (2005). Introduction: Chaos, complexity, curriculum, and culture: Setting up the conversation. In J. William E. Doll, M.J. Fleener, D. Trueit, & J.St. Julien (Eds.), *Chaos, complexity, curriculum, and culture: A conversation* (pp. 305–321). New York: Peter Lang.

Foerster, H.von (1973). On constructing a reality. In F.E. Preiser (Ed.), *Environmental design research* (pp. 35–46). Dowden: Hutchinson and Ross.

Fosnot, C. (1996). *Constructivism: Theory, perspectives, and practice*. New York: Teachers College Press.

Gadamer, H.G. (1960). *Truth and method*. New York: Thomas Crowell.

Gal-Petitfaux, N. (2011). *La leçon d'éducation physique et sportive: formes de travail scolaire, expérience et configurations d'activité collective dans la classe. Contribution à un programme de recherche en anthropologie cognitive*. Habilitation à Diriger des Recherches soutenue à l'université de Clermont-Ferrand, France.

Gal-Petitfaux, N., & Durand, M. (2001). L'enseignement de l'éducation physique comme action située: Propositions pour une approche d'anthropologie cognitive. *STAPS*, *55*, 79–100.

Gal-Petitfaux, N., Sève, C., Cizeron, M., & Adé, D. (2010). Activité et expérience des acteurs en situation: Les apports de l'anthropologie cognitive. In M. Musard, G. Carlier, & M. Loquet (Eds.), *Sciences de l'intervention en EPS et en sport* (pp. 67–85). Paris: Editions Revue EPS.

Geert, P. van (1994). *Dynamic systems of development: Change between complexity and chaos*. New York: Harvester Wheatsheaf.

Geert, P. van (1998). A dynamic system model of basic developmental mechanisms: Piaget, Vygotsky and beyond. *Psychological Review*, *105*(4), 634–677.

Glasersfeld, E. von (1995). *Radical constructivism: A way of knowing and learning*. London: Falmer Press.

Hutchins, E. A. (1995). *Cognition in the wild*. Cambridge, MA: The MIT Press.

Iser, W. (1975). The reading process: A phenomenological approach. *New Literary History*, *3*, 1971–1972.

Iser, W. (1980). *The act of reading*. Baltimore: Johns Hopkins University Press.

Jullien, F. (1996). *Traité de l'efficacité*. Paris: Grasset.

Kirk, D., & Macdonald, D. (1998). Situated learning in physical education. *Journal of Teaching in Physical Education*, *17*, 376–387.

Kuhn, T.S. (1962). *The structure of scientific revolutions*. Chicago, IL: University of Chicago Press.

Lani-Bayle, M. (2008). *La pensée complexe en recherches et en pratique*. *Revue Chemins de Formation*. Paris: Téraèdre.

Lave, J., & Wenger, E. (1991). *Situated learning: Legitimate peripheral participation*. New York: Cambridge University Press.

Le Moigne, J.L. (1984). *La théorie du système général*. Paris: PUF.

Le Moigne, J.L. (1995). *Les épistémologies constructivistes*. Paris: PUF.

Le Moigne, J.L. (2004). *Le constructivisme, modéliser pour comprendre*. Paris: L'Harmattan.

Le Moigne, J.L. & Morin, E. (2007). *Intelligence de la complexité: Épistémologie et pragmatique*. *Colloque de Cerisy*. Paris: Edition de l'Aube.

Lémonie, Y. (2010). *Etude de l'interaction de l'enseignement-apprentissage : le cas de l'enseignement de la natation sportive en EPS* (Unpublished doctoral dissertation). University of Paris XII Val de Marne, Créteil.

Marquardt, M.J. (1999). *Action learning in action*. Palo Alto, CA: Davies-Black.

Maturana, H.R., & Varela, F.J. (1987). *The tree of knowledge: The biological roots of human understanding*. Boston: Shambhala Publications.

McMurtry, A. (2011). The complexities of interdisciplinarity: Integrating two different perspectives on interdisciplinary research and education. *Complicity: An International Journal of Complexity and Education*, *8*(2), 19–35.

Merleau-Ponty, M. (1960). *Signes*. Paris: Gallimard.

Morin, E. (1973). *Le paradigme perdu: La nature humaine*. Paris: Seuil.

Morin, E. (1977–2004). *La Méthode*. Paris: Seuil.

Morin, E. (1990). *Introduction à la pensée complexe*. Paris: Seuil.

Morin, E., & Le Moigne, J.L. (1999). *L'intelligence de la complexité*. Paris: L'Harmattan.

Olssen, M. (2008). Foucault as complexity theorist: Overcoming the problems of classical philosophical analysis. *Educational Philosophy and Theory*, *40*(1), 96–117.

Pastré, P. (2002). L'analyse du travail en didactique professionnelle. *Revue Française de Pédagogie, 138*, 9–17.

Pena Vega, A. & Proutheau, S. (2011). *Edgar Morin, aux risques d'une pensée libre*. Paris: CNRS.

Piaget, J. (1937). *La construction du réel chez l'enfant*. Lausanne: Delachaux & Niestlé.

Poincaré, R. (1892). *Les méthodes nouvelles de la mécanique céleste*. Paris: Gauthiers-Villars.

Ricoeur, P. (1989). *The conflict of interpretations*. London: Athlone Press.

Schiffrin, D., Tannen, D., & Hamilton, H.E. (2001). *The handbook of discourse analysis*. Oxford: Blackwell Publishing.

Schön, D.A. (1983). *The reflective practitioner: How professionals think in action*. New York: Basic Books.

Schön, D.A. (1991). *The reflective turn: Case studies in and on educational practice*. New York: Columbia Teachers College.

Searle, J.R. (1983). *L'Intentionnalité*. Editions de Minuit: Paris.

Sen, A. (2003). *Ethique et économie*. Paris: PUF.

Sensevy, G. (2007). *Agir ensemble. L'action didactique conjointe du professeur et des élèves*. Rennes: PUR.

Shannon, C.E., & Weaver, W. (1949). *The mathematical theory of communication*. Urbana, IL: University of Illinois Press.

Sperber, D. (2011). A naturalistic ontology for mechanistic explanations in the social sciences. In P. Demeulenaere (Ed.), *Analytical sociology and social mechanisms* (pp. 480–496). Cambridge: Cambridge University Press.

Sperber, D., & Wilson, D. (1989). *La pertinence. Communication et cognition*. Paris: Minuit.

Suchman, L. (1987). *Plans and situated actions: The problem of human-machine communication*. Cambridge: Cambridge University Press.

Terhart, E. (2003). Constructivism and teaching: A new paradigm in general didactics? *Journal of Curriculum Studies, 35*(1), 25–44.

Thelen, E. (1992). Development as a dynamic system. *Current Directions in Psychological Science, 1*, 189–193.

Theureau, J. (2006). *Le cours d'action: Méthode développée*. Toulouse: Octares.

Varela, F., Thompson, E., & Rosch, E. (1991). *The embodied mind: Cognitive science and human experience*. Cambridge, MA: MIT Press.

Vermersch, P. (2000). *L'entretien d'explicitation* (3ème ed.). Paris: ESF.

Von Neumann, J., & Morgenstern, O. (1944). *Theory of games and economic behavior*. Princeton, NJ: Princeton University Press.

Vygotsky, L.S. (1962). *Thought and language*. Cambridge, MA: MIT Press.

Wallian, N. (2010). Pluri-sémioticité et plurisémiot®icité en Éducation Physique et Sportive. In A. Rabatel (Ed.), *Les reformulations pluri-sémiotiques en contexte de formation* (pp. 204–232). Besançon: PUFC.

Wallian, N., & Chang, C.W. (2006). Development and learning of motor skill competencies. In D. Kirk (Ed.), *Handbook of research in PE* (pp. 282–311). London: Sage.

Wallian, N., Poggi, M.P., & Chauvin-Vileno, A. (2012). *Action, interaction, intervention: A la croisée du langage, de la pratique et des savoirs*. Bern: Peter Lang (Collection Transversales).

Wiener, N. (1948). *Cybernetics or control and communication in the animal and the machine*. Paris: Hermann.

14 Modification by adaptation

Proposing another pedagogical principle for TGfU

Karen Pagnano Richardson, Deborah Sheehy and Tim Hopper

This chapter presents a scholarship of teaching and learning (SoTL) study focused on how games taught in physical education can draw on game-based learning in video games where conditions are created in the game for the constraints on the player to change depending on the outcome of a previous game encounter. Hopper (2011) and Hopper, Sanford, and Clarke (2009) have called this game modification by adaptation. As stated by Hopper (2011)

> In modification by adaptation the game is modified to increase the challenge to the player who was successful on the previous game encounter. Changes can be made in relation to the constraints of the game, such as space, scoring, rules conditioning play or number of players, in order to ensure the outcome of the game is close, and for the unanticipated to happen during game play (p. 6).

This modification by adaptation connects to a concept in video game play that Gee (2003) calls game-as-teacher. As noted by Gee (2003), video game designers have largely addressed an ongoing dilemma for educators of "how to get people, often young people, to learn and master something that is long and challenging—and to enjoy it" (p. 1). In this chapter, we suggest that when physical education teachers modify the constraints of a game, using the principle of adaptation, it is possible to present students with increasing levels of challenge as they progress in their game play, creating the idea of game-as-teacher. Modification by adaptation provides both challenge and engagement for all learners. From a constraints-led perspective (Davids, Button, & Bennett, 2008; Renshaw, Yi Chow, Davids, & Hammond, 2010), the notion of the 'game-as-teacher' can be used to understand how games can be constructed as an engaging learning context with and for young people (Hopper, 2011).

This chapter will be organized into three major sections. The first section explores how complexity thinking can inform learning through adaptation games. The key premise here is that complexity thinking focuses on the adaptive self-organizing systems in which learning emerges from experiences that activate transformation in the learner (Davis & Sumara, 2006). The second section advocates and provides support for Hopper, Sanford, and Clarke's (2009) and

Hopper's (2011) position that game modification by adaptation represents another modification principle of TGfU in addition to Bunker and Thorpe's (1986) modification by representation and modification by exaggeration. The third section explores how pre-service teachers, as students in a games course, experienced instruction that was informed by game modification by adaptation and, more broadly, the 'game-as-teacher' as they learned (or re-learned) how game learning develops. The purpose of this study was to examine a key premise that this approach creates a complex adaptive system, with enabling constraints as a guideline, of players who engage in a game that is close, where play engulfs them with the delight of good play (Kretchmar, 2005).

Complexity thinking qualities relating to games

First, as complex learning system is unpredictable, meaning that learning occurs when learners adapt to one another, forming a collective that adapts to conditions impacting the system. Adaptation games can provide optimal conditions for learning within which the role of the teacher is changed as the game becomes more central to the learning process. Next, three of the complexity thinking qualities will be explored related to games learning that include adaptation, self-organizing and emergence. Finally, how enabling constraints facilitate learning in the adaptation games will be explored.

Adaptation

First, as a complex system, games require that each player has the potential for adaptation as a result of their involvement in the game (Storey & Butler, 2010). Through nonlinear and dynamic interactions the game serves as a catalyst for change in players' actions (i.e., learning). Learning involves an experience that disturbs the learner's existing understanding, and, through the process of adaptation (adjusting actions to the game situation), leads to the construction of new knowing. Cognitive equilibrium is a product of this new knowing (Light, 2009). During a game, each player continuously tries to gain control of their role in the game. The interaction of each player, with other players, creates a continuous state of disequilibrium where each player tries to regain equilibrium that leads to a sense of control in the game. Critical to the player is their ability to construe their role with others in the game (see Davis, Sumara, & Luce-Kapler, 2008). The construal process creates the adaptive dynamics of the players to the constraints of the game (Davids, Button, & Bennett, 2008; Renshaw *et al.*, 2010). In modification by adaptation, the game structure, by virtue of constraints shifting in response to the outcome of players' engagements in the game, encourages players to make adjustments "through processes of recognition, adaptive decision-making or … on-line corrections" (Rossi & Carroll, 2012, p. 2). The increased advantage to one player balances to the prior ability advantage of the other, creating a situation that requires both players to seek 'new' equilibrium.

Self-organizing

Second, complex learning during game play is self-organizing. Therefore, games organized by the principle of game modification by adaptation can be played spontaneously in the absence of a centralized controller (i.e., the teacher). Based on the diversity of players within a team, the team will "demonstrate self-organizing behaviour as they respond to their opponents and to each other in an effort to have continued success in the game" (Storey & Butler, 2010, p. 145). An example of self-organizing within an adaptation game is evident as each team makes decisions about the constraints of their game that will allow the game to unfold in an unpredictable way. Constraints in a game that adapt to the players' engagement with the game challenge stable patterns of play where one team or player can continuously win with their superior ability. As noted by Button, Chow, Travassos, Vilar, and Araújo (2012), "teachers may in fact circumvent the inherent self-organizing tendencies that exist in social collectives" (p. 14) by creating constraints in the game that focus players on certain desired skill patterns and strategic actions. For example, in pickleball, as an opponent is successful, their court size increases; the player soon realizes to hit to open space in order to take advantage of the shifting game structure.

Emergence

Third, learning is emergent from game experiences. An adaptation game is inherently an unstable system as, by design, the enabling constraints change after each game. Disturbances in an adaptation game are anticipated by the teacher or arise spontaneously as a result of game play. Disequilibrium sets conditions for learning to emerge from game experiences. In addition to the disturbances inherent in adaptation games, each time there is improvement in the skill or tactics of one player or team, this creates disequilibrium for team-mates and opponents, forcing further adaptation and learning (Storey & Butler, 2010). Each time a student makes an adjustment, such as learning to direct the ball toward a touch-line in soccer, a contribution is made as a "recursive elaboration" to the learning process (Davis, Sumara, & Luce-Kapler, 2008, p. 168) that changes the system. Now, surrounding players must also adapt to this increased understanding of ball placement and skill execution. Similarly, Renshaw et al. (2010) explain that, "through self-organization processes, inherent to many biological systems including human movement systems, constraints can shape the emergence of movement patterns, cognitions and decision making processes in learners" (p. 120). Due to the interconnected nature of this learning process, small changes in one part of the system can lead to major changes emerging throughout the system. Therefore, changes in adaptation games made by players as to how they play or changes to the game constraints have the potential to foster emergent learning as players seek to gain cognitive equilibrium and control over the game.

Enabling constraints

Finally, three of the qualities of a complex system—'adaptation, self-organizing and emergence'—form critical elements that allow a system to develop in a nonlinear process (see Chapter 1, Ovens, Hopper, & Butler, 2012). For the complex system to form, it must develop an interaction with the environment so that, when conditions are just right, an 'autocatakinetic' process starts where the system draws on available resources in a self-sustaining exchange. For this to happen in adaptation games, the conditions in the environment need to offer 'enabling constraints' that limit what the system can do to prevent it from being overwhelmed but at the same time offer an openness to possibilities of which the complex system can take advantage. Therefore, adaptation games are designed with constraints in such a way as to scaffold learning at a rate that each player can manage the information–movement coupling demands (Davids, Shuttleworth, Araújo, & Renshaw, 2003). In adaptation games, the role of the teacher is to provide the enabling constraints as guidelines for emergent engagement by students. Rather than being prescriptive, the enabling constraints orient the learner to what might happen in the game, rather than what must happen (Davis & Sumara, 2010). 'Enabling constraints' of the game include rules that allow for changing space, equipment and conditions of play from which students make their own selections. These 'enabling constraints' allow players to develop skills that create more embodied understanding of the game rules (Hopper, 2011). As the game structure changes, the player has to reorient their play to the new tactical demands. If, for example, a player is defending a large court in pickleball, she needs to send the ball with more height over the net to allow more time for recovery to cover the opponent's target area. She may be playing the same opponent but her way of playing has to shift in response to the constraints of the game, thus she learns to play a more defensive game.

Teaching Games for Understanding: principles for game modification

Three decades ago, the approach known as Teaching Games for Understanding (TGfU) was conceptualized. Educators were concerned that children were not experiencing the thrill associated with games, and that they and adults had little understanding of games (Almond, 2010). Thorpe, Bunker, and Almond (1986) proposed two ways to modify games: representation and exaggeration. Modification by representation refers to mini-games developed with the key features and tactical problems of the adult game but played with modifications to suit the learner's size, age and ability. For example, in modified tennis students would play in a smaller area represented by the service boxes and would use a sponge ball. Modification by exaggeration uses the constraints of the game to focus on tactical problems associated with the adult games played in society. For example, in badminton students might play on a long, narrow court to emphasize deep shots and drop shots.

The principle of 'modification by adaptation' adds another dimension to these pedagogical principles. Now the game is modified to increase the challenge to a successful player based on the outcome of the previous game (changes to space, scoring, rules conditioning play or number of players). These conditions of play are triggered as a result of a winning outcome to the game so that the winner is faced with an increased challenge. Multiple game outcomes allow the game to adapt to the ability of the players. An example is provided by a volleyball-like game called 'space adapt' which is played in a quarter of a badminton court. After one student scores two points, the other student increases the opponent's play area, changing the boundaries and increasing space by adding on a quadrant of the badminton court. The students play again. The student who does not win then increases the opponent's play space or decreases their own space and then the students play again. Adaptation allows students even with disparities in skill to engage in meaningful, yet unpredictable game play (Hopper, 2011).

According to Storey and Butler (2010), modification of games by exaggeration and representation each create conditions for bringing perceptions and actions together—creating perception–action couplings (Davids, Button, & Bennett, 2008). The significance in recognizing modification by adaptation as another principle of game modification lies in the unique perception–action coupling that occurs as students experience adaptation games as they learn to manipulate their decision-making actions to the changing constraints of the game.

TGfU in pre-service teacher education

Teacher educators have responded to the need to teach about game modification and to enhance understanding of game play by restructuring activity courses (Storey & Lunn, 2009). Sport activity courses in teacher education programmes, informed by theory and taught through practice, can model innovative ideas to teaching physical education. It is our contention that the experiences of pre-service teachers provide insights into how the adaptation game serves as a critical tool to create what complexity thinkers refer to as an autocatalytic space (Barab *et al.*, 1999; Mason, 2008). In this study we asked, "How do pre-service teachers describe their experiences in modification by adaptation games?" Teaching using adaptation games meant that learning in a game for the pre-service teacher emerged from interactions with each other, the rules, space and equipment and continuously adapting as the system maintained disequilibrium in its ability to enable play.

Method

The research project included two physical education teacher educators (first and second authors) and 19 pre-service teachers concurrently enrolled in a two-credit game theory course and a six-credit advanced methods course. Human subject approval was granted and informed consent provided.

Data collection and analysis

Qualitative data collection from the 19 participants included (a) a pre-instruction open response questionnaire, (b) exit cards, (c) a video-recording and (d) a 45–60-minute audio-recorded, semi-structured focus group interview. Data were analysed using constant comparison (Strauss & Corbin, 1998) between interview data, written documents and artefacts, observations and video-recordings. Categories were created, merged and adjusted as the analysis proceeded, and emergent themes were identified which related to teaching and learning as a part of the inductive reasoning process (Goetz & LeCompte, 1981).

Description of curricular setting

The research was conducted in a games course at a midsize state university in the eastern United States. The course is an early programme requirement designed to develop pedagogical content knowledge (Shulman, 1986) focused on understanding and implementing TGfU. The two-credit course introduces pre-service teachers to TGfU and its theoretical underpinnings and provides opportunities to teach. A four-credit methods course follows, where pre-service teachers plan and implement middle school TGfU lessons. A final six-credit advanced methods course that combines planning, implementation and assessment of TGfU provides opportunities for pre-service teachers to teach a mini-unit in a diverse urban context with the support of the university faculty. Later, pre-service teachers plan and implement TGfU lessons in a public school-based, pre-practicum experience and finally plan and implement a unit of instruction during practicum.

Description of integrated course experience

The teacher educators collaborated to design learning tasks that pre-service teachers engaged in through two course experiences. We realized that, if we can teach pre-service teachers broadly about 'game-as-teacher', we move them beyond replication of the Tactical Games Model (Mitchell, Oslin, & Griffin, 2006) toward a broader understanding of game-centred teaching. Initial exploration of adaptation was led by teacher educators in their respective classes and included: (a) in-depth discussion of readings, (b) viewing modified games on YouTube played by pre-service teachers from the University of Victoria, British Columbia, (c) participation in an adaptation game led by each course teacher educator at the research site. An extension assignment was designed for selected pre-service teachers who were concurrently enrolled in the games course and the advanced methods course. The selected pre-service teachers were put into leadership roles where they taught adaptation games to their peers.

Pre-service teachers were immersed in game modification over several weeks through the two course experiences. The selected pre-service teachers piloted the adaptation games during the upper-level methods class. The pilot experience was a synergetic one-for-all (pre-service teachers and teacher educators) that provided an opportunity for trial/adapt/re-trial in adaptation games. Pre-service teachers refined games and developed lesson plans, visual aids and guiding questions to promote tactical awareness. Next, they presented games at the 'adaptation celebration' to peers in the games course. The final step in the advanced methods class occurred when participants taught adaptation games in an urban high school. Positive responses from the high school students further fuelled pre-service teachers' enthusiasm for adaptation games.

Results

Three themes were identified in the data which highlight how pre-service teachers were changed by their experiences in games designed by the pedagogical principle of game modification by adaptation. The three themes were equalizing power, catalysts for learning and pre-service teacher change.

Equalizing power

The first theme is equalizing power. As participants engaged in adaptation games, they identified how this elicited emotional responses based on their past experiences in games. The adaptation game also quickly became the pre-service teachers' game as some spontaneously developed and refined their own enabling constraints to create games that they perceived fitted their needs.

Levelling the playing field. Pre-service teachers spoke about how the changing constraints of adaptation games levelled the playing field as they engaged in game play. The results were close games, evenly matched and competitive games. Alex said, "I noticed in badminton that some of the people who would normally dominate ... didn't necessarily dominate in the adaptation game, so it levelled the playing field in that way" (interview). Stephanie stated, "I felt like I didn't have to worry whether or not the game would be competitive because the utilization of the adaptation would ensure that the playing field was even" (exit card).

Choice to the underdog/challenge to the winner. Pre-service teachers identified that a unique characteristic of adaptation games was that the student who didn't win had the power to make decisions about the constraints of the next game, which served to equalize the power dynamic between the winner and loser. Holly, a skilled gymnast, described her experiences playing an adaptation game, "it gave you a little more hope, and a little more encouragement" (interview). Kyle stated, "It [adaptation game] privileges the loser of the game while challenging the winner. What it basically does is to make the game equal for both players" (interview). Stan focused on the losing team, "It helps the losing team by having the opportunity to still compete, but on more favourable terms—it allows the team to still participate as the game was intended and is still challenging for higher skilled players" (interview). Differences, however, were evident in how pre-service teachers perceived the adaptation based on their past history with a game, as evident in the next categories.

Empowering game experience. By definition, 'empower' means to authorize, to allow or to sanction. For some pre-service teachers who felt less secure in their ability to play certain games, the use of modification by adaptation gave a sense of empowerment. Natalie said, "It reminded me back at high school when I wasn't good at certain games and I was sitting there [thinking] I don't want to play—this is embarrassing. The adaptation game gave you confidence ... I might not be good at this but the adaptation gives you the chance to be good at it" (interview). The unpredictability of the outcome served to equalize power. Holly said, "The same people weren't losing every time and it increases the challenge for the team that already won" (interview).

Affirmative action for games. For pre-service teachers who self-identify as highly skilled, changing game constraints was viewed as 'affirmative action' for games, but not for them. To them, the adaptation seemed unnecessary and only appropriate for their lower-skilled opponents of unequal status. Hillary said, "I feel that if it's a close game and they felt like they had that chance to win without the adaptation, I don't know if it's always necessary" (interview). Lia said, "I didn't like an adaptation because I am so competitive—I don't want to win that way" (interview). Bo explained in an interview that winning a game adaptation just didn't fit his conception of competition as a skilled athlete and would be most appropriate for the lower skilled.

With changing constraints, the adaptation game equalized power and tempered some of the childhood baggage or privilege that pre-service teachers bring to the game and pushed them to be in the present moment that was the game at hand. For the pre-service teachers who, throughout their lifetime, were accustomed to feeling powerful from games, this equalizing feature was unsettling, while the pre-service teachers who have rarely experienced power during game play felt a renewed interest in playing that game.

Catalysts for learning

Although the pre-service teachers described a level playing field in the adaptation game, the constraints kept changing, thus keeping the game vibrant. Within the adaptation game, power was shifted from the fixed, individual characteristics of the game, which Stephanie described as "what you come to the game with—skills, decisions, experiences … I always win and you always lose" (interview), to the ever-changing constraints. The moment that the adaptation game was different occurred when the game changed for both players and the challenge was reset. Either the winner will have more difficult constraints or the loser will have easier constraints, thus giving both players a new, possibly more evenly-matched, challenge that ultimately becomes a 'just-right challenge' for those game players. "The power keeps shifting during the game" (Natalie, interview).

As power shifted between players and the game took on a life of its own, a change began to occur in how and what pre-service teachers were learning. For this group of pre-service teachers, the catalysts for learning were a convergence of factors that included the ones described in more detail below: 'the teacher takes a back seat'; opportunities for pre-service teachers to play a series of sub-games; and pauses in the game.

'Teacher takes a back seat'. The 'teacher takes a back seat' refers to decentralized control whereby the teacher initially sets the broad constraints of the game. Pre-service teachers play the game independently, making decisions based on the interactions between the players involved. Natalie said, "It [the adaptation game] is student-directed, so it gives the teacher a back seat in the gym and it's really primarily run by students" (interview).

Pre-service teachers described the freedom they experienced when the teacher did not attempt to control the game. Celeste described her appreciation for autonomy—"I was able to make the decision and choose the path of the game instead of having it defined for me" (interview). David echoed this sentiment, "The countless ways to adapt the game and essentially control it ourselves, an independent feeling which makes the role of the student a very powerful one" (exit card). In the absence of teacher control, pre-service teachers took responsibility for decisions during game play.

Series of sub-games. Short games were appealing to pre-service teachers. Bryan said, "I really enjoyed the scoring because it made the games close. The flow of the game went well because we knew the rules and picked up strategies to be successful, which made for a better game" (interview). Carl agreed, "At the beginning we were struggling and struggling and we couldn't get it. Eventually [after a game series], we worked as a team and had a system" (interview).

Pauses in the game. The game outcome provided immediate feedback about strengths and weaknesses of self and opponent. Pre-service teachers utilized the point at which the game was re-set to stop, reflect and make the decision for adaptation. For example, Natalie said, "It put a pause in the game and you had to critically think, 'What do I want to do here? Do I want to make it easier for me?' " Carl also described the pause in the game—"It [the adaptation] gives the person who loses the game normally a few options of what they can do. So, if they are struggling … [they can choose to] make [the game] easier for them or if they feel their opponent is really excelling at something, they can make it harder for them [the opponent]" (interview).

At the pause in the game, pre-service teachers realized that they had to make an important decision about the next game. Hence, student decision-making was fore-grounded, providing a catalyst for transformation when the 'teacher took a backseat' as pre-service teachers played a series of sub-games.

Pre-service teacher change

The final theme is that of teacher change. Pre-service teachers increased their tactical awareness through improved decision-making, skill execution and off-ball movements while engaged in adaptation games. Often, their attention shifted away from themselves and their skill execution to their opponent and the game conditions as they were engulfed in the game.

Tactical awareness. Through trial/adapt and interaction with each other, pre-service teachers solved tactical problems. Appropriate decisions were evident in Lia's statement, "It's cool because it [adaptation game] helps you know to aim it [the volleyball] and try to keep it away from your opponent" (interview). Lia continued, "It really emphasized pushing your opponent back and when you did, in the short court game, that worked really well for me" (interview). David wrote, "You had to keep your opponent in mind. It was very important to read their body positioning and anticipate where their shot would go in order to give yourself more time for your shot." Sandra attended to the placement of her opponent's shots, "[I was focused] where Stephanie was hitting, and being in position after reading her passes" (exit card). Game conditions created opportunities for pre-service teachers to improve their skill execution in the context of game play, with many repetitions, at an appropriate level of difficulty.

Game enjoyment. Pre-service teachers described positive feelings experienced during games. Doug wrote, "it was challenging enough that I felt that I was actively part of the game" (exit card). Kim explained, "It felt good to play the game with the adaptation because it challenged us when we were winning and made it less frustrating when we lost. Overall, we were more involved and it was more enjoyable"(exit card). Jackie said, "I remember playing with Alex, and we would go back and forth but we ended up having a very low scoring game. That is what kept it interesting" (interview). Carl said, "Every single game was competitive, even a game that I wasn't as skilled in. The first game, I lost, but the [2nd] game was easier because we spread out the cones to make a bigger space ... and that was fun" (interview).

Discussion

Study findings point to the critical role of the enabling constraints as an important aspect of adaptation games, which support the idea that modification through adaptation is an additional pedagogical principle of game modification in TGfU. It is the unique contribution of the changing enabling constraints in the adaptation game that allows for the flow of energy and a resultant 'game-play action space' (Gee, 2007). The game-play action space created conditions for exciting challenges that allowed learning to emerge through game play for all ability levels.

The original TGfU approach advocated a game-centred approach using game modification through representation and exaggeration (Thorpe, Bunker, & Almond, 1986). The current study supports a game-as-teacher approach, expanding upon the ideas in TGfU and the notion that adaptation games are a critical site for learning due to their unique changing constraints (Hopper, 2011). Participants identified that their own improved skill and decision-making was scaffolded by the enabling constraints. Due to the changing nature of the enabling constraints, the game eventually matched the rate at which the learner could manage the information–movement coupling demands (e.g., "the cones were further apart I had more time"), which allowed players to engage in game play at an appropriate level of complexity as they progressed through a series of sub-games with opponents. Further, games scores were close and unpredictable and pre-service teachers became immersed in the game-play action space.

Results from the current study highlight how the appeal of the unpredictable nature of adaptation games contributes to student engagement in game play. It was the adapting constraints that created disequilibrium. Disequilibrium created the conditions for learning to emerge by allowing players to interact with each other as they tried to gain control of their roles in the game (Hopper, 2011). It was the small adjustments to individual movement responses, task rules, equipment or space constraints in the adaptation game that allowed for changes in movement patterns as well as decision-making to occur. Learners adjusted their movements to essential information sources through practice (e.g., trial and adapt), thus establishing strong, information–movement couplings to guide their behaviour (Handford, 2006). The pre-service teachers struggled during game play, which challenged them and kept them engaged. Because pre-service teachers experienced prolonged involvement in the games, they were able to utilize an approach to solving problems that included a trial and adapt process. Researchers have identified that movement variability is an intrinsic feature of adaptive movement behaviour as it provides the flexibility required to consistently achieve a movement goal in dynamic sport environments (Davids *et al.*, 2003; Williams, Davids, & Williams, 1999). Hence, the adaptation games provided 'repetition without repetition' (Bernstein, 1967), allowing learners ongoing opportunities to practise solutions to the specific tactical problems presented in the game.

The findings from this study underscore the notion that games can be designed to adapt to the players, thus creating an autocatalytic space within which complex learning can occur. While pre-service teachers engaged in adaptation games, the shifting constraints created a catalytic process that enabled a play space to form where the difference in ability between players did not prevent game play; rather, it enabled the exchange of energy between players and the game structure. As noted by Renshaw *et al.* (2010), by definition, constraints are boundaries that serve to shape the emergence of behaviour and the interaction of different constraints forces the learner to seek stable and effective movement patterns, and to shape decision-making through the self-organization process related to the constraints of the game. They have argued that order is not something that the teacher educator brings to the learner; rather, it continuously emerges through an autocatakinetic process within the learner–task–environment system. During adaptation games and essential to the autocatakinetic processes, the learner is placed at the centre of the process as movements and decisions are made based on the unique interaction of individuals, tasks and environmental constraints.

Game modification by adaptation also has important psychological benefits as it facilitated pre-service teachers' achievement at a level that met their needs as a 'just-right challenge' (Kretchmar, 2005). When presented with a series of 'just-right challenges', all games players can participate in enjoyable games. Adaptation games allowed pre-service teachers to learn to make good decisions based on an understanding of their own capabilities, which provided a sense of confidence as a games player. Because players' actions were altered by how they perceived the game, our findings suggested that changing the focus from winning a game to winning a close game allowed all pre-service teachers (even the more competitive still enjoyed the game) to share the real delight of a well-played game.

Physical educators need to adopt a 'game-as-teacher' approach if they value creating delightful games that engage learners of all abilities. The use of game modification by adaptation is a key pedagogical tool for physical educators. Adaptation games create the opportunity for pre-service teachers to engage in and with each other in meaningful game play, matched to their own level of competency, where the flow of the game play engulfs the players.

References

Almond, L. (2010). Forward: Revisiting the TGfU brand. In J. Butler & L. Griffin (Eds.), *More teaching games for understanding: Moving globally* (pp. vii–x). Windsor: Human Kinetics.

Barab, S.A., Cherkes-Julkowski, M., Swenson, R., Garrett, S., Shaw, R.E., & Young, M. (1999). Principles of self-organization: Learning as participation in autocatakinetic systems. *Journal of the Learning Sciences, 8*(3), 349–390.

Bernstein, N.A. (1967). *The co-ordination and regulation of movements.* Oxford: Pergamon Press.

Bunker, B., & Thorpe, R. (1986). The curriculum model. In R. Thorpe, D. Bunker, & L. Almond (Eds.), *Rethinking games teaching* (pp. 7–10). Loughborough: Loughborough University of Technology.

Button, C., Chow, J., Travassos, B., Vilar, L., & Araújo, D. (2012). A nonlinear pedagogy for sports teams as social neurobiological systems: How teams can harness self-organization tendencies. In A. Ovens, T. Hopper, & J. Butler (Eds.), *Complexity in physical education: Reframing curriculum pedagogy and research.* London: Routledge.

Davids, K., Button, C., & Bennett, S. (2008). *Dynamics of skill acquisition: A constraints led approach.* Windsor, ON: Human Kinetics.

Davids, K., Shuttleworth, R., Araújo, D., & Renshaw, I. (2003). *Understanding constraints on physical activity: Implications for motor learning theory.* Proceedings of the Second World Congress on Science of Physical Activity and Sports, University of Granada Press, Granada, Spain.

Davis, B., & Sumara, D. (2006). *Complexity and education: Inquiries into learning, teaching and research.* London: Lawrence Erlbaum Associates.

Davis, B., & Sumara, D. (2010). Enabling constraints: Using complexity research to structure collective learning. In J. Butler & L. Griffin (Eds.), *Teaching games for understanding: Moving globally* (pp. 105–120). Champaign, IL: Human Kinetics.

Davis, B., Sumara, D., & Luce-Kapler, R. (2008). *Engaging minds: Changing teaching in complex times* (2nd ed.). New York: Routledge.

Gee, J. (2003). *What video games have to teach us about learning and literacy.* New York: Palgrave, Macmillian.

Gee, J. (2007). *Good video games and good learning.* New York: Peter Lang.

Goetz, J.P., & LeCompte, M.D. (1981). Ethnographic research and the problem of data reduction. *Anthropology Education Quarterly, 12*(1), 51–70.

Handford, C.H. (2006). Serving up variability and stability. In K. Davids, C. Button, & K. Newell (Eds.), *Movement system variability* (pp. 73–83). Champaign, IL: Human Kinetics.

Hopper, T. (2011). Game-as-teacher: Modification by adaptation in learning through game-play. *Asia-Pacific Journal of Health, Sport and Physical Education, 2*(2), 18–22.

Hopper, T., Sanford, K., & Clarke, A. (2009). Game-as-teacher and game-play: Complex learning in TGfU and video games. In T. Hooper, J. Butler, & B. Storey (Eds.), *TGfU… simply good pedagogy: Understanding a complex challenge* (p. 246). Ottawa, ON: Physical Health Education.

Kretchmar, S. (2005). Teaching games for understanding and the delights of human activity. In L. Griffin & J. Butler (Eds.), *Teaching games for understanding: Theory, research, and practice* (pp. 199–212). Champaign, IL: Human Kinetics.

Light, R. (2009). Understanding and enhancing learning in TGfU through complex learning theory. In T. Hopper, J. Butler, & B. Storey (Eds.), *TGfU…simply good pedagogy: Understanding a complex challenge* (pp. 23–33). Ottawa, Canada: Physical Health Education.

Mason, M. (2008). What is complexity theory and what are its implications for educational change? *Educational Philosophy and Theory, 40*(1), 35–49.

Mitchell, S., Oslin, J., & Griffin, L. (2006). *Teaching sport concepts and skills: A tactical games approach* (2nd ed.). Champaign, IL: Human Kinetics.

Ovens, A., Hopper, T., & Butler, J. (2012). *Complexity in physical education: Reframing curriculum pedagogy and research*. London: Routledge.

Renshaw, I., Yi Chow, J., Davids, K., & Hammond, J. (2010). A constraints-led perspective to understanding skill acquisition and game play: A basis for integration of motor learning theory and physical education praxis. *Physical Education & Sport Pedagogy, 15*(2), 117–137.

Rossi, T., & Carroll, T. (2012). Ongoing adaptation as a feature of complexity: Further thoughts and possible ideas for pedagogy in physical activity. In A. Ovens, T. Hopper & J. Butler (Eds.), *Complexity in physical education: Reframing curriculum pedagogy and research*. London: Routledge.

Shulman, L. (1986). Those who understand: Knowledge growth in teaching. *Educational Researcher, 15*, 4–14.

Storey, B., & Butler, J. (2010). Ecological thinking and TGfU: Understanding games as complex adaptive systems. In J. Butler & L. Griffin (Eds.), *More teaching games for understanding: Moving globally* (pp. 139–148). Champaign, IL: Human Kinetics.

Storey, B., & Lunn, E. (2009). Learning TGfU and instructional skills in a complex environment: Undergraduates teaching games. In T. Hopper, J. Butler, & B. Storey (Eds.), *TGfU...simply good pedagogy: Understanding a complex challenge* (pp. 189–199). Ottawa, ON: Physical Health Education.

Strauss, A., & Corbin, J. (1998). *Basics of qualitative research: Techniques and procedures for developing grounded theory* (2nd ed.). Thousand Oaks, CA: SAGE Publications.

Thorpe, R., Bunker, D., & Almond, L. (Eds.). (1986). *Rethinking games teaching*. Loughborough: Loughborough University of Technology.

Williams, A.M., Davids, K., & Williams, J.G. (1999). *Visual perception and action in sport*. New York: Routledge.

15 Thinking about complexity thinking for physical education

Richard Tinning and Anthony Rossi

If we accept the tenets of complexity theory, then there is a beautiful irony played out in the classrooms, gyms and on the playing fields of our schools on a daily basis. Schools, stubbornly modernist in character and structured by Taylorism[1] in their operationalization, would seem to be entirely inconsistent with how learning appears to take place. This paradox has been some 150 or so years in the making (in the developed world) since the institutionalization of mass education. However, notwithstanding how linear we view the limits of some educational research and the knowledge it has generated, we have come to understand some things about what the term 'learning' means, and how it might be brought about. Importantly, such advances in our understanding do not appear to have been matched by advances in how the State delivers education. As a consequence we are left with what Biesta (2010) refers to as a gap between educational inputs (schooling, curriculum, pedagogy, assessment) and output (learning). We suggest that things are no different for physical education. However, we want to stress, as do others in the field of education (see Biesta, 2010), that this should not be judged on the old binary scale of good/bad. Rather it is an inevitable outcome given the contours of schooling shaped as they are by structural edict through legislation, structural design from an industrial model and a burgeoning audit culture (Avis, 2003; Ball, 2003) aimed at measuring slimmed down educational expectations and teacher performance (or perhaps compliance is a better word). Indeed, as Avis (2003) suggests when talking about targets and prescribed teacher performance:

> These targets and performance indicators finally confront the classroom teacher or lecturer, thereby defining the terrain upon which practitioners operate, albeit that these may have been mediated through staff appraisal. Although these performative practices set the terrain upon which teachers labour, they are subject to appropriation and mediation as they pass through institutional levels.
>
> (p. 321)

It may well be that the structure of performativity drives the form of teacher performance that more resembles linearity than it does emergence, nonlinearity or diversity of action. As a consequence we are drawn to ask whether complexity thinking (as defined in the introductory chapter) has an impact of *any* significance on the way teachers either think or go about their teaching within the contexts of physical education lessons and programmes of study. This is not to suggest that 'complexity' as a concept has no place in physical education. Rather, we wonder if the idea of complexity is better recruited as a *metaphor* that might provide a lens through which to consider the work of physical education and physical education teachers.

In this chapter we attempt to think about complexity thinking with regard to different forms of physical education pedagogy that have captured the attention of physical education teachers and researchers over the years. Specifically, we consider Mosston's (1966) famous spectrum of teaching styles, Teaching Games for Understanding (TGfU) (Bunker & Thorpe, 1982, and many after) and sport education (as per Siedentop, 1994). In so doing we are interested to see if complexity thinking can provide a generative way of theorizing pedagogy in physical education in ways that are advantageous over other ways of theorizing physical education pedagogy. We acknowledge that this potentially sets up an unwelcome binary that may be challenged. However, we position ourselves, initially at least, as sceptics with a view not to discard complexity thinking but rather to seek its most viable attributes to help shape pedagogical practice in physical education. We then return to the idea of complexity as a metaphor and finally ask whether the attractiveness (usefulness) of complexity thinking might be understood by considering it as a meme (the cultural equivalent of a gene) that happens to have gained attention at this particular point in time.

The limits to certainty ... and a persistent reliance on it

Nonlinearity, unpredictability and recursivity are central concerns of complexity. As Mainzer (2004) suggests, they are central features in the evolution of matter, life and even human society. This is a powerful proclamation and Mainzer strengthens his claim by suggesting, "the social sciences are recognizing that the main problems of mankind are global, complex, nonlinear, and often random" (p. 1). He continues, "Linear thinking and the belief that the whole is only the sum of its parts are evidently obsolete" (p. 1). Certainly this claim is not new. If we believe the arguments of social analysts such as Beck (1992), Bauman (2001), Giddens (1991) and many others, certainty is illusory in contemporary times. Elias (1991) used stronger language describing certainty as deceptive. But even this is pre-dated by Marshall McLuhan who in 1964 claimed that

> In the electric age, when our central nervous system is technologically extended to involve us in the whole of mankind and to incorporate the whole of mankind in us, we necessarily participate, in depth, in the consequences of our every action.
>
> (2002 reprint: pp. 4–5, original 1964)

Thirty years after McLuhan, Giddens (1994) talked about inter-connectedness as being a global phenomenon; globalization, he argued, was not a single process but "a mixture of processes, which often act in contradictory ways" (p. 5). Though the idea of complexity has a solid lineage originally drawn from physical mathematics and cybernetics, there is also a philosophical legacy apparent in the social sciences further extended to include the humanities more recently (see Davis & Sumara, 2006). Stewart (2001) suggests that the way 'complexity' is used is more to do with the purposes being served by its use. He goes on to suggest that, for the most part, definitions of (and indeed use of) the term complexity are invariably inadequate and he includes here definitions of social complexity. Among the reasons Stewart (2001) gives for this is drawing upon complexity to define (and understand) the social, which has created a "partly complementary, partly contradictory hetero-geneous field" (p. 324). Moreover, he considers the nature of social complexity to be very much open to debate, arguing that complexity ends up being more a matter of perspective or framing and level of detail and is inevitably contingent upon the phenomenon/object being observed and how it is perceived by the observer. Allen (1994) argues that complexities within human systems cannot be accounted for through mechanistic determinism because the governance of these systems do not follow physical laws but are shaped by the decisions that individuals make within the context of environmental constraints. In the short term, human systems may appear to behave according to physical laws but, over time, such systems evolve and this process appears to be less 'certain'. As Allen (1994) suggests:

> Because of this uncertainty in the longer term, we cannot know what actions are best in the present. Even if an individual knows exactly what he would like to achieve, then because he cannot know with certainty how everyone else will respond, he can never calculate exactly what the outcome will be. He must make his decision, and see what happens, being ready to take corrective actions, if necessary. Since, in business, on the road and in the shopping centre [and in the physical education class] we are all making these kinds of decisions, simultaneously, all the time, it is not surprising that occasionally there are accidents, or that such systems run in a "non-mechanical" way. An important point to remember here is, of course, that human beings have evolved within such a system and therefore that the capacity to live with such permanent uncertainty is quite natural to us. It may even be what characterizes the living. However, it also implies that much of what we do may be inexplicable in rational terms.
>
> (p. 588)

In this context, according to Bauman (2001) the most important learning for individuals in postmodernity is the capacity of the learner to unlearn and 'adapt to uncertainty'. Increasingly, however, in both schools and universities there is an expectation that we teach for specific, *predictable* learning outcomes as demanded by the audit culture, alluded to above. This linear, modernist orientation to pedagogy and learning (and teachers' work more generally) is now institutionalized. In our view it is, at best, only modestly informed by the arguments of complexity thinking and, at worst, ignores the arguments altogether.

Complexity theory, with its nonlinear orientation to antecedents and events, recognizes that the pedagogical encounter (between task, teacher and learner) is inherently complex and unpredictable and also views learning as 'emergent' and mostly contingent on interconnected networks and the modes of interaction within them (Jorg, 2009). This presents a new "reality" of education as a "domain of possibilities and potentialities" (Jorg, 2009, p. 16). This pedagogical 'pot of soup' (Tinning, 1995) cannot be easily understood and, focusing on the relationship between any two dimensions (e.g., teacher and task) while bracketing out the other (e.g., the student) will inevitably result in an incomplete and largely unsatisfactory account. These elements interact in complex and unpredictable ways, yet the education system expects that certain *essential learnings* or outcomes can be pre-identified and then 'produced' through the pedagogical act. This simply emphasizes the gap as described by Biesta (2010), which suggests that the pedagogical work done in any pedagogical encounter may 'capture' some expected outcomes, but undoubtedly others (both desirable and undesirable) will be 'missed' because they lie outside the description of 'essential' or are simply ignored as collateral and unimportant.

Physical education in a world of complexity

In this section we will briefly discuss two well-recognized models of teaching in physical education (sport education and TGfU) from the perspective of complexity thinking. In addition, we will also consider Mosston's spectrum of teaching styles, which might be better thought of as some sort of 'meta-model', from the perspective of complexity thinking. In particular we are interested in considering if complexity thinking adds something to the way these models of pedagogy might be understood. We also consider the enduring nature of a pedagogical strategy (method or style) that is rather ubiquitous across physical education and sport coaching contexts and how this strategy persists in the face of complexity thinking.

Sport education

Sport education was conceived by Siedentop in 1994 and was later trialled extensively in New Zealand (e.g., Grant, 1992), Australia (e.g., Alexander, Taggart, & Thorpe, 1996) and the UK (e.g., Penny, Clarke, Quill, & Kinchin, 2005). Sport education was a response to what Siedentop saw as the de-contextualized nature of physical education classes. In Siedentop's view, in most physical education classes, sports skills are the dominant, subject-matter content and they are introduced and practised in a decontextualized manner without a realistic 'connection' to the context in which they would have to be applied. It was a similar criticism that motivated the development of TGfU about a decade earlier. The context of sport in its more advanced form (adult format, full competition, leagues, fixtures or schedules) is the 'end state', and is reached through the structures of the games/sport itself.

Importantly, however, contextualizing is not the same as making something more complex. It seems to us that the main principle underpinning sport education is authenticity and meaning. In other words, how can the experiences that are afforded by the broad concept of sport (participation, performance, consumption, observation, understanding, measuring, etc.) be reproduced within the contexts of physical education classes such that the experiences of sport are made more meaningful to learners? Siedentop was concerned that both authenticity and meaning were missing from the typical physical education lesson based on sport skills. Certainly sport education offers the student a potentially more complex learning environment than, for example, a skill-drill practice. Moreover, in the sport or game itself there is greater uncertainty and unpredictability. However, the aim of sport education is not to make a more complex learning environment but rather to make a more authentic one. Some readers might consider this to be a pedantic distraction and would claim that a more *authentic* form of sport must inevitably be more *complex*. However, this surely misses the point. Siedentop's position on the use of sport education to teach sport (in its broadest, cultural sense) was to make it less abstract and therefore, one assumes, easier to understand and learn. So, paradoxically, while the complexity of the context is increased, the demands of understanding the place of the skills required to play and participate in the sport are made simpler, though not necessarily more linear. Whether this means that this form of physical education should be considered as being informed by complexity thinking is perhaps a task for the reader to undertake. It does seem to us though that sport education was regarded as an attractive option for structuring physical education experiences prior to being theorized using complexity thinking, and seemingly for very justifiable reasons. The question that warrants asking is, does complexity theorizing inform sport education in ways that make a difference to its practice or are we merely able to 'explain' sport education in seemingly more sophisticated ways? Accordingly we are not arguing that this form of physical education practice is informed or underpinned by complexity thinking (even if unintentionally).

While Siedentop's sport education owes much to his commitment to play theory, the recognition of the significance of creating a context more like the 'real' game does resonate with what we now understand as 'situated learning theory' (see Kirk & Macdonald, 1998). In our view, thinking about sport education through the lens of complexity thinking offers little practical or theoretical advantage beyond that already offered by situated learning theory. Should the reader regard situation learning theory as a type of or composite part of complexity theorizing, then the distinction may be moot. Moreover, we wonder what might be gained by considering it so.

Teaching Games for Understanding

In the 30 years since the landmark paper by Bunker and Thorpe (1982) appeared advocating an alternative approach to games teaching and coaching, TGfU has become something of a pedagogical 'movement' with its own advocates, devotees and even conferences. Since that original paper, the TGfU 'movement' has taken on various guises and manifestations in different places around the world. Examples include Griffin, Mitchell, and Oslin's (1997) Teaching of Sport Concepts and

Skills in the United States, the notion of Games Sense developed by the Australian Sports Commission (den Duyn, 1997), Launder's (2001) notion of Play Practice in Australia, Kirk and Macdonald's (1998) work on situated learning, and Kirk and MacPhail's (2002) further work in reconceptualizing the original model in the UK. In Singapore this approach to games teaching is known as the Games Concept Approach (GCA) and is even mandated practice for physical education in schools (Rossi, Fry, McNeill, & Tan, 2007).

What is interesting about the TGfU movement is not so much its success or otherwise in changing physical education practice in schools, laudable though that might be, but in the degree to which it has become theorized. Since its first appearance (there were probably other ideas that approximated to TGfU but were not explicitly explained in the same way), TGfU has been theorized using information processing and schema theory, situated learning, ecological psychology, dynamical systems theory, constructivism(s) and, more latterly, complexity theory (Jess, Atencio, & Thorburn, 2008; Light, 2008 make this connection). While most of these post-hoc, theoretical explanations of TGfU seem to have had some usefulness, can we say the same for complexity thinking applied to TGfU? Does complexity theory offer any new explanatory power to understand the nature of TGfU, and/or should insights from complexity thinking actually guide the practice of TGfU?

We note here that (see Davis & Sumara, 2006) complexity thinking should not be regarded as a meta-theory to be imported and imposed on other structures with the intent of explanation. However, in physical education this is sometimes how it is used. For example, Light (2008) claims that both TGfU and sport education are "examples of approaches in physical education that are consistent with complex learning theory" (p. 31). In our view, while this seems to be the case for TGfU, providing an explanatory account is not the purpose of complexity thinking and TGfU can be 'explained' just as well by a number of other theoretical positions. We have already argued that there is little about the pedagogy of sport education that is consistent with complexity thinking. Complexity thinking, as a way to advance some of the better known pedagogical models in physical education, may not be of great benefit. We offer this not as a criticism of either TGfU or sport education, but rather as an acknowledgement that, in both cases, the rationale and practices inherent in these modes can, and often are, informed by different theorizing.

Mosston's spectrum for teaching physical education

Mosston (1966) provided a useful framework for thinking about the strategy and purpose of pedagogy for physical activity. Although there is modest empirical support for its efficacy (see Byra, 2006), it has almost universal recognition in the field of physical education. Most physical education teacher education students learn about Mosston's spectrum of styles in their undergraduate programme and his framework, further developed by Sarah Ashworth (see Mosston & Ashworth, 1994), has had a central role in shaping the way in which many physical education teachers think about their teaching of physical activity. According to Mosston

(1966), pedagogical methods or strategies can be understood as representing a continuum that characterizes the degree of involvement which teacher and pupil have in creating the conditions for the learning environment.

The central premise of the continuum (or spectrum) is that, as the learner becomes progressively more involved in and responsible for the decision-making processes, there is a general move to more discovered forms of learning, increased responsibility for its success and greater independence for how it is shaped. If one were to take the spectrum (initially termed "From Command to Discovery") and overlay it with a continuum of complexity (simple at one end, complex at the other), it would stand to reason that complexity thinking (and learning) would be located at the discovery end of Mosston's spectrum. We acknowledge that this is potentially simplistic, but at a generative level, it is not unreasonable. It is not too much of a leap to suggest that different types of learning 'emerge' at different points in the spectrum, leading to different outcomes—most probably in the developmental channels to which Mosston refers. This stands to reason (and indeed was Mosston's intention). However, Mosston theorized this relationship in ways that perhaps are only modestly enhanced by complexity thinking. Importantly, teachers seldom employ pedagogical methods in a pristine fashion or according to a particular definition. They will usually teach with more of a hybrid method. In pragmatic terms it needs to be remembered that the various points along Mosston's spectrum are better considered caricatures of pedagogies than exact replicas of reality.

The question for us is whether or not complexity theorizing the relationship between any kind of learning (be it discovery or problem-solving or stimulus response approaches) and the pedagogy identified in Mosston's spectrum offers any further *useful* insights. At this point we remain sceptical.

A certain linearity and the challenge of complexity thinking

It is important to note that research into sport education (e.g., Alexander & Penney, 2005), TGfU (see collection by Griffin & Butler, 2005) and Mosston's spectrum of styles (e.g., Byra, 2000) all have legitimate intentions. They are focused on improving physical education pedagogy. However, all this research tends to reinforce a certain linearity—a certain predictable link between the pedagogy and certain, intended outcomes (even if one of those outcomes is discovery or inquiry-based learning). It tends to focus on issues of efficacy and effect.

In complexity thinking, however, we are asked to embrace the idea that educational practice needs to be positioned as teetering on the 'edge of chaos'. The reasons (discussed elsewhere in this collection) are that life in the postmodern world is unpredictable and uncertain and learning in this postmodern context reflects this state of affairs (see Jess et al., 2008). For example, complexity theory advocates in education argue that richer learning experiences happen through self-organization and adaptation and this can be brought about through the ideas of connectivity, developing networks and exchanging information. As Jess and colleagues suggest:

learning is a collaborative endeavour reflecting the complex interactions within the different groups of children, teachers, head teachers, local authority managers and politicians who make up the education system and also across the different "nested" levels of this system. That is, learning *emerges* through the relationships that develop between these constituent "elements," which are themselves considered shifting, dynamic and diverse.

(p. 180, our emphasis)

It would seem to us that considering learning as *emergent* precludes the idea of predictability. Therefore, complexity thinking seems incompatible with many forms of pedagogical thinking in physical education. Pedagogies in physical education are typically thought of as something akin to a 'tool-box'. This technicist metaphor perhaps has little appeal to many in the field (us included) and others will be resolutely hostile. However, the idea that a teacher, possessing an understanding of various pedagogical strategies (or styles), simply chooses the most appropriate one from their 'tool-box' and then employs it in the pursuit of certain, predetermined learning outcomes is a common convention, regardless of its veracity. However, this plug-in/process-out thinking is far from dead and a simple perusal through Teach for America (and indeed Teach for Australia) policies would reveal its prevalence. As to whether such an approach is heresy depends more on where you sit in the broader, socio-political, pedagogical discourse than probably anything else.

Notwithstanding the implicit linearity of this process (selection of pedagogical 'tool' and its application to achieve certain outcomes), it is interesting to note that across many pedagogical settings (e.g., school physical education classes, junior sport sessions, senior sport coaching) and across numerous forms of physical activities, from golf to tennis, from skiing to the martial arts, from rugby to basketball, we should not be surprised to find the form of pedagogy characterized by the sequence of demonstration, explanation and practice (DEP).

Forty years ago Shirl Hoffman (1971) delivered a strong critique of what he called 'traditional methodology' characterized by demonstration, explanation and practice (DEP). He believed that 'traditional methodology', as the most widely used pedagogical method in physical education, is what most learners are exposed to in their school physical education classes and therefore the *model of teaching* that student teachers bring with them to their beginning teaching experiences. For many teachers and pupils alike, the 'traditional method' is *the* way to teach physical activity.

Given that DEP might not be the most appropriate method in all (or most) cases, then why should it be so widespread across most forms of instruction in physical activity? In the face of considerable advocacy and research support for methods that facilitate 'discovery', 'problem-solving' and 'social' frameworks for pupil learning, why is DEP such a dominant pedagogical form? Hoffman (1971) suggested that the method had little to do with any claims to idealism and argued that its origins were "not in science or even theory, but in the unglamorous realities of life" (p. 57). In other words, it is largely contingency-shaped. Certainly the 'unglamorous realities' of a large class of energetic, unruly children spread out across a large playing field may make the traditional DEP method look extremely attractive to the primary/elementary teacher who has to take his/ her class for physical education a few times each week.

Hoffman's observations are now some 40 years old and it is reasonable to ask why they might still be relevant within the exigencies of the performative audit culture of the early twenty-first century. In the contemporary school culture, with its prescribed learnings considered to be indispensible (look at any national curriculum document), dealing with complexity and diversity represents a considerable challenge for the teacher. Any method that structures pedagogy in tightly defined and easily controlled ways might be attractive. This might have the effect of greatly reducing the degrees of freedom within a system (the pedagogical encounter, for example) and reducing potential outcomes. What is also of interest is that the phenomenon of the linearity of learning experiences as being characteristic of pedagogy is widespread. Doll (1993) argued that in the United States, the modernist expression of curriculum that still prevails in American schools is, what he calls, a 'closed-system'. In such a system emphasis is on linear, stable, objective and product-oriented approaches to teaching and learning. Moreover, in a comprehensive review of the literature, Nelson and Harper (2006) noted that within the context of the reductionist models of education so prevalent in the United States, emphasis is placed on speed and efficiency and not thinking and learning and, by drawing on many well-known 'wait time' studies, confirmed that teachers tend to allow almost no thinking time for students, instead preferring to provide the 'right' answer almost instantly upon asking the question. It is not clear to us why we would expect physical education teachers not to display such a proclivity.

Reducing complexity: a contingency-shaped pedagogical choice

In proposing his ecological approach to research on teaching, Walter Doyle (1977) argued that both teachers and students are engaged in attempts to manage complexity by actually trying to reduce it. While Doyle was not speaking of complexity specifically in the sense of complexity thinking, the observation he made was powerful. It is an observation that has currency in contemporary literature on complexity and education for the reasons we alluded to above. Control and order are watchwords in contemporary education and, as Biesta and Osberg (2010) suggest, this creates a paradox in the education enterprise. However, these authors also suggest that the recruitment of complexity as an organizing principle for education is not about the denial of order; rather it is about seeing order differently. In their words order should be considered as emergent and generative. A behaviourist view of human behaviour might suggest that, if we knew everything about an individual's life history, including the antecedents and consequences of each act (see, for example, Moxley, 1982), then we could accurately predict the future behaviour of the individual. There is a reliance on 'certainty' here that perhaps captures some of the limitations of behaviourism, however, there is a certain degree of practical wisdom in this claim. The best predictor (that we have) of future behaviour continues to be past behaviour. Hence, for the behaviourist, order is not contingent upon emergence but a state that can be established through an awareness (or predictability) of the likely behaviours that learners will manifest.

Certainly to exist as a functioning human being we must apply something akin to this behavioural maxim. As a teacher it is important that we have a good sense of how certain things we might do might bring about certain behavioural outcomes (e.g., learning to read or kick a ball). To send pupils on a warm-up of three laps around the school field might reasonably be predicted to frustrate and annoy some pupils in the class. For others it would make them sweat, get out of breath and relieve them of excess energy. This might be an issue related to health, but it also might be a discipline and class control issue, or, dare we say it, a cathartic one! Much of physical education pedagogy is an attempt to produce (a degree of) certainty of outcomes (e.g., pupils in the class will develop a love for physical activity, or will get fitter, or will become more skilful) in part by controlling variables and reducing complexity. It is the response to complexity that shapes much teacher behaviour in physical education. In other words DEP is contingency shaped in response to the many possible outcomes of a particular pedagogical strategy.

As Biesta (2010) suggests, however, complexity reduction should not be seen as a good or bad thing. In his analysis he argues that the educative process available through contemporary schooling is itself an example of complexity reduction. This occurs primarily through the systems of assessment because this is the medium through which the outcomes of learning 'count' and the way we 'judge' a child's progress against prescribed standards. Standards are part of the educational lexicon and a powerful political intervention into complexity reduction. By prescribing standards we are actually eliminating other possible outcomes that might be of value. In a sense this is where Biesta takes his argument. At first glance assessment might be seen as *retrospective complexity reduction* (2010, p. 9); however, he continues by saying it is the planned responses to meet the demands of expected essential learnings or outcomes measured by assessment that actually have the effect of *prospective complexity reduction*. In other words, in anticipation of what it is that needs to be measured (that is, what stands for school knowledge), that which is considered essential is necessarily reduced in complexity. Moreover, there are fears across many education systems that a virulent kind of teaching to the test is emerging in response to standardized testing regimes. To enhance its educational justification, physical education slips into this assessment space, a space that, at its worst, is more like a vortex.

Complexity theorizing as metaphor

Gough (2010) finds it difficult to accept the principles of complexity as they are described in the natural sciences as being especially helpful within the social milieu of schooling, unless they are considered as a 'metaphor'. We share this view and accordingly consider complexity in a metaphoric sense—as a way to think about physical education pedagogy.

A metaphor is generally considered to be a literary figure of speech that uses an image, story or some tangible thing to represent a less tangible thing or some intangible quality or idea. What then, in this case, is the tangible thing that is used to represent a less tangible thing? This potentially gets us into a linguistic tangle, in part because the word complexity as a noun or an adverb is not especially helpful. Hence, the nomenclature that sits under the moniker 'complexity'—uncertainty, nonlinearity, emergence, self-organization—provides the image for what we consider the social world (and therefore the world of learning) to be like. We can then arrive at the point of drawing on 'complexity thinking' to consider how pedagogy might be arranged to bring learning about.

In this sense Tovstiadi (2004) is forthright when he claims that "[c]omplexity shows that linear prediction, even in the simplest situations, sometimes fails miserably" (p. 3). It might be important to note that Tovstiadi is not exactly unequivocal in his claim; the use of the adverb 'sometimes' plays into the very proclamations of uncertainty said to underpin complexity. If we are uncertain about uncertainty then one can only assume linearity and predictability still have their place. In many respects Biesta (2010) acknowledges this also.

Tovstiadi's (2004) main argument is that (in his field of communication) scholars have not yet succeeded (as have colleagues in biology, chemistry, physics and mathematics) in using complexity theory beyond the rhetorical and metaphorical level. "The theory and its main conclusions are used by communication and organizational scholars as coherent narratives that provide good explanations for human behavior" (p. 4). Unlike physicists and mathematicians, communication (and for our purposes we might add education/sport pedagogy here) researchers do not support their conclusions with experimentations and formulas. They use complexity theory as a paradigm for understanding human behaviour. Tovstiadi goes on to suggest that using complexity and its terminology as a *metaphor* has been by far the most prominent line of its applications to the social sciences (Abell & Simmons, 1999; Merali, 2000; Petzinger, 1999; Stacey, 2000; Wilkinson, 2003). It is, to all intents and purposes, a rhetorical device. Tovstiadi (2004) argues that, at the current stage, metaphors have both strengths and weaknesses. On the one hand, new labels invite new approaches and creativity, yet, on the other hand, creative explanations can co-exist with "inapt analogies and overstretched applications" (Petzinger, 1999, p. 194). Indeed, Abell and Simmons, (1999, p. 190), in their review of the current literature regarding complexity and business, claim that "the books have already said more than can reasonably be said at this stage, and probably more than is supportable."

We are compelled to ask then where physical education fits into all of this. We might ask first where is there a sparkle of creativity in physical education? If, as other authors suggest, we are caught in a behaviourist time-warp (see Jess, 2008; Light, 2008), then the sparkle of creativity in physical education pedagogy is but a twinkle in somebody's eye. It also poses some serious challenges.

Our suggestion is that, even though there is widespread agreement in the non-linear world of the physical education class that outcomes can be achieved via different routes, the audit of these outcomes tends to be judged in linear terms. Remember, as we have already argued, in education the goals of the system (certain essential learnings or outcomes or whatever) are to be facilitated by the actions of teachers and schools. This is a fundamentally linear relationship. Reducing complexity of the system makes it more predictable ... exactly what most teachers (and ironically our contemporary education systems) seem to want (see Biesta, 2010).

Often books on complexity applications fail to "distinguish between metaphorical explorations and scientific investigations" (Petzinger, 1999, p. 193). For Tovstiadi (2004), some of these explorations give results that are so general that their value is doubtful; for example, how can one follow the advice of Kupers (2001) that organizational leaders should use complexity insights to "tun[e] his or her intuition" (p. 18)? How can one therefore follow Lumley's (1997) call for a nonlinear approach to creative problem-solving? We are drawn to ask whether, under the conditions under which teachers must operate—the level of accountability in their lives and the overwhelming constraints of performativity (Ball, 2003)—such advice is rather ineffectual.

Complexity thinking catches on

If we consider complexity thinking to be an idea that is spreading in much the same way that scientific ideas spread (Dawkins, 1976), then rather than being concerned with its truth or otherwise, we might need to consider what the conditions that facilitate and restrict its spread are. Also, in a metaphoric sense, complexity thinking can be considered to be a meme—a term first coined by evolutionary biologist Richard Dawkins in his book *The Selfish Gene* (1976) and claimed to be the cultural equivalent of a gene and the unit of cultural transmission. Memes are selected in a process not unlike biological selection. Some memes thrive and others die off or become unused.

Memes differ in their degree of 'fitness', i.e., adaptedness to the socio-cultural environment in which they propagate. 'Fitter' memes will be more successful in being communicated—'infecting' more individuals and thus spreading over a larger population. Whilst a biological analogy may be distasteful to some, it does allow us to apply Darwinian concepts and theories to model cultural evolution. In any given cultural context there are many competing memes. Some memes are more reinforcing for their 'hosts' (people) and they gain a competitive edge and are more likely to be replicated or passed on.

In examining the issue of political decision-making from an evolutionary and memetics perspective, de Jong (1999) argues the case for survival of the institutionally fittest concepts. Ideas that best fit the institutional agenda will win. So what might be the institutional context that is receptive to complexity thinking? And which institutions are we talking about? Certainly the modernist institution of schooling (which we mentioned in the introduction) would seem less receptive to this meme than perhaps the university context in which ideas are a form of currency.

With regard to this, memes, according to de Jong (1999), are mainly replicated because of their ability to make individual actors understand and solve problems.

Accordingly we ask what particular problems might be solved by the meme of complexity thinking? When the memes prove no longer useful in dealing with particular problems, there might be slight modifications, equivalent to slight mutations, or rarely, there might be a complete replacement of the conceptual framework (set of ideas) by another set of ideas. This later event we would recognize as a paradigm shift.

We contend that, while complexity thinking might represent a paradigm shift in thinking for science, for physical education complexity thinking may be of more limited usefulness in dealing with particular *practical* problems and, accordingly, this may threaten its survival. As Sarder and Rave (1994) ask, is complexity the future or simply another fad to be later replaced by another fad? We make no judgement on this question; we do see though, why it might be asked.

A parting thought

Although the idea (or meme) of complexity thinking in physical education has 'caught on' in some institutional contexts, as this collection bears testimony, at this point in time we consider its current practical impact as modest and perhaps future studies will illuminate the physical education community further. In the face of messy, unruly, boisterous classes of school children and the expectation to deliver predictable, explicit, educational outcomes, teachers of physical education are likely to continue to attempt to reduce complexity and have their pedagogy shaped more by practical contingencies rather than complexity thinking. It may well be that ideas that sit under the broad banner of complexity such as self-organization, nonlinearity, adaptability and others provide *images* of how the social world functions rather than providing models to work from in practice. This, in itself, may encourage alternative pedagogical thinking as the world awaits further research studies.

Note

1   The ideas of the efficiency expert, Frederick Winslow Taylor, became very important to the remodelling of the education system during the 20th Century. The tennets of Taylorism are centered on increasing outputs through the standardisation and system-isation to the production process. The effects of this on education can be seen in a number of ways from how schools are strucutured through to how lessons are planned.

References

Abell, B., & Simmons, L. (1999). Review of the reviews. *Emergence*, 1, 190–192.

Alexander, K., & Penney, D. (2005). Teaching under the influence: Feeding games for understanding into the sport education development-refinement cycle. *Physical Education and Sport Pedagogy*, 10(3), 287–301.

Alexander, K., Taggart, A., & Thorpe, S. (1996). A spring in their steps? Possibilities for professional renewal through sport education in Australian schools. *Sport, Education & Society*, 1(1), 23–46.

Allen, P.M. (1994). Coherence, chaos and evolution in the social context. *Futures*, 26(6), 583–597.

Avis, J. (2003). Re-thinking trust in a performative culture: The case of education. *Journal of Education Policy*, 18(3), 315–332.

Ball, S. (2003). The teacher's soul and the terrors of performativity. *Journal of Educational Policy*, 18(2), 215–228.

Bauman, Z. (2001). *The individualized society*. Cambridge, UK: Polity.

Beck, U. (1992). *Risk society: Towards a new modernity*. London: Sage.

Biesta, G. (2010). Five theses on complexity reduction and its politics. In D. Osberg & G. Biesta (Eds.), *Complexity theory and the politics of education* (pp. 5–14). Rotterdam: Sense Publishers.

Biesta, G., & Osberg, D. (2010). Complexity, education and politics from the inside-out and the outside-in. In D. Osberg & G. Biesta (Eds.), *Complexity theory and the politics of education* (pp. 1–3). Rotterdam: Sense Publishers.

Bunker, D., & Thorpe, R. (1982). A model for the teaching of games in secondary schools. *Bulletin of Physical Education*, 18(1), 5–8.

Byra, M. (2000). A review of spectrum research: The contributions of two eras. *Quest, 52*, 229–245.

Byra, M. (2006). *Handbook of research in physical education*. London: Sage.

Davis, B., & Sumara, D. (2006). *Complexity and education*. Mahwah, NJ: Lawrence Erlbaum Associates.

Dawkins, R. (1976). *The selfish gene*. Oxford: Oxford University Press.

de Jong, M. (1999). Survival of the institutionally fittest concepts. *Journal of Memetics, 3*.

den Duyn, N. (1997) *Game sense: Developing thinking players*. Canberra: Australian Coaching Council.

Doll, W. (1993). *A postmodern perspective on curriculum*. New York: Teachers College Press.

Doyle, W. (1977). Learning in the classroom environment: An ecological analysis. *Journal of Teacher Education*, 28(6), 51–55.

Elias, N. (1991). *The society of individuals*. New York: Continuum.

Giddens, A. (1991). *Self-identity and modernity*. Cambridge: Polity Press.

Giddens, A. (1994). *Beyond left and right*. Cambridge: Polity Press.

Gough, N. (2010). Lost children and anxious adults: Responding to complexity in Australian education and society. In D. Osberg & G. Biesta (Eds.), *Complexity theory and the politics of education* (pp. 39–55). Rotterdam: Sense Publishers.

Grant, B. (1992). Integrating sport into the physical education education curriculum in New Zealand secondary schools. *Quest*, 44(3), 304–316.

Griffin, L., & Butler, J. (2005). *Teaching games for understanding: Theory, research, and practice*. Champaign, IL: Human Kinetics.

Griffin, L., Mitchell, S.A., & Oslin, J.L. (1997). *Teaching sport concepts and skills: A tactical games approach*. Champaign, IL: Human Kinetics.

Hoffman, S. (1971). Traditional methodology: Prospects for change. *Quest, 15*, 55–57.

Jess, M., Atencio, M., & Thorburn, M. (2008, November). *Complexity theory: Supporting curriculum & pedagogy developments in Scottish physical education*. Paper presented at the Australian Association of Research in Education, Brisbane, Australia.

Jörg, T. (2009). Thinking in complexity about learning and education: A programmatic view. *Complicity: An International Journal of Complexity and Education*, 6(1), 1–22.

Kirk, D., & Macdonald, D. (1998). Situated learning in physical education. *Journal of Teaching in Physical Education*, 17(3), 376–387.

Kirk, D., & MacPhail, A. (2002) Teaching games for understanding and situated learning: Rethinking the Bunker-Thorpe model. *Journal of Teaching in Physical Education, 21*, 177–192.

Kupers, R. (2001). What organizational leaders should know about the new science of complexity. *Complexity*, 6, 14–19.

Launder, A. (2001). *Play practice: The games approach to teaching and coaching sports*. Adelaide: Human Kinetics.

Light, R. (2008). Complex learning theory—its epistemology and its assumptions about learning: Implications for physical education. *Journal of Teaching Physical Education*, 27(1), 21–37.

Lumley, T. (1997). Complexity and the learning organization. *Complexity*, 2, 14–22.

Mainzer, K. (2004). *Thinking in complexity*. London: Springer.

McLuhan, M. (2002). *Understanding media*. London: Routledge.

Merali, Y. (2000). The organic metaphor in knowledge management. *Emergence*, 2, 14–22.

Mosston M. (1966). *Teaching: From command to discovery*. Belmont, Ca.: Wadsworth Publishing.

Mosston, M., & Ashworth, S. (1994). *Teaching physical education*. New York: Macmillan.

Moxley, R. (1982). Graphics from three term contingencies. *The Behaviour Analyst*, 51(1), 45–53.

Nelson, C., & Harper, V. (2006). A pedagogy of difficulty: Preparing teachers to understand and integrate complexity in teaching and learning. *Teacher Education Quarterly*, 33(2), 7–21.

Penny, D., Clarke, C., Quill, M., & Kinchin, G. (Eds.). (2005). *Sport Education in Physical Education: Research based practice*. London: Routledge.

Petzinger, T. (1999). Review of the reviews. *Emergence*, 1, 193–194.

Rossi, T. Fry, J.M., McNeill, M., & Tan, C.W.K. (2007). The Games Concept Approach (GCA) as a mandated practice: Views of Singaporean teachers. *Sport, Education and Society*, 12(1), 93–111.

Sardar, Z., & Ravetz, J.R. (1994). Complexity: Fad or future?. *Futures*, 26(6), 563–567.

Siedentop, D. (1994). *Sport education: Quality PE through positive sport experiences* Champaign, IL: Human Kinetics.

Stacey, R. (2000). The emergence of knowledge in organizations. *Emergence*, 2, 23–39.

Stewart, P. (2001). Complexity theories, social theory, and the question of social complexity. *Philosophy of the Social Sciences*, 31, 323–360.

Tinning, R. (1995). We have ways of making you think. Or do we? Reflections on 'training' in reflective teaching. In C. Paré (Ed.), *Better teaching in physical education? Think about it!* (pp. 21–52). Canada: Université du Quebéc à Trois-Rivières.

Tovstiadi, K. (2004, November). Complexity as a metaphor: Applications for communication theory. Paper presented at the Annual Convention of the National Communication Association, Chicago.

Wilkinson, D. (2003). Civilizations as networks: Trade, war, diplomacy, and command-control. *Complexity*, 8, 82–86.

Glossary

Adaptation Adaptation refers to the capacity of an organism to manage changing environments, in other words to adapt to constantly changing conditions. Motor skill adaptation is tolerable by an organism based on increased experience and feedback systems that are able to minimize the 'costs' associated with movement to address a challenge from the environment.

Affordances In sport affordances can be defined as a relationship between players' capabilities and the physical conditions of the performance environment to achieve a certain goal. A team's affordance is based on the players' game performance in relation to each other and the opposition and is grounded on the players' ability to identify and actualize opportunities to act for themselves and for others based on interpersonal spatial-temporal relations.[1]

Affordance network The collection of material, social and human capital, taken with respect to an individual, that is distributed across time and space and is necessary for the satisfaction of a particular goal set. The individual components that become enacted as part of an individual's affordance network may include people, technical knowledge, tools, methods, equipment, concepts and practices.[2]

Agent Something that takes part in an interaction and is itself subsequently changed: a person, a society, a molecule, a plant, a nerve cell, a PE student, a teacher, etc. Individual agents interact at the local level and cannot know the system as a whole nor does a central agent have responsibility for overall control of the system.

Attractor An attractor is a trajectory of a pattern or activity in time in a region of space that 'appears' to draw the energy of a system to it. It is a pattern of behaviour exhibited by a complex adaptive system over time. A helpful metaphor is a basin or a lake in a valley into which rain water flows after making its way down the various possible pathways of a surrounding mountain range. The water is said to be attracted to the basin or lake. One of four emergent patterns are noted in attractors.[3]

(1) All the parts of the system move toward the same endpoint. This is a point attractor. An example occurs at quitting time—everyone in the building moves toward the exit, so the pattern of motion is toward a single endpoint.

(2) The parts of the system repeat the same behaviours at regular intervals. This is a periodic attractor. A payroll system is a good example of a periodic attractor because the same behaviours are repeated at regular intervals.

(3) The behaviour of the system stays within observable bounds, but within those bounds anything is possible. This is called a strange attractor. A game of soccer can be seen as an example of a strange attractor. The acceptable bounds of behaviour are known through rules and past playing experiences, but within those bounds, individual players have freedom to make choices.

(4) The parts of the system seem to move without connection to or regard for other parts of the system. This is called a random attractor. It is hard to think of examples of true random attractors in human systems because people are almost always connected to each other in some way. A class of five-year-old children might be considered more random than other types of classes as these children are just learning the ways of operating in a school setting. Who knows what a five-year-old is wondering and what they might say?

Autocatakinetic This describes a process where a system, drawing on available resources, develops a self-sustaining exchange with the environment.

Bifurcation A relatively abrupt change that occurs when some parameter(s) reaches a critical level (far from equilibrium at the edge of chaos) resulting in the emergence of a new state and pattern (a new attractor). The action potential of a neuron, the onset of puberty, a teaching cue that enables a motor skill pattern to flow and pressure build-up that leads to an earthquake, are examples.

Chaos The apparent absence of order in a system that is highly sensitive to initial conditions (small fluctuations that disturbed the system lead to big changes). The weather is a chaotic system in which particular specific states are unpredictable—yet the broad range of those states is predictable.

Co-evolution Co-evolution refers to the coordinated and independent evolution of two or more systems. Participating agents change, evolve, as a result of their interaction. Curriculum and assessment co-evolve, one influencing the other. The teacher–student or coach–player relationship co-evolves as one interacts with the other. Learners co-evolve through the exchange of differences.

Collective variable (order parameter) A condition or state in which many agents interacting in an uncoordinated way coalesce into an ordered or coordinated pattern. People at a dance party are milling around. When the music begins, they pair up or dance in groups forming coordinated patterns. A collective variable represents a decrease in the degrees of freedom among numerous agents. The spin of hydrogen atoms becomes coordinated under the influence of a magnetic field in magnetic resonance imaging. A wave of fans in a football stadium is a collective variable.

Complex adaptive systems "A collection of individual agents who have 'the freedom to act in ways that are not always totally predictable, and whose actions are interconnected such that one agent's actions change the context for other agents" (Plsek, 2003, p. 3)'.[4] Nerve cells, the immune system, the stock market, players in a team, a class of students, communities and schools are complex adaptive systems. A complex adaptive system adapts (learns) in response to changing conditions and thus can be said to have a history.

Complexity science   A collection of concepts and principles for the study of open systems that have nonlinear dynamical, self-organizing and emergent properties. Complexity science is the study of the dynamics of patterns and relationships rather than objects and substance in systems that are open and far from equilibrium. Complexity science focuses on processes and interactions of local agents that result in the emergence of new patterns as a whole. In addition, complexity science is the scientific study of complex systems, systems with many parts that interact to produce global behaviour that cannot easily be explained in terms of interactions between the individual constituent elements.[5]

Constraints-led approach   This approach is drawn from Newell's (1986)[6] ecological task analysis model that classified constraints into three distinct categories performer (learner), environment and task. These constraints interact to shape degrees of freedom in learning within a nonlinear process. This means that motor learning in particular is an ongoing dynamic process involving a search for and stabilization of specific and appropriate movement patterns across the perceptual–motor landscape as each individual adapts to a variety of changing constraints.

Curriculum   A fluid, interactive and unpredictable process oriented towards the expansion of the space of the possible knowing/acting at both individual and collective levels. The notion of curriculum aims to nurture dynamic learning processes and set enabling constraints that prompt learners to engage with subject matter—but it never purports to predict or control learning. This is because knowledge cannot be simply transmitted to students and because education and learning are part of the world—by intervening in the lives of learners, teachers help change the very world they are supposed to be preparing students for.[7]

Deterministic systems   A system in which particular states follow from, or are determined by, previous ones. Deterministic systems are in contrast to stochastic systems where future behaviour is independent of previous behaviour.

Dynamical system   A complex interactive system evolving over time through multiple modes of behaviour and following certain rules. The concept of a dynamical system has its origins in Newtonian mechanics[8] where through an iterative process and given an initial point it is possible to determine all its future positions of a system. Physiological systems such as the heart and the brain are dynamical.

Dynamical systems theory   This theory connects to chaos theory and deals with the long-term qualitative behaviour of dynamical systems. The focus in this theory is not on finding precise solutions to describe the behaviour of dynamical systems, but rather to study questions such as when will the system settle down to a steady state and for how long?—or, to understand how long-term behaviour of the system depends on its initial condition.

Edge of chaos   A critical phase that occurs where it is not possible to predict outcomes with certainty. The possibility for the emergence of new, adaptive patterns is at a maximum at the edge of chaos. A critical threshold where self-organization and emergence are heightened. This phrase has come to refer to a metaphor that some physical, biological, economic and social systems operate in a region between order and either complete randomness or chaos, where the complexity is maximal.

Emergence   The arising of new, unexpected structures, patterns, properties or processes in a self-organizing system. Emergent phenomena exist on a higher level than the lower-level components that give rise to the emergence. For example, fertilization gives rise to a new emergent structure. A well-played move between players on a team in basketball emerges in a game situation or the music that emerges from the coordinated inter-action and exchanges among musicians in a jazz group.

Equilibrium   A system that tends to remain at the status quo, for example, school timetables or a procedure of cutting children who try-out for a school team.

Far from equilibrium   A system in which energy is exchanged across open (indeterminate, fuzzy) boundaries. Far-from-equilibrium states are an essential prerequisite condition for self-organization. Living systems exist at the edge of chaos. Examples include situated cognition, metabolism, a new set of organizational rules.

Fuzzy boundaries   A demarcation, barrier or separation that is open and permeable allowing the exchange of energy between systems and between a system and its environment. A cell membrane, ground rules for group interaction, positional play on a team, culture, ethics and a conceptual framework are some examples.

Linear system   A system in which the relationship between variables can be plotted as a straight line. Small changes result in small effects and large changes result in large effects. Linear systems typically exhibit features and properties that are much simpler than the nonlinear cases. Linear systems are those in which the results of a change are usually predictable, for example, a thermostat re-setting a heater in response to a change in temperature, or applying more force to the ground results in more force being pushed back.

Nonlinear system   A system in which small changes can result in large effects and large changes may result in no or small effects. In nonlinear systems, the results of changing one factor are unpredictable yet may still be replicable. For example, the weather, the stock market, the release of neurotransmitters, the election of a new president, the striking of a golf ball.

Optimal feedback control (OFC)   A key feature of OFC theory is the idea that human capacity for on-line (real time) movement corrections allows ultra-fast heuristics that facilitate feed-forward decision-making in movement. It is this capacity that enables adaptation by a player in a tennis game where he or she adapts a skill such as a forehand drive to the speed, bounce, flight and positioning of an opponent's shot to execute an effective response.

Parametric control   A process that suggests that by manipulating certain parameters such as space, task and equipment, physical educators can guide learners to explore various functional organizational states within a learning context. For example, the manipulation of instructions to focus on different intents in a task or the change in equipment, such as a slower bouncing ball, enables learners to display new or different movement behaviours in learning situations.

Perception–action coupling   The reciprocal relationship that exists between an animal's perception of their environment and the way they move. American psychologist James Gibson proposed that an animal must move to perceive and also must perceive in order to move. Skilled performers have developed a sophisticated capacity to coordinate perception of information and action in a continuous fashion.

Perturbance   A social process in which people respond to turbulence by considering organizational practice. As such, it is possible to have turbulence that does not become a perturbance if it is not processed by people.

Propensities   This concept is based on the belief that the world is always open to events that may or may not happen. As such it refers to how any organic system is open to a range of potential outcomes dependent on the nature of the interactions between the organisms that make up that system. Properties of actions for an organism therefore lack certainty as a consequence of the degrees of freedom inherent in the possible interactions within the system.

Random   Systems in which the results of any action are unpredictable are said to be random. If the exact starting circumstances were recreated in a random system, the result at any given subsequent time would be different: for example, rolling a pair of dice.

Self-organization   A process in a complex system whereby new structures, patterns and properties arise (emerge) without being externally imposed on the system. There is no 'self' in self-organization and there is not a central hierarchical command and control centre. Examples include a flock of birds flying in formation, the pattern of the daily arrival of food throughout a major city, learning, the daily stock market values, and a game that starts to flow as the opposing players match, adapt and respond to each other.

Self-regulated spontaneous learning   This describes how a system is able to spontaneously self-organize based on its ability to connect to its own structure as it engages in environmental challenges, allowing the system to adapt with adjustments to its behaviour to meet environmental challenges.

Self-similarity   A pattern that exhibits identical or similar characteristics at different scales or orders of magnitude. Examples include the branching structure of trees and lungs, the geographic patterns of a coastline, modified games that contain key features of adult games. Fractals are an example of self-similarity.

Social network   Networks can be defined as social structures made up of individuals (or organizations) that are tied together (connected) by one or more specific types of interdependency. Social networks exist as a result of friendships, common interest or through a relationship of beliefs, knowledge or prestige.

Textbook Briefly, textbooks are books used explicitly for learning. An important element of textbooks however is the question of epistemology, or of the knowledge contained in the textbook. Textbooks are presented by authors, by publishers, and often by educators as authoritative 'voices' encapsulating the knowledge necessary for learners at particular and specific stages of their education process; but, underlying textbook knowledge are serious questions about the construction, reproduction and manipulation of power and ideology. PE textbooks traditionally have included a firm grounding in anatomical, physiological and health-related science, principles of programme administration suitable for various institutions, and recommended pedagogical practices and principles that often reflect the common social and/or cultural mores of the era.

Turbulence is the perception of potentially disruptive forces in an organization's environment or operating conditions.

Ultrafast heuristics An heuristic is an experience-based technique for problem solving, learning and discovery. Ultrafast heuristics allow a person to make quick adjustments with techniques to address a skill-based challenge in a situation where a considered search for a solution is impractical.

Notes

1 Araújo, D., Davids, K., & Hristovski, R. (2006). The ecological dynamics of decision making in sport. *Psychology of Sport and Exercise, 7*, 653–676.
2 Barab, S. A., & Roth, W.-M. (2006). Curriculum-based ecosystems: supporting knowing from an ecological perspective. *Educational Researcher, 35*(5), 3–13. doi: 10.3102/0013189x035005003.
3 Eoyang, G., Olson, E., & Kennedy, J. (2006). Complexity 101: Concepts and tools for OD practitioners. *Self-published.* Retrieved May 16, 2011, from www.search-institute.org/system/files/Complexity+101.pdf
4 Plsek, P. (2003) Complexity and the adoption of innovations in healthcare. In Accelerating Quality Improvement in Health Care Strategies to Speed the Diffusion of Evidence-Based Innovations. Washington, DC: National Institute for Health Care Management Foundation. National Committee for Quality Health Care.
5 Adapted from http://www.complexity.ecs.soton.ac.uk/.
6 Newell, K. M. (1986). Constraints on the development of coordination. In Motor development in children. In M. Wade & H. Whiting (Eds.), *Aspects of coordination and control* (pp. 341–360). Dordrecht The Netherlands: Martinus Nijhoff.
7 Taken from http://www.complexityandeducation.ualberta.ca/glossary/g_curriculum.htm
8 Taken from http://en.wikipedia.org/wiki/Dynamical_system.
9 Beabout, B. (2012). Turbulence, perturbance, and educational change. *Complicity: An International Journal of Complexity and Education, 9*(2), 15–29.

Index

The following index has been developed with consideration of key terms listed in the glossary. Each major concept is listed with sub-concepts indented with page numbers.